"In prose both graceful and unsentimental, Nancy McCabe tells the story of the search for identity and the yearning for connection that is at the core of the mother-daughter relationship. As she returns to her adoptive daughter's birthplace, as she struggles with the cultural divide she sees at home, as she watches her daughter, a budding gymnast, 'throw herself into empty space toward the high bar,' McCabe learns both to love and to let go. This is a book for every mother, adoptive and biological, who watches her daughter with love, awe—and bated breath."

—LAUREN KESSLER, AUTHOR OF
MY TEENAGE WEREWOLF: A MOTHER, A DAUGHTER, A JOURNEY THROUGH THE THICKET OF ADOLESCENCE

"With lyrical sensitivity and frank humor, the author of *Meeting Sophie* explores the myriad logistical and emotional facets of international adoption. Nancy McCabe is keenly aware of the challenge in reconciling her daughter's American and Chinese identities as they travel to Sophie's birthplace—a journey that's less a closure than an aperture. *Crossing the Blue Willow Bridge* is a brave, balanced, nuanced narrative, offering a complex answer to the simple question: what is home?"

—SARAH SAFFIAN, AUTHOR OF
ITHAKA: A DAUGHTER'S MEMOIR OF BEING FOUND

"In this heartfelt memoir, McCabe shares a touching journey as she travels to China to introduce her adopted daughter to the places and people from her past. The resulting story radiates wisdom about cross-cultural connections, while acknowledging the struggles of child-rearing. *Crossing the Blue Willow Bridge* offers lessons in love and patience that will apply not only to mothers and fathers of adopted children, but to all parents."

—LAURA BRODIE, AUTHOR OF
*ONE GOOD YEAR: A MOTHER AND DAUGHTER'S
EDUCATIONAL ADVENTURE*

"Nancy McCabe has written one of the most compelling books I've ever read. I read it on the plane, on the train, on vacation, at every opportunity till I'd gobbled it up. Here is a truthful story for every parent and child about their love, hope, and frustration with one another."

—SENA JETER NASLUND, AUTHOR OF
AHAB'S WIFE AND *ABUNDANCE, A NOVEL
OF MARIE ANTOINETTE*

Crossing the Blue Willow Bridge

Crossing the Blue Willow Bridge

A Journey to My Daughter's Birthplace in China

Nancy McCabe

University of Missouri Press
Columbia and London

Copyright © 2011 by
The Curators of the University of Missouri
University of Missouri Press, Columbia, Missouri 65201
Printed and bound in the United States of America
All rights reserved
5 4 3 2 1   15 14 13 12 11

Cataloging-in-Publication data available from the Library of Congress.
ISBN 978-0-8262-1942-8

♾™ This paper meets the requirements of the
American National Standard for Permanence of Paper
for Printed Library Materials, Z39.48, 1984.

Jacket designer: Susan Ferber
Text designer: Stephanie Foley
Typesetter: FoleyDesign
Printer and binder: Thomson-Shore, Inc.
Typefaces: Adobe Garamond and Humana

For Sophie, as always

Acknowledgments

When it comes to writing a memoir, there are a lot of people to thank: those whose presence and support were indispensable during the living of the experience as well as those who helped me write about it. And many people fall into both categories. My old friend Angela Salas read an early draft of the manuscript and gave me positive feedback that kept me going, and several wonderful writers and friends gave me feedback in record time when I was on a tight deadline: Dianne Aprile, Terri Brown Davidson, Liza Greville, and Jody Lisberger. Joyce McDonald and Jill Storey offered me valuable critiques on other manuscripts that ended up helping me with this one as well.

Others have been supportive of my work, provided lively conversations about books and parenting and life, offered babysitting, carpooling and dog-sitting, and fed us: Rekha, Gaj, Mahita, and Manu Gajanan, Michele Hoover, Carol and Harold Newman, Kimberly Weinberg, Scott and Carys Evans Corrales, Helene and Larry Lawson, Eddie Lueken, Tim Ziaukas, Karen Hindhede and Jim Kaisen, and Rachel and Mike Meit. Nor could we have gotten by without the help of our international supernanny and dear friend Micquel Little. For the last thirty years, I've benefitted from the wisdom and inspiration of Anna Smith. Sara King's humor and insight always give me perspective. Since childhood, Ruth Yoon has remained a good friend, and since I became a mother, she has been my most valuable resource on parenting an Asian daughter. I'm also grateful for having an energetic role model and enthusiastic supporter in my former teacher Heather Ross Miller, who still encourages us all thirty years later.

The support of my late parents made it possible for me to be Sophie's mom in the first place, and I'm grateful that they both got to be a part of her life along with my late aunt, Gena Shipley, whom I still wish I could call to ask for advice. No acknowledgments would be complete without mentioning Jody Shipley, Joe Shipley, Jim and Arlene McCabe, and Jeff, Bob, Sidney, Treven, and Megan McCabe.

I am grateful to Sena Jeter Naslund for inviting me to be a part of the amazing Spalding brief-residency MFA program. Sena and the rest of the program's dedicated staff—Karen Mann, Kathleen Driskell, Katy Yocum, and Gayle Hanratty—manage to create an inspiring, warm atmosphere where faculty are nurtured and challenged as much as we nurture and challenge our students.

The Hewlitt Foundation, the Pennsylvania Arts Council, the University of Pittsburgh at Bradford Faculty Development Committee, and the Division of Communication and the Arts all offered funding that assisted with my expenses. Special thanks to Jeff Guterman, Steve Hardin, and Sharie Radzavich. I'd also like to thank Jane Liedtke and her now-defunct Our Chinese Daughters Foundation, who organized our tour and took care of us along the way.

I also want to acknowledge the many people who've been an important part of Sophie's journey, especially Sarah Tingley and Patsy Arrowsmith at School Street Elementary. Michelle Feldman and the entire Bradford Flames coaching staff are an incomparable bunch who put in much underpaid and unpaid time to teach gymnastics skills—and to make our kids feel valued as individuals.

Several magazines published pieces that appear in this book in somewhat altered form: "Threads," *Prairie Schooner,* Fall 2011; "The Art of Losing," *Colorado Review,* Spring 2010; "Notes on a Dancing Daughter," *Fourth Genre,* Spring 2010; "Still Dancing," *Gulf Coast,* Spring 2009; "Running away from Home," *Louisville Review,* Spring 2008; "Bats in the Attic," *Hayden's Ferry Review,* Fall/Winter 2006; and "The Animals in the Walls," *Crab Orchard Review,* Winter/Spring 2005.

I've had the privilege of working with the University of Missouri Press twice. I'd like to recognize those who ushered *Meeting Sophie* so efficiently through the publication process when I had no idea what I was doing as well as those who contributed to making this a better book: Sara Davis, Jennifer Gravley, Clair Willcox, Julie Schroeder, Beth Chandler, Susan Ferber, and Stephanie Foley.

Most of all, I'd like to thank my daughter, Sophie, who has enriched my life beyond measure. Her willingness to speak out, her pride in her heritage, her endless wisdom, and her enthusiasm for this project have provided inspiration and motivation. To some extent, this book was a collaborative effort; Sophie read or listened to most of this book and offered additions, corrections, and changes when she thought I got it wrong or left out something important. She also had veto power over anything that might be embarrassing, which she exercised very sparingly. Nevertheless, writing about your child can be a perilous undertaking, especially when she is entering adolescence.

While my daughter is proud to be a part of my writing right now, while it has reinforced her pride, openness, and confidence in her own story during her elementary school years, I know that that might change. I hope that she and readers will understand that despite her valuable help, this book represents my perspective—in most cases my perspective during a brief period when she was ten years old—and someday she may decide that I got some of it wrong. I do not purport to speak for her; she might tell the story entirely differently. I hope that she will not only always feel free to tell her story in her own way, but that she will also see my effort as the love letter it is meant to be.

Crossing the Blue Willow Bridge

Prologue
October 2008

This is not going well. The orphanage director folds his hands on the table before him; his back is so upright it doesn't touch the chair. His face remains unsmiling, his eyes inscrutable behind sunglasses. He is not here, it turns out, because of his love of children. It is his poor eyesight that has doomed him to this position as director of the Chinese social welfare institute where my daughter once lived.

Mr. Li first took his seat without introducing himself or welcoming us, and our interpreter, Grace, immediately fired off a question: can we see my daughter's file, as promised by a previous director almost ten years ago? I lean forward, anxious. I had planned to build to this subject over time, after a little friendly small talk. But now the question has bulleted across the table, and Mr. Li responds with what sounds like a firm and final pronouncement.

Neither Sophie nor I speak much Chinese. She has taken classes for a month and can say, "This is my nose." I took a class many years ago and retain little except the sentence, "I am not a doctor": "*Wa bu shi daifu.*" I remember this so well because Gubo, the guy on the language tape, spat out the words as if furiously offended that anyone would dare to mistake him for a doctor. I can still imitate his tones and inflections, which I did a bit hesitantly for our guide in Beijing a few days ago when she asked me if I spoke any Chinese. I half-expected her to rear back at my unnecessarily forceful rejection of the medical profession, but instead she looked impressed and made me repeat it for a guide at a silk factory, who also looked impressed. "We can understand you," they both said approvingly. Since then, Sophie and I have been proudly throwing around our Chinese, getting endless mileage out of this one sentence: "I'd help people who are suffering, but wa bu shi daifu," Sophie might announce casually, to which I'd reply, "I would have started us on the antibiotics sooner, but wa bu shi daifu."

When it comes to Chinese, it's not just the words that I don't understand. I also have trouble deciphering moods and attitudes. Later, I will understand

1

this better after reading in *China Survival Guide* that while English has the same tones as Mandarin, "how we intone a word in English doesn't completely change the definition of the word, only the feeling behind it."

No wonder falling tones often sound to my American ears like vehemence, decisiveness, even anger, while rising tones seem to convey hesitation, uncertainty, or anxiety. The speaker could be saying, "Look at the beautiful white geese winging overhead," but if there are falling tones involved, I am likely to tense up and even feel mildly insulted. And if, in rising tones, someone said to me, "This is a stickup. Put your hands in the air and don't make any sudden moves," I might very well be seized by an overpowering urge to pat him reassuringly, and possibly fatally, on the arm.

So when Mr. Li utters a few harsh syllables and shakes his head fiercely, I am instantly discouraged. Not Grace. She machine-guns back a string of phrases. Mr. Li responds at length.

My daughter sags in the leather seat next to me, her mouth a network of wires and bands, the bands red this month in honor of China. She loves being in a country where she blends in, where no one stares at her. She tries not to smile too much, showing the braces that announce, in a country where dental care is often prohibitively expensive, that she is American. Her gaze drifts to the elaborate grates over windows that look out across a courtyard to the baby room where she once slept. She is zoning out at this important, long-awaited meeting, still recovering from the stomach bug that stranded us in Chengdu an extra day.

Trying to stay alert for both of us, I listen intently as if I can follow the conversation. Grace speaks, then Mr. Li, Grace, Mr. Li. I have become adept at watching Chinese soap operas and making up dialogue for Sophie's entertainment. Yesterday, a woman in a red negligee was clearly angry at her handsome bedmate. She delicately brushed a tear from her cheek while he removed a large rock from a hotel minibar and examined it.

"Give me my rock back," she seemed to be pleading. Or "Please don't bash me with that rock." My daughter laughed and laughed.

"Go on," she said.

A negotiation appears to be unfolding, and hope rises in me like a balloon floating over the shiny conference table, expanding, lifting: maybe Grace will coax from Mr. Li a piece of my daughter's past. But then Grace turns to us and reduces ten minutes of conversation to three words: "He says no." I release a pent-up breath. While hope spins away in a rapid, dizzily twirling gust, Grace says, with no transition, "Show him the picture."

I'm not ready. So much rides on this picture. I haven't steeled myself yet for more pleas or arguments, head shakes or buttoned lips. But I nod at

Sophie, and she slides the picture, sealed in a Ziploc bag, across the table. It's us almost ten years ago, me, a red-cheeked baby, and a man, a nameless man we've always referred to as *the Man*. In the picture, we are all smiling. I'm ducking into the edge of the frame like an interloper. The man holds the baby and shakes a plastic rattle, a colorful cage enclosing jingle bells that bounce up and down. They make the music of an approaching sleigh.

I have shown this picture to Sophie many times, telling her the story: the Man, probably a member of the orphanage staff, had brought her on a train to me at my hotel in Hangzhou. She'd clung to him tightly. Gently, he'd peeled her fist from his shirt and thrust her into my arms. Huge tears pooled in her eyes. As he retreated, her hands strained urgently toward him, fingers twitching, and I felt like a kidnapper. All night she howled operatically, her quick dark eyes distrustful. In the morning when the Man came to say good-bye, she tucked her head joyfully into his shoulder. He jingled the rattle and her laughter trilled, itself like little bells.

The Man was the one I wanted to talk to when the interpreter was free. Who are you? I wanted to ask. Why are you so important to her? But the Man stepped aside for my interview with the orphanage director, filled with vague pleasantries about good sleeping habits and favorite foods. It became distressingly clear that the director didn't know a single particular about my sleepless baby with only two teeth. Then, in the chaos of paperwork, baby foot- and handprints stamped in ink on thin paper, an appearance before a judge in which I vowed to provide for this baby and never abuse or abandon her, I lost sight of the Man.

Current laws in China mean that even if it were possible to track down birthparents, doing so could get them into trouble. So the story of the Man may always be one of the few delicate threads we have connecting my daughter to her past. I have used the picture as my fragile bit of evidence that someone loved her the first few months of her life. Should we risk new information that might reconfigure this story? What if the Man was a stranger who only smelled familiar to her, like sticky white rice and jasmine tea and cigarettes? What if he was just some man who was good with babies? What if he is only a comforting myth I invented? After all, I have a picture of the orphanage staff that I have examined carefully, unable to find him.

The orphanage director snaps the picture off the table like a playing card and deals it back to us with only a cursory glance. His answer is quicker this time. All the staff has changed in the last ten years. The Man's face is not familiar.

And with that, it seems, our quest is over. With that, finally and for-ever, our myths are intact, but so much I wish I could know has been lost:

when my daughter first smiled, the first time she rolled over, crammed her fist into her mouth, laughed, cut a tooth, gripped a caretaker's finger and guided it to her mouth to slobber and gnaw. With the words of the orphanage director, all of those missing moments have been fully erased.

At the other end of the table, where plates of oranges and small crisp green fruits like tiny apples are laid out, Mr. Yu, our driver, leaps up from his chair. He strides from the room. Cigarette break, I think. Mr. Li waits in his characteristic formal silence for my next question.

We are like unprepared hikers at high altitudes. My daughter's eyes glaze. I feel sluggish and droopy. I ask Sophie if she has any questions. She shakes her head. I don't know if she really doesn't, or if she's just too bored or intimidated to ask. I frame obligatory, impersonal ones and avoid looking at my watch as I try to prolong the interview to a respectable length.

It would seem impolite not to show an interest in the orphanage, even if the answers to my generic questions could probably be found online. How many children live in the orphanage, what are their ages, how many will be adopted, where do the older ones go to school? What else can I ask, and how soon can we gracefully move on to visiting the baby room, leave to shop for items to donate, and return to our hotel? Mr. Li answers each question briskly, without elaboration. Only five minutes have ticked past by the time I run out of topics.

Then, mercifully, Mr. Yu bursts back into the room. He speaks no more English than we do Chinese, but Sophie and I understand some of his sign language. When he shakes his head at Sophie and encircles his wrist with his fingers, it's clear he's enjoining her to put some meat on her bones. When he works his fingers in the air, he's obviously suggesting improvement to her chopstick technique. When he pounds the steering wheel and unleashes a torrent of words, Sophie interprets under her breath: "Move it, old man!" "Hey, Lady, get out of my way!" I'm guessing that she's pretty close, although there are probably also obscenities involved. I like the paternal affection he shows toward Sophie, telling her through our interpreter that she looks just like a Chinese pop star named Wei Wei. And now he's talking fast, smiling big enough to show his nicotine-stained teeth.

The director stiffens. Grace blinks. Her eyes open wider. She leans forward. Sophie and I glance at each other, waiting for a translation, but now everybody's talking at once. We will just have to wait.

～

A few days ago, on a soft sleeper train from Beijing to Xi'an, I woke early to quiet, only the sounds of the soft breaths of the others in the compartment, the rhythmic clicks of the train over rails. But then everyone began to stir, men waking and descending from the upper bunks, footsteps in the hall, compartment doors sliding open, voices, a seamless switch from peaceful silence and sleepy confusion to a chaos of activity. Whatever is going on now in the orphanage meeting room has nudged everyone into a similar state of wide-awake animation. They all pitch forward like passengers about to reach their station. Mr. Yu's words sizzle and crackle, sparklers igniting Grace and even Mr. Li, who are talking at the same time. Mr. Yu repeatedly pounds his arm with the heel of his hand. Sophie whispers, "I think he's saying, 'Cut off my arm! Just cut off my arm!'"

But it turns out that he does not require an emergency amputation, nor is he threatening to sacrifice a limb if the director doesn't try a little harder. It turns out that Mr. Yu has taken matters into his own hands and gone to talk to the staff. There's a disabled girl who grew up here, who was ten or so when my daughter left, who helped care for her, who remembers her. And someone else identified the Man. They know his wife. But the Man and his wife have both retired to the countryside, far away. Grace sounds regretful. It is unlikely that we will find the man, she says. I had hoped to find out his name for future reference, but my expectations were low. I didn't really think we'd be able to meet him on this trip. I'd just thought if we had his name, we could track him down someday. Sophie stares dreamily at nothing, politely bored.

"Wait here," Grace says, and she and Mr. Yu and Mr. Li retreat to an office down the hall. Soon they are back with a colorful laminated map and four more members of the staff. Everyone's interrupting, overlapping, gesturing, and peering over Mr. Yu's shoulder as he stabs at locations on the map and traces distances with his finger.

"It is very far," Grace says. Small worry lines furrow her brow. "Do you really want to go look for the man?"

Three months ago, my mother died. She collapsed while visiting me in Pennsylvania and spent a week in the hospital in Erie before flying home to a hospital in Kansas. Nurses came and went, velcroing bands around her arm while intently watching a dial, then reporting drops in blood pressure: "112 over 26," they'd say, matter-of-factly, as if this were normal. They brought small paper cups of water for her pills. They remembered, unlike the doctors, that she lived in Kansas. But I'll bet that if I went back now and asked them what they recalled about my mother, they would hem apologetically, remind me how many patients they see every day.

So why would it be any different with orphanage workers who came and went ten years ago, overtaxed workers who cared for thirty babies at a time? I wanted this trip to help Sophie feel connected to her past, but maybe just being here in China will have to be enough, the sense of belonging she feels that I can't fully understand.

I take for granted the many souvenirs we have from my mother's life: her wedding ring, her thimble collection, and the memory of the feel of her skin when we hugged her, putting her on a plane three days before she died. Sophie whispered to me, awed, "Her skin is so soft."

My mother, my aunt, my father, all gone now, proudly told stories about Sophie as a baby, laughed at her toddler antics, bragged about her elementary-school achievements. I want it to be enough that she belongs to a family that has doted on her, that she and I share Grace as a middle name with my grandmother and my great-grandmother, that she is a part of my line now, set to inherit the crystal bowl passed down to all the Graces in my family. But the recent losses make it feel even more crucial to answer her questions about her past.

It seems auspicious that the western name of our interpreter here in Yiwu is also Grace. Maybe my daughter will never know who her birthmother or birthfather are, what they look like, what they have endured. But maybe, just maybe, there are other things she can know. So when Grace says, "Do you really want to go look for the man?" and Sophie shifts out of her daydream to answer, "Yes," I nod my assent.

And with that, the day spins entirely out of my control. We pile into the van, Sophie and me, Grace and Mr. Yu, and a young orphanage worker named Mr. Feng who knows a shortcut. Infectious with laughter and anticipation and goodwill, we go careening down the highway so fast that my pictures out the window, even using the motion stabilizer, are blurred.

This landscape is closer than any I've seen so far on this trip to my childhood image of China, which came straight from the Blue Willow china pattern. On the plates, a path leads to a pagoda with a curved roof, doves hover in the sky, a crooked fence zigzags along, and three people cross a bridge. I loved that picture, the way I could feel the shade of the willows, hear the bubbling of the stream, be calmed by the suggestion of mist, of peace, of the bright blue of sky and ocean. It was like a picture you could walk right into and be at home.

So as we fly down the highway, I snap picture after picture, recording this countryside that feels as once familiar and foreign: rows of small colored flags flying from roofs; people on bikes pulling wooden wagons; road work-ers in wide-brimmed straw hats; mulberry, camphor, and willow trees; fields of sugarcane and rice; red lanterns hanging from stores; farmers' houses with towers and turrets and shiny windows, carefully detailed and freshly painted, looking cut from gingerbread. And ducks on a pond, haystacks tied at the top like witches' brooms, an occasional pagoda on a hill, mountains folding over each other in the distance.

Dusty heat blows through the van, and everyone shouts words I don't understand with a cadence and volume and pitch I do, words wrought with a touching eagerness to offer something to this skinny American girl in braces and a faded T-shirt from a gymnastics meet.

For an hour, Mr. Yu zips along the highway and brakes erratically in traf-fic. He forces the van between two cars as confidently as if our vehicle were a motorbike. The cars part to create a third lane on the two-lane highway. We bounce along in our newly created lane, off on an adventure or maybe a fool's errand, in search of a mythical face in a picture, someone who might remember the girl nodding off in the backseat: a man who once loosened her small fingers from his shirt and placed her hand gently in my hand as if to say, *here, she is yours now,* while his eyes flickered as if with regretful deter-mination. Based on expressions and gestures I might have misread, based on a baby's giggle and grip ten years ago, we are flying down the highway to locate a stranger, veering down another road and into the countryside in search of the Man.

Chapter One

Ten Days Earlier

11:30 A.M.

When we board a plane for China carrying that picture of the Man, I know it's unlikely that we'll unearth much information about my daughter's past. In fact, by the time we finally hand our boarding passes over to the agent and head down the tunnel, I've almost forgotten why it seemed so important to go back to China, why I saved and prepared for this trip for years.

Events have ganged up over the last few months to suggest that perhaps this isn't the best time for a homeland tour. My mother died, the economy tanked, prices soared in Beijing during the Olympics, and no one else signed up for the tour. Sophie has been mercurial and volatile the last few weeks, excited but easily frustrated, happy one moment, irrationally angry the next. My credit card was refused at Dulles, and I spent a four-hour layover on the phone straightening things out with the bank, who'd put a hold on the card after I'd used it in Buffalo this morning to buy food and magazines. I'd often used a credit card in Buffalo, but at 6:00 A.M.? Unheard of. I have to admire the alertness of the credit card company, even while I feel a weird dread that this whole trip might be a bad idea, even while I feel unmoored as I always do the first few days away from the house that anchors me.

And now there is another problem: we have been ticketed to sit five seats apart, which might as well be on opposite sides of the moon, the jetliner is so vast, and Sophie has no intention of sitting down until we are given seats together. She fiercely clutches my jacket sleeve, both of us standing jammed behind the last row in the first-class cabin. Others pass in an orderly shuffle: a British guy in black dress shoes with no socks, cell phone glued to his ear; an Asian student turtled by a bulging backpack; white businessmen swinging weathered leather briefcases. They all stare straight ahead, flinching at the sobbing ten-year-old. They heave luggage into overhead bins and slide into seats.

"Mommy!" Sophie cries, her voice ragged, edging toward hysteria.

"Just ask someone to switch with you," the ticket agent had told us earlier. But when I did, the elderly woman in the seat next to mine set her jaw and stared straight ahead, unbudging, not to be guilted from her aisle seat. I was equally reluctant to give up my window seat. It seemed important for Sophie and me to be able to look out together to see China come into focus.

"Just sit down," a flight attendant yelled at us. Sophie refused. I saw her point. Sitting down would be akin to giving in. We remained in the aisle. "Excuse me," other passengers said politely, at first. "Get out of the way," they finally started hissing.

Which is how we've ended up the recipients of the glares of first-class passengers, reclining with their martinis while my child fists her hand around my wrist like a shackle and implores me not to leave her. Here we are, on the brink of our long-awaited, long-saved-for trip to my daughter's birthplace, with no place to sit.

At ten, Sophie has started sneaking eyeliner and polishing her nails black. She normally hides under skater caps and hoodies with grinning rows of toothless skulls. Strangers flinch at this child who labels herself like a box of poison, and I wish they would look closer at the skulls, some with hearts for eyes, some with bunny ears. I wish they would look closer, period.

Even while I defend her, my daughter often peers at me through smoky eyes, cap pulled low, looking defiantly, prematurely adolescent. She is unpredictable, slipping in moments from argument to hug, cuddle to bristle, independent sophisticate to needy small child.

Like now. Makeup free, skulls left at home lest the images be even more misunderstood in the culture of her birth, she resembles the sharp-eyed, chubby-cheeked baby I met in China almost ten years ago. All morning, I've been remembering that angry, cranky baby who never slept and dissolved abruptly into wails or giggles. All morning, since she rose at 4:30, Sophie has been chattery and ebullient, preoccupied with thoughts of the birthparents she might never know and places she can't remember. "I'm going home!" she has said again and again.

It jars me to hear her say that, especially so close on the heels of my mother's death. I still don't quite believe that my mother is gone. Oh, yeah, I'll think. She died. The words seem so stark, the fact of them raw, startling. That loss is too close. How can I possibly give any part of my daughter back to China right now? Is it really the best time to encourage the part of her identity that is rooted in a whole different culture and country?

From the time I met her, she has had difficulty handling separation from me, her one and only parent, her only family in a thousand miles. And though I fought the total loss of independence that single parenthood necessitated, I gradually came to accept that I don't like to be apart from her either, that professional goals and other personal relationships have to go on the back burner for now. "Are there many other single faculty?" a new colleague recently asked me, and for a second I was confused. Other besides who? I wondered, then realized she meant me.

Though I'm unmarried, I exist in the plural. Even more so than divorced parents or families with helpful relatives living nearby, I always come with an attachment. And my life is so full and busy, sometimes it feels like there is more than one of me. There has to be to maintain two jobs, raise a child, and take care of a house. I've been known to refer to myself as "We," as in "We're trying to decide when to go back to China." Then I think, who is we? Did I just turn royal? Am I really including a child in such a big decision? But the fact is, I have to do so much, decide so much, I sometimes forget that I am, in fact, doing this alone.

But right this minute? Right now—wedged behind a bunch of seats, unable to reassure Sophie or fix the problem—I am fully aware that I am the lone adult responsible for my daughter's welfare, and feel, irrationally, that I'm about to lose everything. Before the seating crisis, this day was Sophie's dream come true. She has yearned for as long as she can remember to see China. Some very young children returning to their homelands are afraid that their parents mean to leave them there. Sophie is old enough to understand that this is just a visit, that we are a family forever. I'm the one who's scared— scared that she won't want to come back. And now that she's upset at the idea of our being separated, my dread gives way to a touch of relief: she's not, after all, ready to do without me.

11:38 A.M.

If your child is going to melt down while boarding a plane and no one will help you, the first-class cabin is a strategic choice of location. The overworked, seemingly indifferent flight attendant is coaxed to rescue us by the annoyance of those who've paid for comfort and quiet. She whisks us off the plane. Back at the ticket counter, everyone is eager to repair damage and offer reassurance. A few clicks on a computer keyboard, the whir of a printer, and we have new seats, by a window.

We retreat gratefully to our places, still a little shaken. Will we have to fight this whole trip to prove that we belong together? Earlier today, in the airport, someone asked me if Sophie's father was Chinese. The correct answer, of course, is yes; my favorite answer is, "I don't know. I never saw him." But I knew what the stranger was really asking, so I replied, "I adopted her from China." At the gate, an agent inquired if Sophie had a Chinese passport. Already this morning the bond we take for granted seems more precarious than usual in the eyes of others.

This kind of thing occurs far less frequently in the area where we live, where people know us. But every now and then it happens there, too, like once at the library we frequent in Olean, New York, when an Asian woman reported that she couldn't find her twelve-year-old daughter. At that moment, Sophie, then six, emerged from the picture book stacks, prompting employees to cry out, "Here she is!"

"This is *my* daughter." I hastened over. The other mother went off to search the carrels along the wall. But one employee narrowed her eyes at me and called in a triumphantly insistent tone to the other mother, "But we've found her! This is her!" She watched Sophie and me all the way out of the library, gaze darting to the phone as if she were considering calling the police to report me for kidnapping.

We laughed about this later. We've also laughed at restaurants with our Korean-American friend Ruth, Manjit from Malaysia, Flora from Taiwan, and Kyoko from Japan; waitstaff inevitably get annoyed when they ask if Sophie needs a kid's menu or what she wants to drink and I'm the one who answers. Last summer, when I was in Prince Edward Island, pretending that my companions Micquel, Mahita, and Sophie were all my daughters, a fellow tourist wrecked my fantasy by assuming that fifteen-year-old Mahita, whose parents are from India, was my ten-year-old daughter's mother.

Mostly we roll our eyes at the expectation that real families have to match, because whatever anyone else thinks, we know we are a real family. Sometimes I wear one white sock and one brown one, my little protest. But in China, our differences will be even more visible. I don't know whether that will affirm our connection or create a rift. Maybe a little of both.

12:00 P.M.

Even settled in our seats, the backs so high it's like we're in our own little cell, Sophie keeps a bone-crushing grip on my hand, which is still partly numb and starting to tingle from our minor crisis. All morning she's held onto me, grasping at my sleeve, inadvertently pinching my arm instead, fisting out blindly like she did as a baby. Ten years ago on the plane home from China, she had to hang tightly to a wad of my sleeve before she could go to sleep, claiming me, converting me to a security object, like a blanket or a stuffed animal.

"Ow," I say now. "You're pinching me."

She briefly releases her hold but goes on chattering. As our plane takes off, unmooring us from time and our own familiar language, we pass gossip magazines back and forth. They report on Paul Newman's death, Heather Locklear's most recent breakdown, and Taylor Swift's wardrobe. Voices hum and buzz around us, languages indistinguishable over the plane's snoring machinery breath. A map on our TV screens shows us winging over the Queen Elizabeth Islands, North America below us, Alaska off to our right. We watch *Baby Mama* and eat the pretzel we bought at the airport. I write in my journal.

Ten years ago I was flying this same route to become the terrified new mother of an intense, noisy baby with quick eyes, alert and watchful, the eyes of an old soul. She screamed a lot. A rash blossomed across her cheeks when she got too hot. She guarded vigilantly against sleep, against missing anything. Her Chinese name, Ni Qiao Qin, means smart and musical.

The girl next to me still hates to sleep. She practices handstands against the bathroom mirror, handsprings onto the couch, front tucks onto the guest room bed, beam dismounts into swimming pools. She wiggles and jiggles even while lying down. She spikes a fever in hot, crowded places. She yells at me from upstairs when I'm downstairs and downstairs when I'm upstairs and gets mad when I don't turn off the water, lower my book, pause the exercise bike, or set down pots and pans and wait in perfect stillness to absorb her words.

But even when I'm irritable and impatient, I feel lucky to be the mother of this smart and musical daughter who can beat anyone at Mancala, charm all the world's dogs, explain my cell phone and camera to me, and reflect with a combination of ancient wisdom and child logic on race, religion, and culture. She has read all about Harriet Tubman, Rosa Parks, the Little Rock Nine, and Martin Luther King Jr. She reads books about the Holocaust and has declared herself Jewish, except she is also drawn to African American spirituals.

And she can dance. I was shocked to discover this. After all, the first time she was in a dance recital, she just stood under bright lights in a fluffy pink tutu, sucking her finger. Fast forward two years. The music struck up— "Man, I Feel Like a Woman." Six-year-olds in peach leggings and fancy updos flounced out, swaying their hips self-consciously, glancing at one another for cues about what to do next, each movement a confused afterthought. They cut their eyes toward their neighbors, then lifted their hands and feet with careful puzzlement, as if their body parts were breakable souvenirs from distant lands.

All but the girl in the middle, whose arms and hips swung, whose feet were quick and sure. She stared into bright lights and flicked her leg back, confident and sassy, turned sideways and cast a glance over her shoulder, defiant and self-possessed. This was my daughter? I dropped my magazine. I bolted up in my seat. This was my daughter.

I'd been taking tap classes for years, dragging Sophie along to color or do homework in the hall. Up until I saw her perform at that dress rehearsal, I had thought of dancing as my interest. And then, there was my daughter, so beyond me, so fully her own person, not always sure how she fit into the world but clearly at home in her own body, dancing.

Since then, for months following each recital, others ask me, "Where does she train?" "I couldn't take my eyes off her," they say. We routinely praise one another's children; it's a pleasant communal way that we reinforce our pride in them, not to be blown out of proportion. But I really believed these compliments, at least until my half-Korean friend Ruth told me that Sophie's dance performances most likely attracted attention because she looked different. It wasn't her exceptional talent, Ruth said.

How do you know? I wanted to demand. You haven't seen her dance.

7:00 P.M.

Someone behind me has thumped the back of my seat every ten seconds for the last seven hours. I'm used to the jolting the way I'm used to the turbulence as we rock and bump through space. A snack arrives: Chinese noodles with dried carrots, onions, and fish. Alaska is below us, the international date line ahead. I page through the *SkyMall* studying the unimaginable array of luggage, the '40s Marshmallow Bazooka, the Animatronic Singing and Talking Elvis, and the Gravity Defying Boots.

Sophie is too wired to read a book. She keeps flipping channels on her TV. If I ever doubted the importance of taking her to China, I see now how right the decision was, how much it means to her to be going. "She's American now," people often say, puzzled, when I talk about her need to connect to her roots. Most parents have been influenced by the cultural checklist of duties that comes with having children, the injunctions we've absorbed about how to promote our children's healthy development. But interracial and intercountry adoption comes with even more obligations.

Most of us stick safety plugs in electrical sockets and gate off the stairs when our babies become mobile. We tick off developmental milestones during the first few years, eventually sign up our children for swimming lessons and summer soccer, help with homework, attend recitals, concerts, performances, games, and meets, volunteer at the schools. If cultural pressure regarding parental vigilance and involvement isn't stressful enough, adoption-related listservs brim with zealous parents who take it as a given that all of us who adopt from China must enroll our children in Mandarin classes, maybe even Chinese art and dance. At the very least we must find some way to celebrate the Moon Festival and Lunar New Year, seek out lion dances and acrobatic shows and cultural festivals and culture camps. Then there are those overachievers who hire Chinese babysitters, send their children to language-immersion schools, and make repeated return visits to China. Sophie found a story in a magazine about a fourteen-year-old girl who had traveled to China fourteen times. "Fourteen times!" Sophie says periodically. "She gets to go every year. How come she gets to go every year?"

On the flip side are comments I've heard from people I know of Chinese descent. "Why are American parents so concerned about teaching Chinese culture?" they ask, bewildered. After all, as Karin Evans points out in a book I read soon after I brought Sophie home, *The Lost Daughters of China,* children growing up in urban areas of China are often more familiar with American culture than they are traditional Chinese ways, wearing Mickey Mouse watches, eating at Pizza Hut, watching Big Bird on TV, and being introduced to the Chinese folktale "Fu Mulan" through the Disney animated movie.

Even when some expectations seem to be a bit overboard, I've found many articles and listserv arguments to be very convincing. Adoption professionals and adult adoptees emphasize how important understanding the birth culture is to becoming a well-adjusted, balanced, integrated adult, how important it is to the process of gaining perspective and finding a sense of belonging. So I've made long drives to holiday celebrations, remained ever-alert for families who look like ours and for events in our area, and booked flights to culture camp. And I have to admit that as Sophie gets older, the wisdom of the advice I've read becomes more and more evident. I see how essential it is for my daughter, one of a few nonwhite children in our northwestern Pennsylvania small town, to take pride in her heritage, to be knowledgeable about it whether or not she chooses to answer the many questions directed her way, to feel she's not alone, to know that there's a country full of people who look like her.

I often feel like I'm way behind in the race to offer my child proper exposure to Chinese culture, though. Child welfare consultants, adoption social workers, trauma and loss therapists, and professors of pediatrics and child development tend to agree: heritage trips, once strongly recommended, are an essential rite of passage for adopted children, especially those from China. In general, children from China know little about their pasts. A return trip can at least fill in some gaps, help them gain comfort and familiarity with their birth country, and replace their fantasies with a real picture of their original home in all its complexity. Professionals who sing the praises of homeland trips claim that they instill confidence, pride, greater independence, and the ability to build stronger relationships.

I hope that our trip will help my daughter work through her ambivalence about being American. She's uneasy with patriotic rhetoric that assumes American superiority. When teachers say, "In America, anyone can grow up to be president," she thinks, "Not me." Asian immigrants were denied U.S. citizenship as late as the 1940s. My daughter herself came to this country on a green card, which gave her permission, at the age of ten months, to work, and despite new laws that conferred citizenship on children adopted overseas, has never been issued citizenship papers. They were not automatically provided to children retroactively affected by the Child Citizenship Act of 2000. After spending several days and suffering many headaches trying to figure out how to apply for them, I gave up and got Sophie a passport instead, hoping it would suffice as proof of citizenship.

Such complications exist for many internationally adopted children as they come to terms with what it means to be American. Right now, Sophie prefers to be called *Asian,* not *Asian-American.* I hope that going back to China will introduce new perspective and help her become comfortable with both sides of the hyphen, figure out how to be both Chinese and American, together.

Of course, theoretically, she knows that China is a country full of people that look like her, but there is a world of difference between hearing or reading about a place and being there. This hit home to me when, in third grade, Sophie showed me her Columbus Day assignment, to create a drawing of an undiscovered land. What land, we pondered, hadn't been discovered yet?

Outer space, she said. Another planet.

Okay, I answered. Draw it.

Since she didn't remember anything about China, it was, to her, the ultimate undiscovered land. Inspired, she put pencil to paper, then stalled, lead poised on the brink of a line, a curve.

"I don't know what it looks like," she said.

For the first time, it occurred to me that she didn't even have the Blue Willow china pattern as a frame of reference. I slid *A Day in the Life of China* from its permanent home on the bottom shelf of the coffee table. She flipped to the portrait of Mao Tse Tung in Tiananmen Square. "I'm going to draw him," she said, and set to work sketching her undiscovered land, the big bald head of Chairman Mao.

I hid my face behind *Wuthering Heights* while I fended off seizures of laughter. She probably now thinks that Emily Bronte was the author of particularly witty works of chick lit, because I laughed until tears streamed down my cheeks every time I peered around my book to follow the progress of the Communist dictator.

"Mao," she wrote. "A great man."

My heart constricted and my throat swelled. I've never gotten used to that sudden press of tears behind my eyelids, as if parenthood implanted in me some sentimental chip that causes this startling emotional reaction whenever a child I know does something especially brave or poignant. My daughter so trustfully idealized her homeland. She so unquestioningly idealized this man about whom most Chinese say, "70 percent good, 30 percent bad," a great revolutionary who transformed China into a world power, a poet and visionary who also encouraged overpopulation to the point of starvation and instituted a violent cultural revolution that persecuted artists and educators, destroyed traditional cultural heritage, and led to the deaths of millions. But who also said, "Women hold up half the sky" and outlawed prostitution, child marriage, and child concubinage.

I doubted that her teacher would be familiar with the complexity of Mao's legacy, but just the words *communist leader* are enough to make many Americans shudder. Would the teacher respond with horror to Sophie's admiration? Would she dock her for not following directions? I worried, as I often do, pointlessly; her teacher never really looked at the assignment. All week, though, our friends asked Sophie what she'd drawn for Columbus Day just to hear her answer proudly, "Mao Tse Tung." "Mousie Tongue?" they'd say, as if we were talking about the taste buds of a small rodent. Then they'd laugh and laugh.

I want Sophie to come away from China proud of her birth culture, but I wonder if she will also be disillusioned by the realities of oppressive government policies, a lower standard of living, a language barrier. Maybe I secretly hope for this, for a more realistic look at the whole picture. Maybe I secretly hope this will keep her from using China as ammunition against me, wishing for her first home and birthparents whenever she's mad.

8:50 P.M.

We're north of Siberia, Sapporo, Tokyo, and Guam. Beijing appears on the plane's map. Sophie high-fives me. "Soon I'll be home," she says. Her tone is joyful. There is none of the animosity with which she sometimes says, "You're not my real mother." She is bursting with excitement and anticipation.

I feel a pang, but I don't want to discourage honesty, so I just squeeze her hand. She dreamily watches TV. I start jotting in my journal again. I'm not sure I really understand what it means to fit in, to belong, to feel at home. That is not something I've often experienced myself. But of course, even when the people around me don't seem to be from my tribe, I can blend in. I can choose to open my mouth and reveal my differences or walk away unnoticed. I take for granted the cultural heritage into which I was born, reflected with variations everywhere I go in the U.S. Over the years, I've tried to be alert to the ways that my daughter's experience differs from mine, often anxious about it while still fascinated at how the world looks through her eyes.

Once, my friend Ruth, my invaluable resource for insight into what it means to be Asian in a white community, told me a story about her childhood. In 1970, in Wichita, Kansas, she was part of a church children's choir that sang "Jesus Loves the Little Children." They lined up in a straggling row before the congregation, the director marching up and down, adjusting them; at least that is the way I picture it. Soon they were as perfectly aligned as birds perched on a wire, the too-big sleeves of their flowing white gowns drooping like tired wings. The children clasped their hands. "Red and yellow, black and white, they are precious in his sight," they sang, and on *yellow,* the choir director nodded at Ruth. Ruth took a step forward. Even at seven, she felt foolish and embarrassed, standing there alone for the heartbeat it took the choir to reach the word *white.* That was the cue for the rest of the children. They stepped forward to join Ruth.

Maybe it's not always so blatant, Ruth said when she told me this story thirty years later. But a child who is different in a homogenous community will know what it is to feel singled out.

I thought about this often when Sophie was little, as the issue of race inevitably cropped up again and again. Once when she was four, Sophie said to me, "Can you pass me the skin-colored crayon?" She knelt beside the wobbly, loose-legged coffee table, coloring, surrounded by a spill of naked crayons. They were brighter without their paper labels, if harder to grip, and so she instantly stripped each one. I found the curled wraps under couch cushions and between bookshelves, printed with words like *carnation pink, scarlet, dandelion, apricot.*

At first I thought maybe I hadn't heard her right. "The what?" I asked.

"The skin-colored crayon," she said patiently.

"Skin-colored?" I yelped. "What color is that?"

Sophie barely glanced up from filling in Cinderella's blue dress. She groped across the table for the peach crayon, the one that Crayola used to label *flesh.*

I laid the crayon against my arm, then hers. "My skin isn't this color and your skin isn't this color," I said, babbling in my frantic efforts to head off all the unconscious biases, all the thoughtless assumptions, all the unspoken ignorance my daughter would face, so much more difficult to address than outright slights. "How can it be skin-colored if no one's skin is this color? Who has skin this color?"

My daughter gently extracted the crayon from my hand and filled in Cinderella's face.

For weeks afterward, I presented her with bouquets of brown and tan crayons, all shades. "What color is this one?" I quizzed her. "And this one?"

"Skin-colored," she always answered promptly, humoring me.

Sometime during the next year, she stopped equating peach with flesh. Sometime during the next year, she began to drift toward books about black children and photos of black models in catalogues. Driving through Pittsburgh, we passed a woman pushing a stroller along a sidewalk. She popped gentle wheelies over the cracks while her baby laughed.

"There's someone just like me!" Sophie called happily from the backseat. She pointed at the woman and the baby. They were black. In just a few short months, my daughter had gone from imagining her skin as peach-colored to seeing it as a rich dark brown. "There's another one!" Sophie shrieked as we overtook a group of teenagers with loose-limbed swaggers and baggy pants. She was practically jumping out of her car seat with excitement. Hastily I rolled up her window as she pointed and screamed, "There's another one!"

Here I have to backtrack and correct myself. Recently, Sophie declared that she doesn't like the word *black.* She insists on *African-American. Negro* hacks her off. It sounds too close to the racial slur. And her sense of race has grown more complex as she's gotten older. She still feels a strong kinship to African-Americans, but she also wonders how she fits in a country where discussions of race tend to revolve around blacks and whites.

"If I lived before Martin Luther King," she said at dinner with friends once, "would I sit on the black side, or the white side?"

The children at the table, all white, hastily assured her: the white side, of course. Sophie was skeptical. Anyway, she wasn't quite sure she wanted to sit on the white side. In her firm and joyous identification with African-Americans, she does not perceive how, in a white community, she is mostly treated as an honorary white, or as part of a "model minority," a stereotype that, while positive, carries its own pressures. She does not yet see the advantages or liabilities of well-meaning attitudes that both accord her privileges and erase a vital part of her.

"Don't you feel rejected when she identifies with African-Americans, not you?" friends used to ask. It had never occurred to me to feel hurt by this. I'd read articles and books about raising a child of another race in a world where colorblindness and assimilation are no longer regarded as healthy or desirable goals. I'd paid attention to a generation of adult Korean adoptees who caution white parents not to ignore difference. I'd pondered studies showing that around second grade, Asian and black children raised by white parents tend to start wishing they were white, tend to feel white inside and to be surprised by their reflections in the mirror. I did not want this to happen to my child. I embraced her differences, with no plans to feel hurt by her search for the place where she belonged. Every month, I put money into a savings account so we could go to China someday.

The last few months, ever since I paid the tour deposit and we started planning this trip in earnest, Sophie has been more moody and difficult than usual. She mutters "don't care" or worse when she thinks I'm reprimanding her. When she's mad, she bangs her rolling desk chair against other furniture. She can howl and scream like she did back when she was two or three. Was this a mistake, I wondered, planning a trip back? Is it awakening dormant feelings better left alone?

But I kept plowing forward, hopeful as I read about homeland visits on listservs and in blogs and articles, full of testimonials like the ones in the book *From Home to Homeland:* "She emerged from a shell that had held her apart from others." "She smiles more, more radiantly." "She became lighter, happier, as if she had reached some kind of resolution to the questions that had been dogging her all year." "We saw big changes in our daughter. She clearly felt firmly and securely part of our family . . . she became a calmer, more centered person. She knows who she is, where she comes from, and where she belongs."

I read some of these to Sophie, and she rolled her eyes. She has been expert at rolling her eyes since she was about three. I still believe that there's truth to these accounts and am pretty sure that the last few months have been a necessary stage, the fluctuating weather of processing difficult events, the storms that are necessary for calm to return.

～

12:45 A.M.

"When is daytime ever going to end?" Sophie asks as the sun burns on, never setting. We can see the earth below: China. It's not sectioned off like the farmlands of my native Midwest, or heavily forested like the area where we live now. China looks rugged, treeless, carved from rock. In the distance, mountains loom.

Sophie's eyes droop. She's slept in brief spurts, leaning against my arm until it's numb, then wakened, wired and bouncy, jiggling to keep herself from drifting off again. Over the years, the roundness of her toddler cheeks has disappeared, replaced by sculpted cheekbones. Now I feel like already I'm seeing peace steal over her features after a tumultuous year. As tired as she is right now, she looks nothing like the girl who's glared the last few months from dark eyes made darker and more mysterious by skillfully applied eyeliner. Makeup-free, eyes bright with anticipation, she's a little girl again, straining to see out the window. Children, I think, are like kaleidoscopes, cycling through variations of the same patterns, constantly revealing new versions of their complex selves.

Other parents, mostly American-born, have told me that I should forbid makeup. Friends from other countries compliment her. I've never been willing to wage any wars over cosmetics. Until Sophie had braces, I didn't battle over gum chewing, either. I've said nothing negative about the whole sleeve of bracelets that normally jangle on her forearm or the embroidery-floss-and-bead bracelets that armor her ankles, any of the things that make her look grown-up or self sufficient or distant or rebellious or different, so different, from me, her blond, blue-eyed mom too impatient to bother with much makeup or jewelry.

Right now we are united as we lean forward together and look at the ground, watching as it comes closer, this land that changed both of our lives so completely.

1:30 A.M.

We switch places so Sophie can watch our descent, face flattened against the window as Beijing appears. It's 1:30 A.M. our time, but 1:30 P.M. in Beijing. Tall buildings stick up out of the ground in random places, like slabs of gravestones in an old cemetery. We should be hopelessly exhausted, but excitement arcs between us like the sparks of static electricity we exchange in winter.

The plane touches down, bumping onto its wheels. We cruise into a gate, a whole world of knowledge and experience away from the last time I landed here.

We're in China. Sophie is home.

Chapter Two

When Sophie was about six, she first heard Iris DeMent's agnostic anthem, "Let the Mystery Be" on an old tape I was playing in the car: "Everybody keeps wondering what and where they all came from. . ."

"Play that again," Sophie said from the backseat, so I rewound and replayed.

"Again," she said. It's a playful, catchy song, but it surprised me that she kept wanting to hear what was essentially a philosophical examination of religious beliefs about human origins and the afterlife.

Finally, she asked, "Is that song about adoption?" and it all became clear to me. These weren't existential questions for her. She wanted to know, quite literally, what and where she came from.

Not long after, she requested Paul Simon's "Born at the Right Time" over and over again:

> Down among the reeds and rushes, a baby boy was found
> His eyes were clear as centuries, his silky hair was brown. . .

Whenever I heard that song, I thought of my own clear-eyed, dark-haired baby girl, found, according to documents, on the steps of a police station. When I heard the song, I thought of the birth mother hidden somewhere between the lines. I wondered if my daughter also heard echoes of her own story in those words.

The birth mother question looms large for many adopted children. Classmates raise the issue in kindergarten and first-grade taunts: "Your real mother didn't want you!" Before we left for China, strangers and acquaintances were endlessly curious: were we going to see Sophie's family? Track down her birthparents? I can give a talk about race and culture and adoption, and at the end, someone will always ask, "But do you know her family?"

"We are each other's family," I tend to say, but I know what they mean, and the answer is no. In China, it remains illegal to abandon a child, to bear a non-government-approved child in the first place. Those having second, or in some places, third, children face heavy, sometimes crippling fines. There is no legal mechanism for placing a child for adoption. As much as many adopted Chinese children would like to meet their birthparents, we don't know what risks seeking them could pose—even if we could find them in a country of 1.3 billion people.

All we have been promised is a tour of China. Toward the end, we will visit Sophie's orphanage, but it is hard to know what to expect. Most people go with many questions but get few answers. It would be nice to track down some link to my daughter's past, someone who knew and cared for her in the orphanage, someone who can fill in gaps and relieve, at least a little, the acute sense of loss reflected in the questions she sometimes asks. This is why I pack the picture of the man who brought Sophie to me. I know from hearing about the experiences of others that it is unlikely we will be able to track him down, to meet him, to talk to him. I just hope that we can find out who he was.

In my adult life, I have lived in six states and, until now, never spent more than five years anywhere. I often wonder what it feels like to know a place deeply, to live there forever, to have a firm concept of home. So I relate a little to my daughter's feeling of disconnection. I'm not quite sure what we'll find, but we're setting off for China because I believe the past is important. That was something I learned from my childhood friend Stacey.

"Your parents got stuck with you, but mine chose me," Stacey used to fling at me when we were in third grade. Indeed, the story went, Stacey, a beautiful olive-skinned, dark-eyed baby, was born to young married college students. It turns out that many adopted children were told this in the '60s, reassurance that they came from moral, educated people, as if it were too shameful to be the child of unwed high school dropouts. Told that Stacey was likely to be retarded, unable to assume such an overwhelming responsibility, the young couple who'd brought her into the world had magnanimously given her over to a better life.

I used to picture a warehouse lined with cribs containing babies in need of homes, a sort of humane society for orphans. I imagined Stacey's parents solemnly strolling between rows of gurgling babies, suddenly arrested by a cry, a laugh, big dark eyes, a supernatural recognition that this one, Stacey, was the one for them. Only then did they notice the laminated label hanging from the crib, like refrigerator warranty information at Sears. "May be retarded," it said.

"I don't care," said Stacey's mother in her gravelly voice, made rough by years of smoking. "I want this one."

I was a child when I imagined the adoption process as a sort of shopping expedition, but it's an image that remains pervasive, even among adults. I've been asked many times how I chose Sophie out of all those babies in a Chinese orphanage. I didn't. The Center for China Adoption stuck her photo in my file, and I became her mom.

I'll never know if Stacey's first mother drank, or if Stacey was deprived of oxygen during her birth, or what led doctors to predict retardation. But Stacey proved to be quite bright, a fact that added a dimension of tragedy to her story, an element of needless sacrifice. If only her birth parents had known, Stacey told me, sorrier for them than for herself, they could have been spared the great grief of her loss.

Instead, she'd ended up in a family who doted on her. Their triumph and adoration shone on their faces whenever they beheld her. Visiting their house, I always sensed that her mother was comparing me unfavorably to Stacey. She gazed at me with disconcerting narrow-eyed disapproval if I spoke. Then she lit up, smug, when Stacey bested me in any game, banter, or academic subject. Stacey was fond of pointing out that she was smarter and prettier than I was, in addition to being more generally mature and interesting.

Stacey could be warm and funny and vivacious, and up to a point, I forgave her insults. I knew how haunted she was, even when she was very young: I remember her as a wistful child full of wild yearning. At five she'd danced onstage to her brother's band wearing an outfit that included white go-go boots. She stole the show. The audience went crazy, applauding and cheering. For all the years that I knew Stacey, kindergarten up to high school, she wanted that day back, the go-go boots, the confidence, the love and acceptance, applause and compliments.

Stacey's ethnic origins were something that we never talked about. In the third grade, I was shocked and horrified when Stacey said of African-Americans, "They're not like us. We think they should stay in their own neighborhoods and schools and TV shows." At eight, I had never been exposed to racism. My religious parents had always emphasized the equality of all humanity in the eyes of God. I gaped at Stacey, alarmed that she could really believe anything like that. It never occurred to me until adulthood that though she was brought up as white, she herself may have had Latino or mixed-race origins. It never occurred to me that her longing for love and attention, her obsession with her looks, might have had something to do with more than go-go boots.

By third grade, her deep longing landed on a socially approved target: Donny Osmond, a handsome young singer who might have been her brother. Stacey composed fan letters and went all dreamy-eyed when "Go Away Little Girl" played at the skating rink. It puzzled me that she thought he was addressing her yet still didn't get the message that he wanted her to go away.

By seventh grade, Stacey finally accepted the rebuff and transferred her affections to a more manly object: Paul Michael Glaser from the TV show *Starsky and Hutch,* a swarthy actor who could have been her father. In eighth grade, Stacey decided to be more realistic in her pursuit of unrequited love. She took to stalking ninth-grade heartthrobs in the school halls, squealing when they noticed her and writing long accounts about the occasions when her eyes met theirs across the room. Her most high-profile long-term eighth-grade crush was a ninth-grader from a Lebanese background named Paul, so masculine that a curly tangle of black hair burst forth above his collar no matter how high he buttoned his shirt, which wasn't actually very high. Every time she glimpsed it, Stacey swooned.

By high school, Stacey and I moved in different circles. I don't know if she had a favorite class, a best friend, or a boyfriend. I don't know if she ever considered searching for her birth parents. I heard that she was a groupie for some rock band, and I pictured her sometimes dancing on stage with them, maybe even in white go-go boots. At nineteen, long after we'd lost touch, Stacey was killed in a car wreck. She died near the corner of Harry and Greenwich, less than a quarter mile from my house.

The next day, I drove to that stretch of Harry Street, examining it for skid marks or broken glass. I was oddly furious with Stacey, the friend with whom I'd made up secret codes, reenacted Carol Burnett skits, written plays, sung, "I'm Enery the Eighth I am" in bad British accents, rolled my eyes for a whole day when she responded to every mundane comment with "That tickles me pink!" and a trill of manic giggles. Why, why, I wondered, merciless in my anger, had she wasted so much of her life chasing what she couldn't have?

Now, Stacey's yearning makes poignant sense. Now I understand how much her insecurities and longings laid groundwork for me to raise my own adopted child. Now I understand the deep impressions made on me by the adoptions of three cousins. I understand how influenced I was when a Korean girl at my elementary school named Linda spoke to my class about how she'd lived on the streets of Seoul until she was six. I recognize how my friends Julie and Lee and Tina shaped my beliefs about adoption. Every one of them was deeply attached to the family that raised them. But I was frequently exasperated by the compulsions of Lee and Tina to endlessly prove themselves and be the centers of attention, beloved by all. Maybe it was just a coincidence that both had been adopted.

Nevertheless, I went into parenthood with the firm belief that it's normal to want to know about our pasts, that loss inevitably shapes us. I went in with every intention of confronting my daughter's questions head-on and making sure I kept her connected to Chinese culture and other adoptees. But when she asked me, "Is that song about adoption?" I was taken by surprise.

Being prepared turned out to be harder than it looked.

At two, Sophie didn't know what adoption or birth parents were, but I felt a duty to start the conversation, especially when we moved from a southern small town where people knew our story to the Northeast where I was regularly, startlingly deluged with questions. Where was Sophie from? Was I going to tell her she was adopted? Did I know her family? Did she know her family? I answered patiently: China, I think the secret is out, I am her family, but no, most children adopted from China can't know their original families.

The first time I told Sophie that she had had another mother before me, my throat tried to close and trap the words inside. I swallowed hard and they stumbled out anyway, but I didn't really believe them. And yet I felt this other mother, this other sorrowing woman, come between us. Objectively, of course, I don't know that this woman is sorrowful, but I can't help but believe it after reading many accounts that were written or dictated by birth mothers. "People might say that a woman who abandons her baby must have a heart of stone," writes Chinese journalist Xinran, who interviewed many anonymous birth parents for her book *Message from an Unknown Chinese Mother*. "But everything I saw and heard told me this was almost never the case." It irritates me when people assume that Chinese birth parents somehow come from a different, less human, species than Western ones, that they suffer less when they lose a child.

Some of my adopted cousins and friends are fiercely pro-life, believing that their birth mothers didn't want them but at least had the moral courage or generosity not to kill them. Often, as an adoptive parent, I'm presumed to also be against abortion rights even though I'm adamantly pro-choice. I don't believe that, in general, birth parents don't "want" their children. Often they didn't see themselves as having real choices—as they didn't in the U. S. before *Roe v. Wade.*

In accounts by U. S. birth mothers, women and girls who "chose" adoption were largely impoverished, young, single, lacking in family support, deeply anguished and afraid, and/or the objects of familial and institutional coercion. Coercive rhetoric lives on in the conservative Christian agency that handled my own daughter's adoption to a single parent. Their monthly magazine routinely celebrates the inspiring, selfless sacrifices of single, pregnant American women who inevitably understand that their babies would be better off with Christian married couples. In almost every article by a birth mother, the author considers whether being a single mother is in her child's best interest and ultimately concludes that her child deserves two parents, including a mother who stays home full time.

Such articles are always followed by pieces by couples praising God for willing their adopted children to be theirs. Once when I did a quick Internet search using the key words *adoption* and *single parenthood,* I found not information that addressed my situation, but instead articles with titles like, "Adoption Should be Encouraged as an Alternative to Abortion and Single Parenthood." If equating single parenthood with abortion is so prevalent in some circles, I imagine how embedded these single birth mother/adoptive couple dichotomies must have been thirty, forty, fifty years ago, how intensified the rhetoric. In account after account, women report being manipulated into believing that they were inadequate, morally corrupt, or otherwise unqualified for parenthood. Many did not make free or informed choices to relinquish their babies.

When I read these condescending views of the qualifications of unwed and impoverished birth mothers, I understand better a predominant assumption among many adoptive parents, that we are the superior choice to raise our children. At least attitudes have shifted somewhat in the U. S., with open adoption so common. Parents who adopt domestically no longer have to rely so much on speculation. Many maintain enough connection to birth parents to avoid excessively negative or overly romantic portrayals of them, which are recognized not to be in the best interest of our children. But in cases of foreign adoption, where less information is available, there are still many who cling to an image of heartless Chinese birth mothers who coldly reject their children.

In one of my favorite novels, Amy Tan's *Joy Luck Club,* the main character, Jing Mei Woo, learns as a child that her mother once abandoned twin baby girls in China. Jing Mei pictures her mother matter-of-factly unloading two wailing babies under a tree and gallivanting off to a freer life. But when she's an adult, after her mother's death, Jing Mei hears from her father the real, heartbreaking story. In his version, her mother is desperately ill with dysentery as she flees her home during war, then stumbles along with two babies and nowhere to go. Fearing she will be found dead next to her babies, drawing bad luck to them, dooming their futures, she tenderly lays them on the ground, leaving jewelry and a note promising more to the person who finds and returns them to her.

In contrast to the suspicion and disapproval historically attached to birth mothers, adoptive parents have been typically granted a patina of saint-hood as if our desire to raise children somehow exists on a higher plane than the desires of biological parents. But periodically, there's a reversal of this when suspicion of adoption emerges in high-profile news stories that focus on the attachment disorders of some Russian-born children, accu-sations of child trafficking in Guatemala, and celebrities who seem to be bypassing the rules to adopt children, as Madonna did in Malawi, who are not technically orphans. Once-canonized adoptive parents find themselves vilified by some of these stories as questions arise: are white, comparatively wealthy Westerners inadvertently contributing to corruption when they go overseas to adopt? American parents have been shocked to learn that not all Chinese birth mothers willingly give up their babies, that government officials have been known to forcibly remove "illegal" children from loving homes.

But whether government representatives seize babies or "merely" enact a law fining and punishing families who have too many children, there is little real choice in many decisions to abandon babies. Birth mothers in China are coerced every bit as much as those in the U. S. once were, if not more: by laws, by in-laws, by the weight of tradition and fear of the future. What do you do when there's no social security system or son to support you in your old age? In areas where the one-child policy is strictly enforced, Xinran writes, having more than one child can mean "losing your job, your home . . . your entitlement to food and clothing rations, your child's entitlement to school-ing and medical care, and even your chance of finding other work, as no one would dare employ you."

Although nothing approximating open adoption from China currently exists, I resolved that my child would not, if I could help it, be haunted the way I believed that Stacey had been. I resolved that I would find whatever information I could and talk openly about whatever issues arose. I cer-tainly never intended for the birth mother question to become an elephant in the room.

Addressing these issues was easier said than done. Finding a place to live, making another home, became imperative when I rather abruptly lost my job in one state and fled to another. Sophie was two when we landed in Bradford, Pennsylvania, a town of 8,000 in the Tuna Creek Valley, once a prosperous producer of oil and lumber, where in a depressed real estate market an enormous and beautiful if somewhat neglected old house could be had for $70,000.

"What's in Bradford?" a new acquaintance from California once asked me.

"Zippo!" I replied with enthusiasm.

"Oh, I'm sorry," he said, thinking I meant zippo, zilch, nada.

But in fact, I was talking about Zippo lighters, Bradford's enduring claim to fame. Here, near Zippo headquarters, the streetlights are shaped like lighters and a car resembling a large Zippo lighter makes its way down Main Street during every parade. The town annually holds a swap meet where people gather to buy and sell collectible lighters; the daily newspaper has a column tracing sightings of Zippo lighters in movies and on TV; and I routinely take visitors to the quirky, surprisingly charming museum that boasts artwork made from Zippos, historical displays, and exhibits of lighters that have been run over by tractors and crushed in garbage disposals.

Bradford is a working-class town where 16 percent of residents have college educations and many families live below the poverty level. In the early 1930s there were Chinese laundries here and a Jewish population substantial enough to support two synagogues. Now the population is more than 97 percent white, with a scattering of Jews, no more than ten or twelve families. The area is heavily Catholic, with fish fries at every restaurant on Friday night and displays of white first communion dresses in the girls' clothing section at Walmart.

People's lives here revolve around their children, around soccer and baseball games and dance recitals that routinely draw audiences of 1,200 doting family members—more than for any other cultural event in town. On prom night, spectators gather in the high school parking lot to watch teenagers in their finery arrive by limo, scooter, and, it wouldn't surprise me to learn, horse-drawn carriage. Entourages of parents, grandparents, aunts, and uncles are not unusual at the pediatrician's office, assembling for a child's annual checkups. One family I know is related to so many in town that if one of their daughters is interested in a boy, she has to clear it with her mother, who checks to make sure that the two are not distant cousins. As a single parent by choice of an Asian daughter, educated, firmly middle class, brought up Protestant but no longer practicing any religion, I felt early on like a foreigner getting to know a new culture. I knew that our differences would present challenges, as would finding connections to Chinese culture. But for those first few months, our strange house itself presented the biggest obstacles.

There were no elephants in the room, but there was some sort of animal scampering through our walls. I first heard it clicking and swishing four months after we moved in, while I was working intently at my computer, and at first I barely registered it. I imagined the brisk clip of stiletto heels across a parquet floor, the electricity of staticky hair through a comb. Then paws skittered along the wall inches from my feet. I reared up and rammed backward, suddenly fully aware of what I was hearing: the clatter of claws, the brush of fur.

I called an exterminator, who said we had rats. A neighbor thought my walls harbored a chipmunk or a skunk. "I think it's a baby elephant," Sophie volunteered.

Another exterminator told me that it was a red squirrel storing its stock of pinecones inside my walls. He suggested I call a business right over the New York border called Critter Getters.

An animal in my walls, as if I weren't already overwhelmed enough as a single parent in a new job, a new town, and a crumbling monstrosity of a house overlooking the Tuna Creek valley. My daughter didn't remember being torn from a life in China and transplanted to the U. S., but she did recall being ripped from a life in South Carolina, and at two, she was articulate enough to express her unhappiness: "I miss my house, I miss my room, I miss my yard!" she kept wailing.

I was still regularly surprised at where I had landed. China's adoption process is proactive and extremely deliberate. It requires questionnaires and interviews and notarized, state sealed, and translated documents. The process involves fingerprints and photographs; approval from the state, the U.S., and the Chinese governments; support groups and parenting books and bags of gifts and hand-me-downs to fill in the long periods of waiting. To help me get used to the idea of a baby, I set up a shelf of shoes—baby Birkenstocks and high tops and patent leather Sunday school slippers. With the slam of neighbors' doors and shifts of my apartment building, the shoes ended up at odd angles, as if arrested in the middle of a dance.

I couldn't have been more prepared and yet, even two years later, parenthood seemed like it had come about accidentally. It remained both an unfathomable miracle and a complicated morass. Even as I became a parent, the ties to my own parents were unraveling. I'd arrived home from China with my new baby, and only weeks later my dad had died of a cancer that had spread swiftly and silently, unnoticed until the end. I sat beside his bed and listened to his last breaths. Back in Kansas, lost without him, my mother had one small stroke after another.

Then all of a sudden, due to politics I never quite understood, I was facing unemployment. For college professors in the humanities, finding a new job, if it can even be done in most overcrowded fields, means relocating entirely. I had to sell my house, find a new job and a place to live, pack everything, and move—all with a toddler in tow. I knew, buying this house, that I was probably getting in over my head, but it seemed like the sort of place where a child ought to grow up. So far, I hadn't done such a good job of giving my daughter what she ought to have. Things like stability, grandparents, Families with Children from China gatherings, zoos, plays, craft activities, birthday parties. There had been too much stress for any of that.

But here was this storybook house, huge with a lopsided foundation to accommodate the slope of the mountain. That, along with yellow siding and purple trim, gave the exterior a pastel shapelessness reminiscent of a big hideous half-melted piece of candy. Inside there were window seats, gas fireplaces, built-in bookshelves and nightstands wired with small lights, high ceilings, rich woodwork, hardwood floors, and a spectacular landing. There, above the window seat, a sizeable picture window framed by beveled and stained glass turned sunlight to rainbows. Whenever I rounded the curve of banister, I found them splattered everywhere.

"Rainbows," Sophie liked to yell, stomping on them as if to squish them like bugs. Gently they relocated to the tips of her sneakers.

"Expect to replace the roof, furnace, windows, and garage within the next few years," said the inspection report. The hall wallpaper's clusters of pink flowers were as big as cabbages, as big as Sophie's head. The pink-and-green rose-and-trellis wallpaper in the master bedroom peeled off in patches to reveal bare walls, unlike the master bathroom, layered by five generations of green floral patterns. The shower was homemade, its mold and mildew undaunted by the Comet that stripped away the paint.

These were mostly cosmetic, I told myself, and anyway, the house was so cheap. The dishwasher left the kitchen smelling faintly of burnt rubber. The ancient oven threw sparks. The water heater repairman emitted one of those low whistles usually reserved for the discovery of dinosaur bones.

∿

I still occasionally have nightmares that I've bought a house with a whole third floor of rooms I'm afraid to enter. Some people say that houses are metaphors for our minds, that off-limits, haunted rooms represent secrets suppressed by the subconscious. I don't think mine stand for trauma so much as for those things over which we have no control.

Many northwest Pennsylvania homes have rooms their owners never enter. There's one in my basement, floorless except for wood planks, musty and cobwebby. A friend has a basement room with a dirt floor. She once opened the door and saw what appeared to be a bloody rag crumpled in the middle. She slammed the door and has never gone into this room. Mostly she keeps the door closed and pretends the room's not there. We came late to the histories of our houses and have to be alert for evidence of their stories, just as I came late to my daughter's history. And there are things we're not sure we really want to know.

Our first weeks in this house were full of surprises. Doors opened into unexpected spaces. Narrow stairs descended to a craggy basement with fissures in the floor filled by years of dust and dirt. I ducked through its many chambers—a laundry room with a sink, a storage area lined by cabinets labeled "Pigeons and Traps," "Scuba diving gear," "Football and Basketball." Another room with a worktable and tool rack, a tag dangling from an old electrical box: "Ask me about my friend Jesus." A nail hung with a pile of surgical masks, webbed inside by long-dead spiders. Leaning against the wall, someone's discarded painting of a barn. Another room with shelves lined with paint cans and rolls of wallpaper, some yellowed and crumbling. A small walled platform containing nothing but a toilet, once a popular feature for coal miners and oil field workers who could clean up in the basement before entering the rest of the house. Out the back door to the patio, a storage shed tucked under a grill porch. Upstairs again: a cubby in Sophie's bedroom, under the attic stairs, where she promptly dragged her crib mattress so she could sleep in there like Harry Potter. I sometimes heard her rattling the cellophane envelopes of junk mail in there and briefly mistook the sound for our wild animal.

I didn't find the extra closet in the bathroom, previously hidden by the open hall door, until I'd unpacked most of our possessions. And then there it was, another set of empty shelves. Other things were right in front of my eyes but just took me a while to notice. Like the slots in the medicine cabinets below tiny iron plates with raised letters flattened by time, now as difficult to decipher as a weathered tombstone: "Drop used razor blades here." I imagined the insides of the bathroom walls heaped with razor blades and the dust from eighty years' worth of whiskers.

Above the attic's many shelves and closets, doors opened to yet more cupboards. Sometimes it still felt as if I were living in one of those dreams in which there were whole worlds beyond my immediate vision, no longer scary but magical, those secret rooms hidden behind mirrors and walls, chamber after chamber.

I didn't know where to begin to get this house, our lives, in order. But every morning Sophie gave me her ritual hug, kiss, and push out of the preschool's door. She brought home papers on which she had outlined her hands and feet in endless overlapping repetitions. One day, upon hearing the title of a movie I'd rented, she stamped her foot and yelled, "I do not want to watch *The Princess's Diarrhea!*"

Some people think I "saved" my child from an orphanage. In fact, it was she who saved me, every day, in those moments that I understood that our house was like our life: rough around the edges but when it came right down to it, luckily, amazingly, structurally sound and breathtaking in its details.

Or so I thought, still think, hoping that I'm not delusional. Because of course there are always the rotting boards on the porch steps, the animal in the walls, the things you can't see, the words that, despite your best intentions, can't be spoken. Like the time when Sophie was two, and I told her she once had another mother, she clapped her hand over my mouth. She didn't want to hear it. Yet. It wasn't even an elephant in the room. It was safely, if disconcertingly, enclosed away, like the animal behind our walls.

Whenever I heard the animal's movements, I pictured a baby elephant loping along, small trunk curling and thumping from side to side, toenails tapping. As a child, I learned to draw the backside of an elephant: floppy ears, swishing tail, half-circle toenails. This is how I pictured our baby elephant, a cute little Dumbo fisting its trunk around acorns instead of peanuts. Teaching Ernest Hemingway's "Hills like White Elephants," I asked my students what the title suggested. The things we don't really want, they said, like white elephant sales, like the pregnancy in the story that challenges a shallow relationship. The thing in the room nobody talks about, they said.

I marched into international adoption with every intention of confronting head-on whatever arose, the questions and challenges faced by so many adopting from overseas, forming interracial or intercultural families, or parenting alone, without partners. None of these circumstances were any longer remarkable. Adoption was no longer shrouded in mystery, lies, silences, or shame. The existence of birth parents and the grief of adopted children were no longer supposed to be big secrets. Honesty would blaze a path through difficult territory, I thought.

But there was always too much to do. Carpets to take up, broken windows to replace, garage doors to repair, floors to refinish, leaks to fix, ceilings to replaster. There were questions to prepare for. There was heritage to instill when the only available resources were confusing Chinese-language tapes and the occasional traveling troupe of lion dancers or acrobats. There were books to read, CDs to play, trips back to China to save for. There was a name change to apply for, proof of citizenship to establish, a college account to start, a will to write, retirement accounts to build. I was no longer in a state of emergency, but now where did I begin? We read books. We walked to the park pulling behind us Sophie's wagon with her stuffed dog named Ozzie Osbourne. Ozzie had been washed so many times, his flattened fur looked tight as wool, and strangers mistook him for a lamb. Books and walks and meals and baths were all I could manage. Every day I asked Sophie what she did at day care, and she answered, "I was sad, I cried, I missed my mommy." Meaning me.

"She looks like an Indian," said the seven-year-old girl from next door. I darted a quick glance at Sophie, busy yanking a trike free of a tangle of toys in the neighbors' garage.

"She's from China," I said.

Laney's eyes widened. "Why didn't her real parents want her?"

Since that day, we have heard that question many times. Since that day, I've come to understand that not everyone grew up with adopted friends and cousins; not everyone sees adoption as a commonplace alternative way of forming a family. Laney's question was my first glimpse into that future, and it knocked the breath out of me. "That's not the way it works!" I snapped.

Sophie didn't appear to be listening as she tugged and maneuvered the trike. I took a breath and spoke in a level voice, just in case my daughter was really listening, just in case how I responded to this kind of query would shape the way she thought about her background. I explained that I was Sophie's real mom. I explained that your real parents are the ones who raise you.

After that, my explanation went downhill fast. I was lecturing a seven-year-old on a foreign country's complex political, social, and economic circumstances that leave children without families.

As I explained, furrows appeared on Laney's forehead. She didn't like this one-child policy one bit. She had three siblings.

"I'm glad I don't live in *that* country," Laney said.

I was up all night. I read and paced, disproportionately bothered by this conversation. I started some laundry, toppling Sophie's light-up sneakers into the washer with towels and socks. I wondered briefly if it was okay to wash those shoes with lights that flickered on impact.

I didn't understand the technology behind the shoes, but I did know that there was no electricity involved. I still felt as if I were teetering on the edge of risk as I dumped in detergent and turned on the spray of hot water. When we first bought those shoes, Sophie went leaping and bounding down the mall's walkway. The lights pulsed and stuttered. Sophie galloped and skipped and stared at her shoes, heedless of passersby who smiled and darted out of the way.

The shoes gently thumped against the washing machine barrel. And I thought: how could anyone imagine that someone wouldn't want my child?

I remembered my stunned reaction in China the moment I opened her documents and read her abandonment papers. Tears filmed my eyes as I imagined my baby, a fragile newborn, left on the steps of a police station. I tried to picture the person who had left her there, her birth mother or father, a grandparent. Maybe the family was holding out for a boy, or maybe they already had one or more daughters. Research by Kay Ann Johnson, who interviewed many Chinese families, suggests that only about one third of abandoned infant girls were born to families who were childless or already had sons. Most of the parents had already had between one and five daughters, some of whom had also been abandoned. It is statistically less likely, though possible, that my daughter's first mother was unmarried or poor.

At three, my daughter never forgot a song, a saying, or a promise. She was distinctly beautiful with big eyes and even features. She was witty, moody, stubborn, and resilient. She could be headstrong and high-strung. Somewhere in China there was a woman who shared my daughter's beauty, a woman with a quick mind and maybe some remnant of a child's flaring temper and tender heart. I simply couldn't, can't, believe that her first mother doesn't live day after day with a wrenching, unfathomable loss.

The shoes clanged in the washer, threatening to throw it off balance. I opened it to check on them. Pink, yellow, and blue lights flickered through white suds, incongruously festive down here in the middle of the night, like fireworks through the mist that hung low over the mountains early on autumn mornings. After the shoes battered the dryer for a while, I was pleased that they still worked. Except one shoe wouldn't stop lighting up on its own. Pink, yellow, and blue lights chased each other nonstop, like those in a Las Vegas marquee.

Once adoption had seemed simple: uniting a baby who needed a home with a home that needed a baby. That night, rocking and waiting for dawn, my vision started to change. I imagined another mother's losses, putting my toe in the water of my own griefs, filtering anguish into manageable doses of sorrow and compassion. In a bit I would shower, help Sophie get dressed, pour our cereal, and go on like someone not in mourning, someone whose greatest joy might be someone else's greatest sorrow.

At dawn I heard the animal stirring in the ceiling above me, stretching, then scurrying off on its morning patrol of my walls.

At a party, Sophie generously doled out M&Ms to other guests, but she wouldn't give me one. "You won't let your own mommy have an M&M?" I asked.

"Her second mom," the five-year-old daughter of friends corrected me. "You're not her mom, you're her second mom."

Well, yes, I answered, Sophie did have another mother before me, but I wasn't just her second mother, I was the only parent she'd ever known. I was Sophie's mom, I told Amy. Period. And I wondered if these conversations would ever feel less unsettling.

I tried to be patient with children who made these kinds of declarations, to give them latitude: they were literal creatures, trying to make sense of their world. But like many adoptive parents, I sometimes felt touchy about the persistence of outsiders in trying to define us. We felt pretty much like any other family, any other parent and child. It startled me that others didn't always think of us that way.

Only a few days later, our neighbor Laney's six-year-old brother, Abel, confronted me with visible hostility. "She's not yours," he said. "You bought her."

Abel was always calling Sophie names and running off with Ozzie Osbourne. I'd tried to convince Sophie she should tell him that if he was going to be a bully, she wouldn't play with him. Instead, she yelled at him that he was a bowling ball and a cotton ball also, insults that were lost on him.

"She is mine, and it's illegal to buy people," I told Abel. Sophie looked, as always, absorbed, this time in a dandelion bouquet she was collecting. I wondered whether she was as serene as she appeared, how many questions, how much turmoil, would stay hidden from my view.

~

Right after we moved to Pennsylvania, we'd made a trip home to Kansas where my aunt organized a party for Sophie's third birthday. Then my mother ended up in the emergency room with another TIA.

"My daddy had a stroke and died," Sophie had announced the week I first heard the animal in the walls. The canned peach I was dishing up flew from my spoon. It skated across the floor.

"Have you been telling people that?" I asked cautiously.

She closed her mouth tight, smiling her zipped-lip amusement, enjoying baiting me.

Painstakingly matter-of-fact, I asked her if she understood that our family hadn't ever had a daddy.

"I know, Mom," she said, at three already a master of adolescent scorn.

What I was learning was that there was no way to be ready for every question or comment that an unconventional family invites. On Father's Day two years later, the kids of our neighbors Mary and Jim would taunt Sophie: "You wouldn't understand Father's Day because you don't have a father!"

Mary burst anxiously from her kitchen to reprimand her kids and reassure Sophie. "But you do have a father!" she cried. "Your father who art in heaven!"

"Is Jim my father?" Sophie asked me later, confused. Over dinner, as I tried to explain that no, Mary's husband was not Sophie's father, that just as she had a birth mother, she also had a birth father, she announced, "I know why my parents gave me up. It's because they were blind. They couldn't see me." It was as good an explanation as any. How could anyone possibly see this girl and then get along without her?

Another set of neighbors told their son that Sophie's father traveled a lot. "He's too young to understand," the mother confided in me, as if there were something scandalous about a woman traveling, out of wedlock, to China to adopt a baby.

In the fourth grade, Sophie would bring home an assignment to write about her birth. She spent the evening alternately testy, volatile, whiny, accusatory, and tearful, the same cycle of moodiness I was accustomed to around her birthday. I suggested she just switch to a different topic. Instead she glowered at a piece of paper and seesawed her pencil rhythmically, thumping the eraser against the table. Finally she wrote, "I was born in a house while my father was dying."

"Are you sure you want to say that?" I asked, anticipating the hushed voices and sidelong looks I'd get, the tragic widow, or, instead, a renewed swell of hesitant questions about Sophie's Chinese parents.

"I was born in a house where my father was dying," Sophie answered, gleeful. "I was born in a house where my father was dying," she repeated again and again, clearly pleased with herself. Sometimes she still says to me, "Remember, Mom? I was born in a house where my father was dying."

The architecture of my house and my heart felt daily more complex back then. One day when Sophie was three, I realized that from the landing I could trace the progress of our creature. It galloped down my bedroom wall, passed above the landing window, and leapt along the inside of Sophie's bedroom wall. It moved through the expected arteries between our rooms, finding crisscrossing networks, capillaries and veins over doorsills and between windows. It carved out new pathways while I picked up Sophie's books and toys and junk mail and shoes, listening. My walls were one big Habitrail, a series of McDonald's Playland tunnels and slides.

I looked up red squirrels in the set of 1960s World Book Encyclopedias I had inherited from my childhood home. Red squirrels, I learned, can cover three feet in a second. "Proteins, fats, and carbohydrates, all neatly packaged in a peanut shell, get a squirrel's undivided attention," said my encyclopedia. "Fence, branch, and telephone wires are all highways to the lightning-quick and sure-footed little rodents."

Critter Getters made an appointment to come inspect. Then they called back. Turned out they weren't licensed to trap animals in Pennsylvania, only New York.

I found it comforting to imagine the intruder stocking up on pinecones and nuts, leaves and twigs, insulating my walls, then dreaming nearby through the long winter. No, said my alarmed friends. It could bite through electrical wires.

I was pretty sure that the animal's entry point was somewhere above my bedroom, where I frequently heard a tumbling sound and then the thump of a body and the rush of small feet. I considered crawling out a window onto the balcony to leave the trap there. But the windows stuck. When I tried to force them, the wood felt rotted, ready to splinter and snap. I finally set up the trap on the front porch, two storys below the animal's hangout, too far away.

It sat there for days, untouched.

I wrote down a story that Sophie had demanded that I tell again and again, one about a girl named Sophie. It was after bedtime, but the real Sophie was still wide-awake. I settled cross-legged on her bed. "I want to read you a story," I said.

She listened intently to the familiar narrative about a girl who wanted to stay a baby. She jumped in to supply some of the dialogue. When I finished, she said, "Again?"

"Tomorrow," I promised. I tucked her in again and returned to the enclosed porch behind her bedroom.

A while later, Sophie marched in, notebook in hand. She plopped down cross-legged on the coffee table. "I want to read you a story," she said.

She had drawn squiggles across several pages, ink rising and falling like ocean waves, taking flight like small birds, spiking and dipping like a heart monitor. "Once upon a time, there was an animal in the walls," she said.

On cold nights, I slept in the middle bedroom, away from the creature's skittering and scratching. But it, too, discovered the warmth of the middle room, and late one night I heard it scrambling through the walls beside my bed, racing and bounding and leaping and somersaulting. I dreamed of the rasp and scribble of small claws. Cartoon squirrels tumbled merrily head over tail, vaulted over ceiling joists, flipped and dived and cartwheeled. I woke exhausted by all the activity. From under the closed closet door, the lights in Sophie's shoes pulsed like the furthest moon of Jupiter.

September 11. I was teaching when the planes hit. During the next class, the twin towers collapsed. Up and down the hall an eerie stillness presided. Colleagues and students congregated around TVs somewhere. I was new and didn't know where the TV lounges were, but I stood in the Humanities office listening to radio reports. A plane crashed in Pennsylvania and the university shut down.

"Planes crashed into buildings?" Sophie asked whenever I turned on the news in the car. "People died?"

I didn't know how to explain terrorism to a three-year-old. "Planes crashed into buildings," I agreed. "People died."

Back when my dad was dying, everyone in my family stumbled around with faces frozen into a blankness that deflected a barrage of stunned recognition. Now, all day every day, I passed face after face that had been wiped free of expression, animation dissolved into slow, careful navigation of an uncertain world.

And so I forgot about mundane matters like animals in walls until one evening, when I went upstairs to change my clothes, the ceiling was rattling, a small earthquake of metal clanking. In the attic crawl space, the Havahart trap had closed its doors on a frantic red squirrel. It whipped around from one end to the other, lunging with bared teeth at the metal bars. As I carried the trap down to the porch, the animal heaved itself repeatedly against the door. Our friend Kyoko came over to help release the animal before it died of a heart attack. On the edge of campus, I tripped the door and the squirrel shot out, one long muscle, bullet-swift, into the woods. I held Sophie's hand. My tension lifted a little.

"It's getting cold out," Kyoko said. "The squirrel hasn't had a chance to prepare for hibernation. It will probably die anyway."

On Monday, our secretary reported hearing an animal scrambling in the ceiling of our building. Secretly, I hoped it was our squirrel. My secret hope backfired when some small animal devoured an entire bag of Hershey's kisses I left in my desk. The next day, I found a drawerful of silver foil wrapper crumbs. One Saturday, a chipmunk leapt out at my division chair. We spent a week chasing chipmunks out of offices, classrooms, and computer labs.

Caution: Chipmunk Inside, said signs on classroom doors.

Do Not Enter: Chipmunk Inside, said the warning on the bathroom door.

The presence of wild creatures in bathrooms and behind walls would turn out to be nothing in this new life I'd taken on. Neighbors sighted bears and mountain lions in their yards. My trash was routinely overturned by mystery animals. Eventually my house would become infested by bats.

Briefly, though, we were alone in our house. We slept through the night, no longer disturbed by our nocturnal companion.

Back then I could listen to Iris DeMent and Paul Simon without thinking about the questions they might raise. Big things were happening in the world. Faces remained braced for disaster and the news went on about recovery efforts, anthrax, smallpox. When I heard the tick-tock of rain, I scanned the ceiling for leaks. Every time the furnace took a rest, I held my breath, waiting for it to kick on again. Sometimes the swish of my skirt or the plop of a dropped toy on the hall carpet froze me, listening for a new stirring inside my walls. Nothing. Numbly I waited and watched the news.

Eventually I took my Dustbuster to suck up squirrel droppings from the attic crawl space. A friend nailed a board across the chimney's missing brick. And for a clean, triumphant moment, before the squirrels found a new opening, I reclaimed our house. I imagined moving forward into a future where I could do the right things, answer questions, smoothly connect Sophie to her heritage, make us a home.

But still, heavy sadness blanketed us, suffocating at times. Sophie was supposed to be in bed that night as I sat motionless again in front of the news, struggling against the baring of my illusions: that grief could hibernate and stock up provisions against more grief. That the alarmingly ferocious creature parenthood had turned me into was anything but terrifyingly defenseless to protect my child. The news droned on, a trap snapping shut, an airless, sunless shrinking space.

Then an inhuman high-pitched sound emerged from Sophie's room. A thump, then a bang, a staccato screech, laughter. I peered around the corner.

Sophie was wearing a pair of squeaky shoes from China. The pink canvas shoes had sat on the shelf for months. Now I understood where they got their name. With each step, they squeaked like a chorus of angry rubber duckies.

Sophie leapt, stomped, and jumped, intent face collapsing into delight at the variations of squeaks and screeches her feet could make, loud and soft, abrupt and elongated.

I thought of how, when we first moved here, Sophie and I had exchanged wide-eyed looks each time a door opened into another previously undiscovered space. I watched her face now, focused on her shoes. Somewhere in China, I thought, a woman's stretch marks reminded her daily of the baby she had once carried. Not far away, not long ago, hundreds of lives had been obliterated in the instant between a period and a capital letter in a morning e-mail, between a sip and swallow of coffee.

But for this moment, Sophie's shoes could make noise. She sprang onto the bed and off again, vaulting over her toy box and sailing through the air, shoes squealing like happy animals. And for the first time in days, my heart opened up into whole new light-filled rooms I hadn't known about, chamber after chamber.

Chapter Three

October 2008

The day before we left for Beijing, Sophie paged through *A Day in the Life of China,* studying each photo. "He's eight," she said incredulously, pointing at a baby standing in a crib, gripping the railing. "This one is four," she gasped, showing me a tightly swaddled newborn-looking creature.

I only glanced, barely listening. I was making lists of things to do and pack. I absently explained that malnutrition can slow growth and development, making children appear younger than they are. I mentioned a beggar in the street in Hangzhou, a scruffy, scrappy girl as small as an American three-year-old, but probably six or seven. I talked about year-old babies from orphanages who were tiny as four-month-olds and could not sit up or lift their heads.

"She's ten," Sophie said, holding up the book to show me a picture of a wizened old woman. I wanted my daughter to be prepared for whatever she saw in China, but these pictures seemed a little extreme. I tried to sound authoritative, describing how disease and hardship can age people prematurely.

But not *that* much, on second thought.

"Let me see that," I said.

I examined the captions. It turned out to be the photographers, not the subjects, who were eight, four, and ten.

For months I have dreaded the disillusionment that might topple Sophie's idealized view of China but also looked forward to her developing more realistic impressions. But she's ten, and I remember from a psychology class that ten-year-olds largely do not yet recognize logical flaws. You can say to a ten-year-old, "I'm glad I don't like broccoli, because if I did I'd have to eat it all the time, and it's yucky," and the child will inevitably agree. After encountering this example in a textbook, I repeated the statement to all the ten-year-olds of my acquaintance. "I know!" they'd reply. So how can I expect a child still fixed in yucky broccoli logic to easily arrive at a complex understanding of her home country?

And, in fact, my own notions are clearly far from the whole picture, influenced by American stereotypes of impoverished Third-World countries and citizens without real freedoms. I warned Sophie about the poverty she might see, but our own once-prosperous town surrounded by natural beauty is, in contrast to Beijing, more immediately visibly poor with its sagging porches and peeling paint and cracked and broken sidewalks.

From the moment we step out of an airport bathroom, where a sign cautioning against using too many paper towels reads, "Protect the nature," my eyes are dazzled by light. The shiny floors of the new terminal's baggage claim reflect back each of the ceiling lights, become skies full of distant stars, stars mirrored in Sophie's eager eyes. She's in China. This is China.

Our guide is Lily. We somehow find her in an endless snaking line outside of customs, where more than two hundred people stand holding signs. We make sleepy conversation as we head out of the airport to meet our driver. Lily is in her thirties, with a seven-year-old son whose name, she says, is Little Dragon.

Outside, I am startled by the sunlight and the profusion of color—flowers and trees, the yellow and pink and green characters along the store awnings, the blue windows of white high-rise buildings. In the U. S., office windows would typically be closed, allowing the buildings to present cold, imperturbable faces. Here, open windows break the uniformity, hinting at life inside.

As we ride along the highway, I ask Lily what the schools here are like, what parents are like. The children are tested often, she tells me. Parents are fiercely competitive.

Oh, I say. Just like in the U. S.

Mr. Wong is our driver. He speaks about as much English as I do Chinese. "Bee-u-ti-ful," he often says, and, "No problem." He and I will learn to pantomime successfully, but right now he just smiles big at us and shakes his fist and yells at other drivers. We speed down the congested highway, weaving between other vehicles, trucks and economy cars and luxury cars and motorcycles and buses all squeezing close together, and then, on the city streets, bicycles and scooters crowding the edges as well.

He pulls up in front of a state-of-the-art hotel, with a sleek glass entryway and marble countertops. Lily checks us in. "Nancy?" she says, in the same anxious tone our friend Flora uses when she says my name. Are both native speakers tentative about addressing me, I wonder, or is it just that *Nancy* sounds close to a Chinese word that has a rising tone at the end? "There are no laws here like in your country," Lily goes on to say, and actually, she does sound a bit worried. "They cannot control smoking."

I have read that more than 60 percent of Chinese men smoke, which may be why the hotel doesn't put forth much effort to control it. Our nonsmoking room is outfitted with ashtrays and matches, and as we enter I can already smell smoke wafting through the air. Sophie is hyper as we unpack, playing with the fan, the panda bear, and a mysterious piece of cloth in the gift bag from our tour company. She parades back and forth, proffering the Chinese flag like an Olympic athlete. I turn on the lights by fitting my key card into the slot near the door. It's impossible in Chinese hotels to waste electricity by leaving lights on when you're not in the room. I try to figure out the TV's remote control, which is the size of a credit card, while I ponder these contradictions: seemingly little concern about air pollution but a far greater awareness of conserving resources than in the U. S.

We head downstairs for an early dinner. Normally, our tour company has a welcome meal, a session for the group to get acquainted and ask questions and for the company to give instructions and information. But this time, Sophie and I are the whole group. I was told in August that no one else had signed up. I debated briefly but didn't cancel. I had saved for this trip for years, taken a semester's sabbatical, and obtained permission from Sophie's school for her to be gone for two and a half weeks. In the wake of my mother's death, it seemed to me especially important to carry on with our plans. But now our arrival feels a little lonely with no group and no welcome dinner.

Lily promised to order food for us in the hotel restaurant, but the staff stares at us in puzzlement. I mention the name of our tour company as we droop wearily in the empty room of round tables covered by white cloths.

The young woman at the reception desk shakes her head. She glances nervously, desperately toward the kitchen.

"Our guide ordered food?" I try.

Another young woman emerges from the kitchen. They exchange a few words and the receptionist thrusts a Chinese menu at me. She tries to usher us to a table.

"Lily?" I say, automatically stripping nonessential words from my vocabulary. "Tour? Ordered food?"

The two women stare at me. One of them says something. I shake my head. She repeats.

"She said 427," Sophie hisses at me. Our room number.

"Yes!" I nod vigorously. Smiles break out all around. We are led to a small table set with tiny saucer-sized plates and chopsticks. The waitress delivers dishes: beef and noodles, tofu with chicken and peanuts, snow peas.

An instrumental version of "Love Story" plays over the sound system, but Sophie is still put out with me for not understanding the waitress's English.

She doesn't catch my eye or seem to recognize this song, the theme from a movie that was formative for our friend Rekha when she was growing up in India. Sophie's embarrassment is visible as I stare mystified at the table, uncertain how to dine without serving utensils, a fork, or a napkin. When I came to adopt her, it was with a large group of Americans. We usually ate at hotel restaurants with lazy susans, dinner plates, silverware, and a dish of French fries. I was grateful for the forks, too busy feeding and restraining and comforting my baby to try to use chopsticks.

The waitress sees my confusion and rushes over. I point to the soup bowl and our individual bowls. She deftly scoops up noodles with my chopsticks. Then she ladles out broth with my ceramic spoon. "Xie xie," I say, but I'm still puzzled. So we're supposed to use the ceramic spoons to serve ourselves from common dishes?

The song switches to "Memories" and Sophie drops a chopstick on the floor. The waitress rushes over with a replacement. She stations herself a few feet from our table, alert. I can't open my water bottle, and she hurries to my rescue. Sophie stares fixedly at the table, mortified at my lack of Chinese language and international dining skills. She digs into her food, pretending not to know me.

"Moon River" plays in the background. We just watched *Breakfast at Tiffany's*, and this song feels like a little glimpse of home and our shared history. To my relief, Sophie catches my eye and smiles, relenting.

Upstairs, she vows that she is not going to sleep. "I am not tired," she says right before her head lolls forward. She jerks back, shaking herself awake, and starts writing in her journal. Then she stretches out on her stomach to write. Seconds later, she's breathing evenly.

I ease the journal out from under her cheek. "I'm in CHINA!" she has written. "But the bad news is I had to be . . ."

That's where she fell asleep.

We wake at 3:00 A.M. At 4:00 we give up on going back to sleep. Sophie finishes her sentence: "on a plane for hours and hours." She turns on the TV, and we watch British CNN's coverage of the economic crisis and its effect on "football investments." Sophie flips channels, past a televised pool game to some Eddie Murphy movie.

There are no washcloths, and when I splash water on my face, my pajama sleeves get wet. I end up wetting the corner of a towel to swipe my face. Later I will read in *China Survival Guide* that to obtain washcloths, I should have rung housekeeping and requested "little square towels." At least when I take a shower, the controls are straightforward, and I don't scald myself or spray water all over the bathroom. I did this on my adoption trip, soaking all of my clothes.

Waiting for daylight, I turn through the travel memoirs I've brought. First, Polly Evans's *Fried Eggs with Chopsticks: One Woman's Hilarious Adventure into a Country and a Culture Not Her Own,* the story of her solo trip through China, visiting some of the same places we will go. I pause on paragraphs about the rapidly changing position of China in the global economy, the expanding business interests that are ending China's historical insularity. I turn to J. Maarten Troost's *Lost on Planet China: One Man's Attempt to Understand the World's Most Mystifying Nation,* described by reviewer Jon Foro as a book about "a country with its feet suctioned in the clay of traditional culture and a head straining into the polluted stratosphere of unencumbered capitalism." "The center of gravity has moved east," Troost writes. "Business, finance, manufacturing, everything revolves around China." This is what the typical Third-World stereotype ignores, not just the beauty and history of an ancient culture, but the growing importance of this country on the world stage.

Sophie is raring to go have breakfast and then explore. Down at the buffet, we check out a couple of the tables of options: slices of cheese and cold cuts, scrambled eggs, pastries, congee, noodles, and steamed dim sum. I'm not sure if we should eat the fresh fruit—how do we know if it was washed in tap water? And then, as I move on to the next table, I wonder: is it safe to eat yogurt in the wake of the recent scare in China involving melamine in milk products? The plates have droplets of water on them. We've been instructed to swipe our plates with Lysol wipes, but I'm not sure how to go about this without appearing rude.

We try seaweed-wrapped congee and dumplings, huge slabs of bacon, and bland sausage. We skip the three-bean salads and braised fish with black beans. "I want to live in this hotel," Sophie says dreamily, handling her chopsticks adeptly.

Out on the street, she's embarrassed by me again. She hisses at me to put away my camera. I look like a tourist. I snap pictures of the shops across the street, the McDonalds a few blocks down, the hundreds of bikes that crowd a rack. Sophie wants to blend in, and I'm sticking out. I'd stick out even without the camera. And truthfully, so would she, in her braces and T-shirt, the only child among crowds of businessmen in suits and young women in short skirts, stockings, and high heels.

～

It hurt my mother's feelings when, at fourteen, I was mortified to be seen with her at the mall. She never understood that I wasn't embarrassed by her so much as by the fact that I was at the mall with my mother. I was afraid I would look like I didn't have any friends. So I try not to take too personally the way my daughter edges away from me. Even in adulthood, though, I was always edging away from my mother, who often sighed and wished aloud that we could be best friends like some mothers and daughters. Why couldn't we? I always wondered. I complained to my friends that she never listened to me, that she was always trying to mold me into something that I wasn't. But maybe we were just too temperamentally different to really enjoy each other's company.

If I had so little in common with the mother who gave birth to me, whose genes I shared, what are the chances that my daughter and I won't face similar tensions? I hope that the lack of genetic connection means that I can see my daughter as her own person, not as a reflection of me. But after spending the majority of your time for nearly ten years with another person, it's hard not to sometimes see her as an extension of yourself. We talk often about our similarities. "I've lived with you for so long, I've gotten some of your genes," Sophie will say with absolute confidence that that's the way it works.

But now we're in a country of more than a billion people who all appear to share more, genetically, with my daughter than I do, a simple fact that calls into question our connection. I wonder what it feels like to look like everyone else for the first time, to have me be the one who's different.

Sometimes I wish I could know what traits came from Sophie's birth parents, what she picked up from me. Of course someone else gave her straight dark hair, a rich brown others call *black,* even though she corrects them: all hair is really a variation of brown. I like the way her correction connects us: we both have brown hair, even if hers is closer to black, mine to blond. Of course someone else gave her lively eyes and a tiny, flexible body that runs hot, as if she always has a fever. But I gave her my ironic sense of humor, a love of books, goofy songs my dad taught me. From my mom, she briefly took up the habit of licking a finger before turning a page. Somehow, Sophie and I ended up with overlapping allergies, sensitive skin, B positive blood, mild asthma, and inconsistent performance on academic tests.

And there's dance. I like to take responsibility for giving her dance.

An IQ test once identified me as retarded. I I thought I was being screened for speech defects, so I outwitted the counselor by refusing to speak at all. She recorded this as indicative of mental delays, the school accepted the score, and for a good three years thereafter, teachers assumed that I was performing at the top of my ability and should not be pushed or challenged. Last year, Sophie followed in my footsteps by bombing a standardized pretest. She was instantly moved from an advanced to a remedial group, then bounced right back with advanced scores on the real test.

Her teacher said she was having trouble understanding literary concepts like motivation. At home, she was reading children's novels about serious topics like *In the Year of the Boar and Jackie Robinson, Roll of Thunder, Hear My Cry,* and *Number the Stars.* Her classmates deemed these books boring, but they spurred Sophie to ask questions about immigration, the KKK, and Nazis. She related strongly to the protagonists. She got Chinese immigrant Shirley Temple Wong's enthusiasm for African-American baseball player Jackie Robinson. She identified wholeheartedly with Annemarie's family's unquestioning responsibility to save her Jewish best friend from the Nazis. She was enraged that white kids got to ride the bus while black kids had to walk. It seemed to me that we were always talking about motivations. Once, she woke me in the middle of the night. "Mom?" she whispered, standing by my bed. "I just don't understand. Why did people listen to Hitler?"

Another thing my daughter struggled with, her teacher said: figurative language. "I'm like wheat bread and you're like white bread," Sophie announced that evening. Then she hastily amended, "But you're the whole grain kind."

I was pleased by this concession. And relieved: my daughter clearly understood how to make connections. My daughter clearly understood how to make a metaphor, as important a skill as identifying one, I thought. And I saw this as more evidence of how alike we were when I thought of my own history of good grades but discomfort with the little boxes in which schools seemed determined to put students.

My mother, I often felt, tried to remake me in her own likeness and was disappointed when she failed. Maybe all daughters feel that way to some extent. Maybe my daughter will sometimes feel that way about me. Because sometimes I catch myself trying to see her as a reflection of myself. A few years ago, in the Human Body section at Denver's Science and Nature Museum, a mirror reflected our infrared light—mine, Sophie's, and Ruth's. My reflection was yellow, tinged green around the edges, but fiery red under my sweatshirt. Sophie, always hot in crowded places, appeared mostly red, and Ruth, who runs cold, appeared mostly green. In this mirror, I was pleased to see, I resembled my daughter and friend far more than they resembled each other. See, I thought. Under our skin, look how alike we are. Sometimes it's hard to separate my own need for reassurance from hers.

Right now, I understand, I'm the one who wants reassurance. Silent and distant, my daughter isn't thinking about me at all. She's just walking up and down brick sidewalks feeling what it's like to look like everyone else. We stroll past a white building with hot-pink trim, restaurants, advertisements. These are oddly beautiful when you don't read the language and can only admire the shapes of the Chinese characters. I ponder a sign outside McDonald's, a photograph of a sandwich I can't quite identify, one of a biscuit that appears to be stuffed with cheese, bacon, hash browns, and lettuce, a drawing of a coffee cup in the background, steam swirling above it.

What I really want to do is stare at people, an impulse not unlike the one I sometimes have to stare at, say, my niece. It's fascinating how when she faces forward, her long, shapely nose is the same as her mother's but how when she turns to the side her profile becomes mine. Here in China I want to examine people's faces for their similarities to my daughter's, to observe their movements and expressions and features for reflections of hers. Then, I'll think, watching the way she smiles or pivots her head to look in a window or thoughtfully studies passersby, no, she got that from me. It seems miraculous to me, the way children combine so many characteristics and influences to become their own complicated, beautiful, changeable selves.

Some things I can imagine that my daughter got from me, but some—like the ability to roll her tongue—are indisputably from her birth parents. Nobody with whom I share close blood ties can do that. I thought of her birth family regularly when, at eight, she developed a whole series of mouth tricks based on this genetic ability.

"Hard taco," she'd say, sticking out her tongue, folded over like a taco shell.

"Soft taco," she'd announce, rolling her tongue. "Hot dog," she'd continue, forming a soft taco tongue, then laying her pointer finger in the middle.

"Hamburger," she finished, lining up her finger between her lips and closing them like buns. I laughed and imagined that my daughter had a sibling somewhere in China, a child close to her age who looked like her, entertaining the family with dumpling and egg roll and wonton tongue.

I feel like I'm trying to keep a seesaw level, to stay balanced midway between the impulse to look for similarities and the importance of acknowledging differences. Yes, there are differences between us, but I still get pretty testy when my cousin and uncle who collect family history place too much emphasis on genetic heritage. Is family history about bloodlines or values? I ask. Medical information or stories? Are we most interested in diseases and eye color or drama, adversity, tragedy, triumph, the passions and vision passed down from one generation to the next?

But sometimes Sophie envies one of her cousins, whose baby pictures look like mine. She observes that my baby pictures look like my dad's. Sometimes she wants to be one of us, one of the interchangeable, indistinguishable pale blond babies in our family line, except that she's never really wished to be blond; what she really wants is for us to look like her. Even grafted onto the family tree, a little twig right now, she's not always treated like she belongs there. There are kids at school who insistently refer to me as her "stepmom." There are relatives who sometimes leave adopted family members out of photographs, grouping them with in-laws. We've both seen how little twigs get snapped off in high winds, litter our yard, and clog our lawn mower.

As we walk, I have to restrain myself from launching into a stream of chatter, of observations and commentary, from interpreting a world around me that my daughter just wants to quietly absorb. By force of will, I keep silent, but I take lots of pictures.

At a shop window, people line up to order dumplings. We climb three steps to browse in open-front stores, sniffing the air of a bakery, turning through plastic clips in a bin at a hair accessories store, wandering through the aisles of music stores as if we've never seen music stands or violins or flutes. We admire the paper cuts on a wall, pieces of thin paper with designs and characters cut from them.

Crossing the street is harrowing. Cars and buses and motorcycles plow right through crosswalks and park in the middle of intersections, nosing within an inch of pedestrians and plunging forward at the first opportunity, grazing slowpokes. Bicyclists without helmets pedal through traffic. *China Survival Guide* says that crossing streets requires "the watchfulness of an eagle, the agility of a mountain lion, the guile of a fox, and the luck of the Irish" and compares it to a real-life game of Frogger. "Learn from wildebeests or antelope in the Serengeti," it advises—travel in packs. I make sure we're in the thick of a crowd before we attempt heart-stopping dashes across.

In Pennsylvania, there's a law that cars have to stop for any pedestrian who steps off the curb into a crosswalk, even if the light is green, even if the street will be free and clear after your car passes. In Bradford, pedestrians shake their fists at drivers who fail to stop. They jot down license numbers. They glare and pretend to dial 911 on their cell phones. That behavior seems even more provincial in a city like this. Still, I gain new appreciation for orderly crosswalks and lights, for the freedom to cross streets without fear of being mowed down. I also understand how the Chinese stay fit.

"Wouldn't you hate to live in a place this big?" I ask Sophie, who has often expressed an aversion to cities like New York and Chicago.

"I'd like to live *here,*" she says.

Lily, our guide, takes the subway to meet us at 9:00, and we all set out with Mr. Wong for the Panjiayuan Market. There, we pass table after table covered with red umbrellas, displays of bead necklaces, wooden boxes, paintings, silk purses, jade objects, mah jong games, Mao alarm clocks, fans, pajamas, cloth-covered books, boxes of terra-cotta warriors, embroidered cloth, slippers, and rugs. Merchants shove items in our faces. I buy chopsticks for Sophie's classmates.

"They'll just stick them up their noses," she predicts.

If our small town's literal adherence to street-crossing laws seems increasingly ludicrous, so, as we walk through this market, do all of my previous efforts to connect Sophie to her cultural heritage. Our resources have, up till now, been Chinese New Year celebrations with carryout food, red envelopes, and craft projects from kits: making lanterns, painting fans, and stringing jade necklaces.. We have been to the occasional Asian festival, to Chinese Culture Camp in Colorado, to Lucky Market near my mom's apartment in Wichita. Every summer we go there to buy eight dollars' worth of sweets: hairy-looking tamarind candy from Vietnam, gummy fruits from Japan, white rabbit candy from China, Hello Panda biscuits from Singapore, sesame cakes from Thailand.

The tradition began because I was determined to embrace Sophie's birth heritage as fully as I expected her to accept mine—even if the only available representatives were hard candy coated by white hair that looked plucked from the head of someone elderly. On our first expedition, I got back in the car and popped a tamarind candy into my mouth. The hairy exterior was, it turned out, a protective layer that broke down in an instant. The candy released a red hot flame that ignited my tongue and burned my throat. I spat the stuff out, coughing madly. I pulled over for a drink, twisting the candy container to read the ingredient list: tamarind, chili, sugar.

That same summer we traveled to Denver, where my old friend Ruth took us to see dragon-boat races. We sat on the ground eating noodles and sushi from paper plates. Another day, we went out for pad Thai and sticky rice. The next, it was a Korean barbecue, where Ruth cooked meat for us on a grill on the table. Waiters asked Ruth if Sophie could have a cookie or a sucker, if it was okay to give her a butter knife. When I answered, they flinched a little and fixed their stares on Ruth, waiting for her to verify my reply. I wondered if Ruth was secretly pretending to be Sophie's mom the way, before I was a parent, I used to pretend to be my blond, blue-eyed niece's. I wondered if Sophie was pretending to be Ruth's daughter.

My favorite part of the Temple of Heaven is all the people. The park is a historic site, a complex where the emperor used to come to pray, but unlike historic sites I have visited in the U. S., there are no tourists carrying maps or talking in hushed, reverent voices. This is a lively place, a cultural and recreational center. Women twirl long multicolored ribbons. Groups perform tai chi and folk dances on the open sidewalk. Men play a hackeysack game with shuttlecocks. Ballroom dancers promenade, the men in dress pants, the women in white dresses. A group sings opera on a covered walkway once meant for transporting slaughtered animals to be sacrificed.

In cities like Chicago and New York, when street-corner musicians set up shop, they place cups in front of them for tips. When we visit Barcelona a few months later, Sophie's favorite activity will be walking up and down Las Ramblas, strolling through the Gothic Quarter, and climbing up and down the levels of Park Guell, encountering garish living statues. She will love watching Edward Scissorhands, cavemen, and monkeys, artists sketching landscapes, acrobats leaping over the heads of impressed tourists, musicians playing ehrus and drums and guitars, a woman blowing huge bubbles. Sophie will choose her favorites and drop coins in their cups.

But at the Temple of Heaven, there are no cups. These are not largely performances for tourists but people gathering to exercise and have fun. I wish we had parks like this in the U. S. Many people complain that packaged tours don't take them to the places where real citizens go, but in China, many tourist attractions do double as hangouts for locals.

We stop to watch a game that I think of as tai-chi tennis. Players use canvas rackets to cast balls into the air, ribbons attached. The ribbons float and flutter before the next player catches the ball, balancing it gently on his racket. It's a dance, peaceful and graceful, emphasizing balance. A man invites Sophie to play. He teaches her patiently for fifteen minutes. Then he offers to sell us a set.

Okay, so the Temple of Heaven has its touristy side.

We turn to Lily, who always weighs for us whether a purchase is worth it. "Not a good deal," she sometimes says, but this time, she approves: "It's a good deal." And so we buy the game set.

Past the music and dancing and games, families picnic on the steps of the temple, an ornate three-tiered building. We climb up to peer through doorways into empty, echoing halls. We gaze upon bulbous squatting incense burners. We ponder a mysterious red wooden structure that turns out to be a contemporary addition, a loudspeaker.

At lunchtime, we drive to a restaurant bustling with customers. Benches scrape as people come and go, the room perpetually in motion like a subway station at rush hour. With the arrival of each new customer, waiters in royal blue jackets and pants shout in unison. As they clear tables, white dishes clink rhythmically, until, with several waiters joining in this dance of deft arms and hands, the dining room sounds like a roomful of hungry children banging forks on tables to demand their dinner. It's a song of clattering dishes, an opera of calls and responses.

A few months ago, I read aloud a tour-company recommendation to bring plastic dinnerware in case children had trouble with chopsticks. Sophie laughed and laughed. She knew that it was I who had trouble with chop-sticks. And now, as I slip out my plastic fork, our driver laughs and laughs. Friendly ridicule sounds pretty much the same in both English and Chinese, and I deserve it, so I just smile and get busy on the pork, tofu, broccoli, and fresh noodles. Sophie eats much more slowly, having to pause for well-inten-tioned chopstick instructions, communicated through demonstration. Mr. Wong patiently shows her again and again, heaping more food on her plate. Sophie dutifully keeps eating, though her eyes glaze over with exhaustion.

I try a red pepper dish, so hot that my taste buds go numb and my stomach twists. Hot food tends to upset it and lead to painful heartburn. I put down my fork. The driver is anxious. He cocks his head and gestures at the dishes. I pat my stomach: full. Full is politer and easier to explain than nauseated. The driver shakes his head: he doesn't believe me.

Almost ten years ago, I was too jet-lagged and anxious about meeting my baby to get much out of the Forbidden City, where emperors had lived for more than five hundred years. I paid no attention to the tour guide's long rundown of the twenty-four emperors who once lived here. Nor did I absorb any of the interesting facts that I would find later in books like *China Survival Guide;* for example, the Forbidden City supposedly has 9,999 rooms, though I'm not sure anyone has actually counted. Only heaven, it turns out, is allowed to have 10,000 rooms.

On my first trip here, I was too busy staring at children, wondering what mine would look like, to absorb fun facts. This time, instead, I compulsively watch adults, searching their faces for my daughter's features, wondering how she'd be different if she'd grown up here, how she would carry herself, gesture, smile, how I would recognize her in a crowd.

People keep speaking Chinese to her. She studies them gravely as if she understands. The occasional white tourist catches my eye and smiles. In the minority here, suddenly we have a connection. I wonder if this recognition passes between those who are in the minority in rural Pennsylvania, if it is why Sophie has always felt so connected to others who aren't white.

The courtyard swarms with people, most of them part of domestic tour groups wearing matching caps—a red group, a white one, a yellow, and a blue. We admire the bricks that pave the courtyard and walkways, since Lily's husband runs a factory that manufactures these bricks for historic sites.

I remember the majestic buildings with roofs that curl up at the ends so that they look like ships floating above flights of steps. The ceramic tiles are rows of long brown tubes, resembling bamboo. We recognize buildings and courtyards from *The Last Emperor,* which we watched a couple of weeks ago. I'm grateful that Lily avoids long speeches, instead pointing out interesting features like the water heaters, huge vats perched atop stoves, once used to keep water from freezing in case of fire in a city full of wooden buildings. She points out elaborately carved stone walkways and gold statues of mythical beasts. A cypress tree near the exit is called "the couple's tree," she says, because of the way two join into one. The man-made mountains of rocks are from Sophie's home province, leading to a high pagoda. "A single act of carelessness leads to the eternal loss of beauty," says a sign.

Sophie and I cling to a railing, slowly edging forward with the crowd to peer into empty throne rooms. Around us, people push one another and cut in line, one of the Chinese habits that most frustrates foreigners. "They are just pushing and shoving, not waiting their turn," a man says in a disgusted voice and perfect English, and from then on, he is Sophie's champion. Anyone who steps ahead of her gets a tap on the shoulder and a string of scolding Chinese words as the man gestures toward Sophie. Gradually he clears the way for her.

Suddenly, the white-capped tour group surges up the steps with the force of a tidal wave. Its spry elderly members body slam each other, smile big smiles, and practically trample one another and us in their eagerness to gaze into dark, empty halls. I am tall, and I have learned how to stick out my elbows to clear a path while bodily protecting Sophie. We make our escape.

Minutes later an elderly woman in a yellow cap, also grinning, heaves Sophie out of the way as if saving her from an oncoming bus. Sophie stumbles backward.

I'm still surprised by the contrast between Chinese indifference toward strangers and loyalty, warmth, and kindness toward friends and families. And I'm also used to the American expectation that the elderly be meek and silent and allow us to live our lives without benefit of their wisdom or advice. So I can't help but laugh, startled and amused, as the woman, her path now clear, darts on by.

Sophie laughs, too, her determination to love China never wavering, not even in the face of crowds, pollution, smoke, scary traffic, pushing, shoving, or exhaustion. Coming here seems exactly right, now that I see how everything we've done to learn about Chinese culture has been a weak imitation of the real thing, now that I see how happy and connected Sophie feels. But underneath, I'm still uneasy. What if it's not China she becomes disillusioned with? What if it's me?

From the moment I met my baby, Ni Qiao Qin, I could feel her anger. She didn't shiver and withdraw like the other babies in our group. She screamed and howled. Anger had never really scared me. I'd understood that anger is often like a scab providing the only protection for what would otherwise be a raw gaping wound. So I bore with it, with the child who, once ripped from her Chinese caretakers, continued to lash out in age-typical ways, biting at two, hitting and kicking at four, insulting me and slamming doors at six and eight and ten. It has been talking about China, and celebrating birthdays, and attending Chinese New Year gatherings and culture camp, that has most brought out this anger. After such events, Sophie is far more likely to be out of sorts. She is far more likely to say, accusingly, "You aren't my real mother."

Usually, I just shrug. Usually, I just say, "You have another mother who gave birth to you, but I'm your mother now." Anger can be a normal and healthy response to some experiences, so I've always figured that it's my job as a parent not to suppress it, but to help find productive channels for it. And despite the rough patches, I've seen that facing the past and understanding heritage can boost a child's confidence and firm up her sense of identity. I'm determined to weather the storms, though I've sometimes had my doubts.

Like at culture camp in Denver two years ago, where the kids attended an interactive role-playing workshop. It was designed, the program explained, "to process thoughts and feelings about adoption in a safe, supportive camp environment." Sophie arrived afterward for lunch, her stare fixed. She wouldn't speak to me. Out on the lawn, she turned her back. She scootched away from me. She faced a small tree, barely taller than she was, shooting out sparse, shadeless leaves, bark crawling with ants. She chewed her hot dog and stabbed at her watermelon.

In the middle of the private school's lawn, needlelike grass blades pricked my skin. Other families shook out blankets. They fluttered on a light breeze and slapped down flat onto the ground. Parents and children bent over food, too hungry to talk much but still clustered together. I was sweating, not just from the glaring sun that forced me to visor my hand above my eyes, but from my daughter's burning radius of rage that caught me in its sweep. I'd never bought into the common notion that acknowledging adoption issues and my child's separate heritage would alienate her from me. But I'd never seen her quite so angry, nor so muted by her anger. I'd never felt its silent force quite like that, and all of a sudden, I was convinced that I'd been wrong.

Nearby, parents on blankets sliced up hot dogs and anchored napkins with cups of lemonade. They were capable and in control, like mature adults who would never feel wounded or embarrassed if their children sat three feet away, publicly ignoring them. I slid black seeds from my watermelon onto my paper plate. When Sophie was little, there were tasks to occupy me: cutting small bites, daubing up spills. Now all there was to do was eat, take a bite of hot dog, a bite of watermelon, a sip of punch.

Adoptive parents used to believe that love was enough. With love, our children would forget their origins and their differences. Love would make them fully our own. The first wave of Korean adoptees came of age and exposed the fallacies of that. I had tried to follow their wisdom, to validate my daughter's feelings, but that day at culture camp, I started worrying that I was just reminding her of her differences, thrusting her away. I regretted bringing her to the camp. I found myself wishing that I'd tried, at least for a few years, to deceive us both with the myth of the all-soothing power of love.

"So what did you do this morning?" I tried again at lunch, carefully casual, but she replied in her most eviscerating tone, "*Nothing.*" She chewed and chewed, her jaw clenched, chewing more than strictly necessary to grind up small bites. She stared at the tree.

We threw away our paper plates. We walked. Down the sidewalk, into a pretty little village of shops, away from camp. "I hate it here," my daughter said.

"Why?" I was cautious.

"It's boring. Everyone ran wild."

"Was there a session where you talked about adoption and China?"

She folded her arms, lowering them against her chest with a huff. "It was all this dumb stuff about uncomfortable questions like how much did you cost and blah blah blah."

"It sounds like there's some anger going on there," said a workshop facilitator when I approached her later.

"No duh," I didn't say. But I thought it.

"She's probably just starting to process these issues," the other facilitator said.

"I don't think she's just starting," I answered. I'd assumed it was pretty standard for adopted kids to be asked, beginning in kindergarten, how much they cost and why their real mothers didn't want them. I'd assumed it was common for third-graders to pull back their eyes and make jokes about Chinese people eating pet dogs. I was pretty sure that Sophie had journeyed far beyond the beginning of this. And, in fact, those were comparatively minor annoyances next to questions about her roots and where she fit.

The facilitators shrugged. I opened my mouth to tell them that they were underestimating my child. This is your fault, I wanted to say. You're the ones who uncovered all this hostility. You have to fix it, I meant to say.

But the facilitators had already turned away to greet smiling, grateful parents.

I had no heart for tea tasting, scrapbooking, calligraphy, cooking, or mah-jong lessons. I was irritated by an adult adoptee's cozy talk. She said that families formed by adoption were meant to be, as if it had happened by divine intervention. As if God himself had removed children from their birth parents and cultures and given them to us. Whenever I said to Sophie, "What would I do without you?" she rolled her eyes.

"If you didn't have me, you'd have another daughter, and you'd love her, too," she said.

I was stumped. It was true: I would have loved any child who was mine. But once you have a child, it's hard to imagine loving any other quite as completely and fiercely.

Snarled tight with tension after the talk, I opened the schedule. Tomorrow, there was a rehearsal for a Baba dance, which parents performed at the final banquet. The idea of dancing lit me up, the promise of shifting my focus from my sullen, miserable daughter to the meditative peace of repeating sequences of steps.

When Sophie came to meet me, her mood had shifted. She bubbled over with news about the year of the dog stamping activity and the music and especially the dancing. She was dancing, I would dance, and our crisis had slipped away.

On Saturday morning, some of the girls focused intently on their martial arts lesson. Their fists flew out, tightly controlled but fierce. Their legs kicked up, feet slicing the air like knives. Kicking and pounding, they counted in Chinese: *Yi, er, san, si, wu, liu . . .*

Sophie was half a beat behind. Her gaze wandered. She parried and punted with limp disinterest. She yawned. And I remembered what Ruth had said after a dance recital, about Sophie only standing out because she was different. Now I saw that Ruth was right. Among other Chinese girls, my daughter only stood out to me because she was mine.

That day at culture camp, I sneaked out of the Red Butterfly Village, my volunteer assignment. I'd helped children try out an ehru, an abacus, a Chinese yoyo. They'd played with creepy Moon Festival dolls, little pandas that crawled menacingly, eerie music playing, red eyes flashing. They'd exchanged gold coins for Asian sweets, small bags of Hello Pandas and hard pineapple candy. I left the kids making postcards about their imaginary travel to the Red Butterfly Village. I slipped off to the cafeteria to join the Baba dance.

The point of the Baba dance, it turned out, was primarily to make sport of parents. Eight of us were willing to bark, waggle imaginary tails, and flop the fuzzy pink ears that dangled from our black top hats. We practiced for four hours. We leapt, clicked our heels, and dislocated our knees on the landing. We stumbled through a side step, twirling our squeaky canes. We revolved like an irregular and deformed clock. In random order instead of the intended clean progression, we kicked up our canes one by one for our grand finale. We laughed and fretted about forgetting the steps. When our instructor threw in some do-si-dos, I wondered how authentically Chinese this dance really was.

At the closing banquet, Sophie's group bowed as the music started. My daughter's arms swept the air. She dipped low. The group lunged forward. My daughter pointed her toes. Her extension lengthened her limbs.

My objectivity cracked open in the face of her broad, graceful movements. Onstage, my daughter's cheeks were as round as a toddler's, but her shoulders rolled and hips rotated with the challenge of a teenager, the poise of a woman. When my daughter danced she was sassy and witty, rude and sweet. When she danced, I saw the full range of who she was and who she would be.

I wished Ruth were there to see.

Some parents need only look at their children for evidence of what has been passed on: blue eyes, curly hair, double-jointed thumbs, pitching arms, bad eyesight. The source of other traits is more nebulous: musical ability, obsession with sports, a talent for dance. I will always wonder: does my daughter's birth mother dance? Can she curl her leg to touch her foot to her head? Can she sit with legs outstretched and lay her chest flat on the floor? What percentage of Sophie's ability came from her—what portion of flexibility, grace, energy, spontaneity, persistence, or passion?

You might have thought, watching the Baba dance, that none of it came from me. But I told myself that risk was always a starting point. We forgot some of the steps. The CD skipped. The audience howled. Cameras flashed. We barked and primped our fuzzy ears. We took a bow. Our children rushed onto the stage. They snatched flowers from a pile and joined us.

Since the day I'd met my baby, maybe even before that, I've spent a lot of time trying to attain some measure of wisdom about heritage and race, love and family ties, some understanding that will sustain me through my child's teen years, through the inevitable moments of anger and alienation that lie ahead. Maybe that's part of why families make heritage trips to China, to head off some of that by helping our children place their identities in a context. But my own desire for reassurance often ends in uncertainty and turmoil. Maybe I remember the culture camp episode so well because it ended happily. Maybe I remember it for the same reason I fondly recall the days Sophie comes in irritated at the world, then turns on music. She circles me with the agonized expression of a Russian pairs skater, cheeks sucked in, pulling me into her reenactment of the death throes of a long-necked swan. We make up our ridiculous dance and forget about stupid comments.

But other times a complicated, angry stranger glares at me through smoky eyes, and I know what it's like to feel defensive and inadequate by virtue of my race. And those days, I wonder again, with shameful wistfulness: what if we didn't talk about differences so much? What if I'd found some way to head off her premature awareness and air of sophistication? What would have been wrong with a little denial, oversimplification, oblivion on my part?

∽

But back to my happy ending. After the Baba dance, Sophie doubled over, laughing, proud to have a goofy mom willing to make a fool of herself in front of a hundred people. She came to stand beside me. She took my hat and cocked it on her head, batting at the ears. She took my hand. She offered me a rose.

So there, I thought. I'd given her something, some permission to her spirit through my clumsy efforts. But I didn't know who her dancing ability came from.

Only that she took it, and it was hers now.

And so it is with China. I brought her back here, but what could never be mine to begin with is quickly becoming hers. She wants me to know this: China belongs to her, not me. She sees through the eyes of a native. I am a clumsy foreigner.

I am especially conscious of this gap between us as we enter a small upstairs restaurant a block from our hotel, on our own for dinner. A waitress in a brick-red scarf and apron brings an English menu and seats us, speaking in rapid Chinese.

"Only speak English," I say.

She responds in Chinese.

I shake my head again.

The waitress plants her elbows on the table and leans on them, hovering as I turn through the menu. Her relentless attention makes me claustrophobic. She is leaning too close, and I have to resist the impulse to pull back a little. I know that different cultures have different notions of personal space, but still I feel crowded.

"Can I have a few minutes?" I ask.

She shakes her head.

"I need a few minutes," I say.

She leans closer.

"She understands that you need more time but she's not going to go," Sophie says impatiently. She glares at me. The waitress hovers. I'm starting to sweat.

A boy about Sophie's age pops up above the divider that separates our booth from his. He talks to the waitress. She replies.

He turns to me. Straightens up nice and tall, as if preparing for a recitation. "Do you speak any Chinese?" he asks in perfect English. His mother and grandmother sit across the table, beaming proudly. Sophie has just started taking Mandarin at school, so she just looks at him. I struggle to remember something from my long-ago Chinese lessons, but none of the sentences I've retained are particularly useful at this moment: "I am your mother," "I am your father," and "I am *not* a doctor." "No, but can you tell her that I just need a few minutes to look at the menu?" I ask our savior, this miraculous English-speaking Chinese boy who then addresses the waitress, his mother, and his grandmother in Chinese. They look floored by his brilliance.

Gradually it dawns on me that "Do you speak any Chinese?" pretty much exhausted his English-language skills, because we seem to be back where we started, except now he is hovering over me on one side, the waitress on the other, serenely, and it seems, permanently crouched over our table. I flip the laminated pages of the ten-page menu, gazing at pictures, trying to absorb descriptions and convert prices. I feel hemmed in. I wish everyone would back off.

The waitress forcefully stabs her finger at mysterious dishes that look unusually unappetizing or unfamiliar. Desperate, I point at a dish that looks like beef and green beans, one of spinach and meat dumplings, and some rice.

There are no pictures of drinks on the menu, so, remembering writer Polly Evans's method of ordering by pointing at others' meals, I look around the room. But there are no glasses on any table, no cups of tea, even. Later I will learn that many Chinese eat soup in place of a beverage, but for the moment, I am confounded. The waitress points at a picture of milk. I know from my adoption trip that the Chinese think of Americans as obsessed with milk. I hate milk.

"No," I say.

She points at the milk again, more insistently.

"No," I say. "Water?"

She shakes her head fiercely.

The ten-year-old boy stands by, looking important, waiting just in case he needs to ask me again if I speak any Chinese.

"Water?" I say hopefully to him.

The boy says something in Chinese, ending with "water." The blank look on the waitress's face suggests that his translation ran along the lines of, "I have no idea what the meaning is of this exotic English word, *water*."

The mother glows with pride. The waitress stares awestruck at the amazing boy then comes back to earth to deal with me. I'm afraid she will break her finger, the way she pounds it against the picture of the milk again.

"No," I say. I fish out my booklet of translations and point at the word *water*.

"No," she says.

I slide my finger to *ice water*.

"No," she says.

I move down to *cold water*.

"No," she says.

I have trouble accepting that this restaurant has no bottles of drinking water. I have never seen anything but bottled water in restaurants in China but figure if I keep pointing at words that refer to water she'll understand what I am asking for. It is possible that once the waitress first insisted that there was no water, she was then obligated to save face by continuing to deny that there was any water available. What may be a matter of pride to her feels to me like a power struggle. I search for a compromise. I point at *Diet Coke*.

"No," she says. Her finger shifts over to *beer*.

"No," I say. We are no longer attempting to communicate. We are involved in a weird negotiation.

She points at *Coca-cola*.

"Yes," I say. I don't really want a caffeinated, sugary beverage right before bedtime, but it's the best I'm going to do. The waitress departs to place our order, and I can breathe again. I dab at the sweat on my brow. "Wow, that was harrowing," I say. "She was so pushy."

Sophie is silent, staring at the table. She has taken sides against me, turned into a foreigner who exudes a subtle air of disapproval toward me and my strange ways. "We should leave a really big tip," she says. "She worked so hard to understand us."

Chapter Four

"I miss our house," Sophie sometimes says while we are in China. "I don't miss anything else. Just our house. I wish I could move it here and live here."

I imagine our Victorian house, complete with squirrels and bats and mice, a wooden structure with cracked siding, lifted and dropped down here, dwarfed by the slick high-rises of Beijing, out of place among all the steel and concrete. I imagine sitting on our wide front porch and watching traffic tangle and snarl while people walk by, cell phones at their ears. I imagine hanging laundry from our upstairs balcony. Our house is many times larger than the typical Chinese apartment, and would, like me, be an odd sprawling creature among so many compact ones. I imagine instead living in something lighter, smaller, less cumbersome—a pagoda on a hill with willows waving beside a stream.

Sophie's attachment to our house surprises me. Sometimes I do miss being at home, the way time passes differently, more quickly and purposefully, when I'm in my own space. At the same time, it's freeing to be away, even more so because I have no cell phone and little Internet access here in China. So often, the house, like my schedule, has felt to me like a burden, a trap I want to escape, an entanglement that is just too much work. Leaky pipes have necessitated replacing ceilings three times, until I finally just gave up. Now the kitchen ceiling is a checkerboard, square holes cut in it at intervals, offering glimpses of rough wood and snaking pipes above. Every few months, I call contractors or just let problems go, like the patio that is falling apart, the driveway that is breaking up, the unused basement toilet that emits a foul smell, the light switches all over the house that don't work. The house could be a full-time job. The house could be a full-time job, parenting is a full-time job, teaching is a full-time job, and then there's writing and my second teaching job. I have too many jobs. There is no hope for keeping up with them.

~

But for a brief time after I figured out how to deal with the squirrels, it felt like I might get things under control and gradually widen our world. We found a group in Erie called Panda Girls and an international adoption group in Allegheny that held regular gatherings. We both enrolled in dance classes, and Sophie started taking gymnastics. I aimed to make sure that my child was comfortable in her identity, in her body, in her home in ways that I hadn't been when I was young. But at every turn, a family member died or another home repair emergency cropped up. Bats arrived and took over the house. My mother was diagnosed with breast cancer.

For some reason, it was the bat infestation that pitched me to the bottom of Maslow's Hierarchy of Basic Needs. I was too focused on physiological and safety needs like shelter and protection from physical threat to move up the ladder, process more complex issues, and achieve progressively higher states of being, much less self-actualization. So it's a surprise to me that the house that has never felt quite like home to me is, like China to Sophie, a place that she thinks of as home.

Dance and bats were opposite yet somehow complementary forces—yin and yang—making us first more comfortable with ourselves and then more profoundly unsettled, bringing back my own regular vague childhood impulse to flee. I grew up in a family in which no one ever danced or sang. We sat stiffly in the back pew at church, standing awkwardly for hymns, waiting for the music to stop. Even jiggling my foot or swaying felt taboo. Although I'd always liked to dance and took a few ballet classes, I quit altogether in my teen years, swaybacked and self-conscious that the leotard made it more obvious. It was hard for me to stand up entirely straight unless I lifted my knee above my hip. I learned to pull in my stomach and lift my ribcage, but it has always taken work, and sometimes, then and now, I've longed for the freedom not to be expected to focus, at all times, on my carriage.

Every Monday at five P.M. when Sophie and I climbed the narrow staircase between a tattoo parlor and a real estate agency, up to Peggy Johnson's Dance Studio, I imagined that I was steering my own daughter carefully around the pitfalls of my own childhood. For all the feminine stereotypes associated with dance, I believed that there was no better way to instill coordination, musicality, and physical confidence. From a folding metal chair in the hallway, I watched children stream into the studio, bottom-heavy with fat legs and frilly tutus, like Weebles that wobble but don't fall down.

Parents and grandparents watched through the window as our little girls swung their hips to

> I'm a disco dancer
> And I love that disco beat
> It makes me feel so groovy
> Right down to my feet.

While our children learned position number one, moms passed around scrapbooks devoted to their preschoolers' two-month dance careers. At the end of class, the little girls lined up for stickers, which the teacher affixed to their noses as they filed out.

And then it was time for my class. As I buckled my tap shoes, I felt a sense of private triumph that somehow I had gotten past my childhood fears and was setting an example for my daughter. I picked up steps quickly, probably because I practiced so much on the bathroom floor while Sophie splashed in the tub. If I woke in the night, filled with panic and dread because I alone was responsible for a child and a house, visualizing dance routines was calming. It also reinforced the steps in my memory as well as the transitions between steps, always the hardest parts for me.

And then the bats arrived. For months they made me jumpy, too alert, as if I were in the midst of a grief so deep, I could no longer go on living in my own skin. We had to move, I thought after the first one, then the second. I couldn't raise a child in a house where creatures kept flying out of nowhere, whizzing around rooms. I couldn't ever relax.

A lot of people have household bat stories, I eventually discovered, and they are all pretty much alike. They involve sudden startled awareness of wild, reckless flitting and darting before lights, suggesting a presence powerful enough to blot out the sun and leave the world wringing its hands in darkness. They involve jerky motions, ducking, screaming, pins-and-needles scalp sensations, and more often than not, brooms or tennis rackets. They are about violated territory, indignation at invasion, fear of the unpredictable, and a lost sense of ownership—of rooms, of space, of the air we breathe. The First Law of Bat Physics is this: household bats inevitably take up psychic space way out of proportion to the physical area they occupy.

My first bat encounter went along the usual lines. At first, I thought a moth had eclipsed the overhead light, but I looked up from the computer and saw a bird winging by. Across the hall, it whipped low over my sleeping daughter, exhausted from her first day of kindergarten. The bird banked, swooped down again, and landed on the hall carpet. Only then did it become clear that this was not a pale soft-winged night-flying cousin of the butterfly, not a chirping feathery creature who took a wrong turn after a day of gliding picturesquely through sunlit skies. It was a flying rodent that sought out dark places and hung upside down in them.

I screamed, slammed doors, called neighbors. My scalp prickled. Later I read about an experiment in which a researcher wrapped a woman's hair tightly around a bat, but it obstinately kept escaping instead of nesting there. I knew that the thing about bats and hair was an old wives' tale, but my instinct was still to cover my head and picture old wives with pink scalps showing through white hair, so unbearably pink, vulnerable as newborn mice.

A brave neighbor, a bright light, and a shoebox later, we released the bat into the night. Afterward, this became an amusing story, and Sophie was disappointed that she slept through it all. But that's okay: we would have more bat stories, at least seventeen of them, and I would quickly learn that sharing a good bat story could be a bonding ritual. Others commiserated and offered up tales of their own undesired wildlife encounters. But there was the small minority of repelled listeners. With a measuring glance they seemed to convert me instantly to a scary haglike nocturnal creature who lived in a sunless cave or a rickety carnival haunted house with laceworks of cobwebs wafting from every corner, stark, windowless walls, or sagging staircases that lead nowhere, twisting like arthritic hands. I was surprised to see in the mirror that I hadn't suddenly aged fifty years. I was surprised to come home to sunlight shining through lace curtains and stained glass, casting watery patterns on the walls and multiplying into rainbows all over the stairs.

I read up on bats, which on the page and in theory, fascinated me even if, in practice, flying around the house, they completely freaked me out. Our house was infested by little brown bats, a protected species in Pennsylvania. Bats, I learned, once called "flitter mice," have such precise echolocation ability they can detect a single strand of hair in total darkness. On the page, bats seem less supernatural in a creepy horror-movie way, more supernatural in a miraculous, mystical way. Bats are flying metaphors whose ultrasonic waves bounce off obstacles and the objects of their hunger, showing them where they are. I was quite taken with the notion of the sensory equipment and amazing instincts of bats.

This may have been partly because I had such a hard time learning to trust my instincts as a parent. When I adopted Sophie, I knew nothing about babies, and measuring and weighing the advice of others against my own intuition did not come easily. When my baby was handed to me, she had a rash on her face and a tendency to pluck at her onesie where it touched her tummy. I followed the advice of a Chinese doctor and our facilitator, continuing to feed her milk formula, mixing in medication that the doctor had prescribed. But the rash didn't get better. The baby thrashed around, increasingly uncomfortable.

So, despite the disapproval of others, I switched her to soy formula. Lo and behold, she began to improve. The rash disappeared, her stomach stopped gurgling, and she began gulping down heaping spoonfuls of oatmeal. It amazed me that my instincts had been right: she was lactose intolerant.

I became braver. The doctor had given her antihistamines for an upper-respiratory infection, and she was wired all the time, never sleeping. I had always experienced the same symptoms when I was on antihistamines, a reaction opposite to the drowsiness that overtakes many people. Again to criticism from our facilitator, I stopped the antihistamines cold turkey. Sophie settled down, relaxed, and slept.

I would like to say that those incidents made me surer of myself and my decisions. When I put Sophie in day care, it was against not only the prevailing wisdom of many mothers, but also the advice of adoption specialists. For proper attachment, many maintain, parents should bring their babies home and live in isolation, allowing no one outside the immediate family to care for the children so that they will bond with us fully. It was neither possible nor seemingly desirable for either me or Sophie to be cooped up together all day with no source of income or outside stimulation. In time, I was pretty sure, our bond would be solid. In time, it was. But what mother doesn't still doubt herself regularly in a culture that sometimes seems designed to kindle parental doubt?

When Sophie was eight, she asked me, "How old was I when I started walking?" She'd just returned from a friend's house, where the other mother had proudly announced that her children had taken their first steps at eight and nine months, respectively.

Sophie was deflated when I told her the truth: she'd been almost fourteen months old the first time she finally tottered forward without support.

In fact, I'd been awed, watching a baby who'd spent most of her life in a crib suddenly take off like an airplane idling on the runway then shooting abruptly into space, skipping the gradual ascent of its counterparts. When I took her at eleven months to her first doctor's appointment in the U. S., she'd just learned to sit up and she could scoot a little. The doctor was concerned. He recommended physical therapy. If she didn't catch up in six months, I'd consider it, I said. But I wasn't really worried.

And sure enough, over the next three months she'd fast-forwarded through the development she'd missed: she crawled, pulled up, cruised, and walked. She also spoke her first English words. I was proud of my spontaneous moment of wisdom, my confidence that the doctor had been wrong. Now, here Sophie was, eight years old, competing as a YMCA gymnast, dancing beautifully, and feeling somehow lesser because her development had been delayed by a couple of months when she was a baby. And I, who had spent a lot of time struggling to trust myself, faltered for just a second. With physical therapy, would she have walked sooner? Would she now be an elite gymnast or a professional dancer? Did I really care? Would it have mattered one bit?

Influenced by Korean adoptees who grew up in rural areas where they were the only Asians, many white adoptive parents of Asian children believe strongly that it's important to move to diverse areas and send children to schools with students from a variety of ethnic backgrounds. I have repeatedly read on listservs about the extraordinary efforts of many families to relocate or to transfer their children to different schools in order to keep them from feeling alone. Unless I find another job in a difficult market and move us, this is not possible for us. But I find myself perpetually questioning whether staying in our small town is the right thing to do. These questions have kept me from entirely settling in and making Bradford my home, fed my uneasiness about living in this house forever. The bats may have simply compounded a nebulous sense of disquiet that was already there.

Right after the first bat, but before the many sequels, Sophie landed in an emergency room in Alexandria, Virginia. She had survived squirrels and bats in the house, black bears and skunks in the woods, raccoons and mangy dogs in our trash, but now, a couple of days of visiting a city and staying in an apartment with a cat had felled her. Two days before Thanksgiving, she woke and then went right back to sleep. I let her sleep for a few hours. She again briefly came to, and then her eyes rolled back in her head and she slipped back into sleep. I picked her up and only then saw how her whole body labored for oxygen, her chest hollowing when she exhaled, lungs failing to fill when she inhaled. I watched her and finally understood that this was a crisis.

For eleven hours, emergency room staff worked to get her breathing under control; her asthma attack had been complicated by severe dehydration. It was truly the eleventh hour, when the doctor had decided to admit her to the hospital, that she finally began to breathe normally again. I wondered: how do you follow the advice of adoption experts when you are simply trying to survive?

Two weeks later, in another hospital, this time in Kansas, Sophie and I waited through the long hours of my mother's mastectomy. Mom had known it was cancer from the second she found the lump. Her sister had had breast cancer. Their mother had died of it. My father's mother had also died of breast cancer, and this makes me glad that Sophie does not have my genes.

Like happy families and bat stories, I thought, waiting during my mother's surgery, hospital visits were all alike: rows of attached seats and piles of magazines and droning TVS, tension, boredom, beeping monitors, ringing phones, white sheets, flat beds, a loved one's face gone slack in sleep. Sophie was getting used to hospitals. She played with her Barbies and complained that she was bored.

After that, she became fascinated by breasts. The next week, she marched a stark naked Barbie across the floor of my bedroom. "Don't laugh at my breasts," Barbie said in a ridiculously high falsetto. "Yes, I have breasts! I have breasts and you should not laugh at them!"

"Is Barbie talking about her breasts?" I asked.

A sly smile from Sophie. She paraded Barbie off to the next room. "Do not laugh at my breasts!" I heard Barbie proclaim again.

The next day, Sophie announced, "I don't want breasts."

I broke the news. "Well, you're a girl, so chances are, you'll have some."

She looked horrified. "I don't want big breasts like yours," she said.

"You think mine are big?" I tried not to sound incredulous.

"Like a giant!" she replied.

I smiled at this memory as I learned the dance to "Little Rock Getaway," which I misheard the first time as "Little Rat Boy." Even after I knew the correct title, I still thought of it as "Little Rat Boy." My classmates humored me and called it that, too. Whenever our teacher started the music and we kicked and ball-changed forward before segueing into a soft shoe, I pictured little boys during the black plague, leaping away from the rats biting at our heels.

Maybe that picture came to my mind because I'd begun to feel as if I were always running from something, never settled, running from my family legacy of breast cancer, wishing to put down roots but often running away, in my imagination, to a bigger, more diverse place, running from the bats whose visits had become part of a monthly event that included ducking and screaming and calling neighbors. Then there was the bat whose flight we missed altogether. Instead, very late one night, I heard from the window a mysterious, potentially eschatological series of thuds and rattles and crashes, the vibrations of the sky falling, boulders of stars hitting the driveway, cracks opening in the earth, the continents splitting. I stumbled outside expecting debris, shingles, bricks, a neighbor's car door, a ragged chunk of moon but found only a layer of slickened blackened leaves.

Later we discovered the bat in the bottom of the window fan. I was sick as I imagined it flying toward the window and hitting, instead, the fan blade, dropping down to the bottom and rising into the blade again and again as it tried to escape. Bats were, I discovered as I removed screws and lifted off the grill, more mammalian in death than in blurry flight. I got a look up close at the furry little body with its wings folded neatly around it like a malfunctioning parachute.

Much as I admired the instincts of bats, they were not, apparently, so good at detecting the spinning fan blade, since soon after that, we found another one that had taken the same kamikaze route. If I'd heard it hit, I would have turned off the fan. But I was shamefully relieved not to have to face another live bat alone or implore my neighbors for help.

"Mom," Sophie said one night at bedtime, "when a snake eats a mouse, what do you feel the most—bad for the mouse or good for the snake?"

Answers formulated then died away. Predators and prey are just nature, I almost said. And then: maybe I should outline the food chain, emphasizing the custodial rather than dominant role of humans. But no: Sophie's question was really about power and compassion, which impulse should take precedence. So I abandoned the teachable moment and said, "Bad for the mouse," and she beamed and said, "Me, too."

Honestly, I didn't feel all that bad for the mouse. And when a fan killed a bat, I wondered, what did I feel the most: bad for the bat or relieved for me? I didn't want to think too much about this, or how responsible I felt for everyone, even the bats, or how this small death in a fan at night nudged at my fears, at what I myself stood to lose.

I liked listening to the other mothers of daughters in dance. In this working-class community, many parents were determined to give their children better lives, more education and more opportunities than they had had. Though my background was different, though I'd benefited from a lot of education and opportunities, my desires were not unlike theirs. I was happy that my daughter might not have my predisposition to breast cancer. I was happy that we talked openly in ways I would have never talked to my mother, that in the middle of the night, Sophie woke me up with her fears. "I don't think I'm ready for the test," she'd announce sometimes at 3:00 A.M. Or "I'm afraid I'll be seduced by a UFO," mixing up the words *seduced* and *abducted*.

Even in the face of family deaths and illnesses, she saw the humor in the human body. Her outlook was so mercifully different from my own when I was her age, when my fundamentalist Christian upbringing emphasized the spiritual over the physical, condemning vanity and sins of the flesh, leaving me alarmingly out of touch with my own body. And now here we were, laughing until tears trailed down our cheeks when we mistook the largest bra in Target for an oddly shaped purse. Here I was with a daughter whose idea of a great joke was to hang my bra in the landing window to show off to the whole neighborhood. Here I was with a daughter who dissolved into similar hysterics when Anne of Green Gables yearned out loud for a "bosom friend." "Bra-zil," I heard Sophie tell her stuffed dog, "is a country with two large mountains."

Even when she was very little, she was able to see the body as a funny thing. But she was not so sold on feeling ridiculous in dance recital costumes, as she did the first time she performed. I delivered her to a room swarming with tiny girls in tutus large and stiff enough to stand alone and hairstyles that were masterpieces of Byzantine architecture. Volunteers lobbed powder puffs at small cheeks, tied ribbons, and hunted down lost shoes.

I hurried to find my own group, in snug costumes, hair slickly straight or twisted up or unusually curly, faces elegant in understated makeup, eye shadow and lipstick. Our dance was terrifying, standing on a stage where we could see only light, heat and intensity and brightness flooding the stage. There were dark forms beyond, coughs and rustles, but no faces, only rows and rows of faceless forms, surely, I thought, noting our every mistake, and I made a lot of them. Yet the audience responded with thunderous applause.

Sophie, absurdly not herself in her pink tutu, brought tears to my eyes. Just standing there on that stage seemed so difficult and brave. Other women said they cried for us for the same reason. I was pretty sure that my own child would never think of dancing in front of people as such a miracle. But I also knew that no matter how hard we try to protect our children from our own struggles and flaws, they will have their own questions, their own conflicts to confront, and we will still make a million mistakes.

I couldn't just pick up and move to a place with a bigger Asian population and more connections to my child's birth culture without significant trade-offs and sacrifices. Jobs in my field were scarce, particularly those with security and health insurance. How could I know for sure that a move would be worth it? So often I was dubious about the recommendations of experts, like the one from our local health department that advised rabies shots for anyone who'd slept in a room where there was a bat, just in case a bat had bitten us and we didn't know it, just in case that bat might have happened to be rabid. My instincts told me that rabies shots would be a waste of time and money. It seemed to me that we would know if we'd been bitten, and even if we had, our health department had only been sent one rabid bat ever. Statistically, we had a higher chance of winning the state lottery than being bit by a rabid bat. Still, our doctors concurred: we ought to get the shots. They couldn't tell us not to, I reasoned. They were too worried about liability. Against my better judgment, I did what the pediatrician's office suggested and headed to the ER for our first round.

"So you both just got bit by a bat today?" asked an ER receptionist in a guarded, pleasant voice. The room went very still, an eerie pre-tornado sort of stillness. A nurse lowered her chart to peer at me. Another desk clerk's hands hovered, motionless, above her computer keyboard. The two women avoided each other's eyes. I explained about our bats and the health department and the doctors. They all shuddered an appropriate amount and regular motion resumed.

Sophie and I were, understandably, a lower priority than the guy whose chest flamed grotesquely. He said that a red hot brick fell a hundred feet and hit him. This seemed to me a more freakish accident than two members of one family being bit by a rabid bat on the same day, but ER workers rushed to treat him without exchanging sidelong wary glances. A parade of people went ahead of us: a young man with a burnt hand, a feverish child, an elderly man who might have had a heart attack.

For three hours, we waited in an uncomfortable curtained partition. On the suspended TV, a man's voice droned about the curious habits of the amazing bumblebee, then perked up to advertise fishing rods and hunting gear. Sophie was terrified of the shots and clung to me like a little bat pup, but I was feeling very Zen. Here we were in the ER, but nothing was wrong with us. So maybe hospital stories weren't all alike.

Waiting for my mom to wake after surgery a few months before, I had glimpsed death in her loose, waxy face. Two weeks before that, my daughter kept dissolving into sleep in the middle of sentences, eyes rolling back in her head. She'd looked so fragile that night in the Alexandria ER, tubes and tapes and a board like a small splint holding in place an IV, an oxygen monitor clipped to her toe. She'd looked like one of those overpackaged Barbies held fast in its carton by wires, tapes, and cardboard.

My mother, fresh from another test, treatment, or surgery, had often said, "When will it end?" I avoided the obvious answer. And now, here we were in the emergency room, and nothing had ended yet, and nothing was wrong with us. It was a pain, waiting there on an uncomfortable backless stool, trying to read my assignment for the next day's class while Sophie whined, "How much longer?" But I still didn't mind being there, because so easily something could have been wrong but nothing was.

"Is the f-word bad?" Sophie asked.

"Well," I said, caught by surprise. "I don't think it's something you want to go around saying."

"Okay," she agreed readily, which made me suspicious.

"Do you know what the f-word is?' I asked.

She thought for a second, then said, voice hushed, "Stupid?"

"No," I said.

Her eyes widened. She leaned in close. In a whisper, she tried again: "Dead?"

And I laughed. We weren't sick or dying. We just had bats.

I'd like to say that this moment of perspective steeled me for all the lost bats ahead, flying through the house, our bedrooms, my dreams, that from then on I bravely faced them alone, without screams, a pounding heart, or grudgingly helpful neighbors. I would like to say that after constant trips to the hospital for the rest of our rabies series I came to trust my own judgment more or that at some point I stopped wondering if we should move. But those things were not easily achieved.

I would, however, learn to listen for the particular thunk of a bat landing in the dark so I could immediately set it free. I would learn to lure bats outside with patience, an open door, and a porch light. But I would never learn to be calm about it.

Nor, quite honestly, despite seven recitals, would I ever really feel comfortable dancing in front of an audience or wish to see the videos of our dances. When someone insists on playing them, I resolve not to wince the way my mother did when she was my age, seeing herself on film, but who wants to be confronted by such a vivid depiction of all their flaws? My mother survived breast cancer and reminded me every year to go for my mammogram, another version of myself on film. I go. I want to live long enough to know my grandchildren. I would even like to be around long enough to see my daughter become an old woman with white hair. "You're doing everything you can," the kind mammogram technician tells me. "You are doing the best you can."

Sophie's interest in dance class has waxed and waned. She can afford the luxury of disdain: she's strong and graceful and flexible. Dance carries none of the baggage for her that it did for me, so either I have succeeded spectacularly or I never needed to worry in the first place. When she joined the local gymnastics team, Sophie quit dance. I kept going, briefly unlocked from tension and time, ball-changing, pivot-turning, toe-flapping, heel-tapping, as if I could outrun anything that was chasing me.

After another Thanksgiving dinner in Virginia, I gathered plates and glasses and crumpled napkins from my friend Sara's table. Forks and spoons rattled into the sink as I rinsed dishes and loaded the dishwasher. Back and forth from the table to the kitchen, piling, scraping, rinsing, loading. Most of the guests had left. Sara dumped leftovers into Tupperware containers and snapped on the lids. She fitted plastic and foil over the tops of bowls and stacked them in the refrigerator. The kids played in another room.

I had a weird sense of urgency as I piled up dirty dishes from the children's table. My mind prickled with an insistence that there was something that I was supposed to notice, something that would be important later. I dismissed the strange feeling and wiped the countertops.

The next morning when Sophie woke, it was like a rerun of the Thanksgiving before. "I can't get up," she said, and dropped back to sleep. Her breathing was shallow, abdomen caving in on every intake. She took a puff from her inhaler and went back to sleep again, her breath still whistling in her lungs.

I started packing another bag for another ER—sweaters, books, money for snacks. I checked on her again: no improvement. We should go, I thought, but I was reluctant. I felt that strange prickling again, like there was something important I was supposed to remember. I turned on the shower and as water cascaded down and plastic toys swam from one end of the bathtub to congregate around my feet, an image came to me, a full glass of water I'd carried to the kitchen from the children's table.

Sophie hadn't drunk a thing the day before.

During her previous Thanksgiving emergency room visit, she'd had regular nebulizer treatments for asthma, but the IV, I suddenly remembered, had been for dehydration. I snapped into action, jumped out of the shower, towel-dried my hair, and called to my friend, who headed out for some Pedialyte.

Sophie took a few sips and was back on her feet. The inhaler worked. Her energy returned with startling rapidity.

I was in a daze of disbelief, as if I'd just experienced a miracle. A miracle of intuition, of realizing how much my instincts had sharpened over the years, of knowing that I could, after all, trust myself to perceive signals beyond my hearing, beyond my conscious recognition.

It took a couple of years before the bats mostly went away, and during those years, I would often lie awake, a feeling of doom hanging over me, my heart beating out the words: *I have bats, I have bats.* The month before my mother died, four months before we left for China, we got a new roof, and that pretty much took care of them. For a while, trapped pups wandered into the house and we'd find them splayed like five-cornered leaves on the insides of window screens, moving throughout the day to escape sunlight, huddled from the afternoon sun down at the corner of the sill, slowly unfolding again after dusk. Three trapped pups matured, and in their attempt to escape flew down into the basement, into the same tall narrow box. A boxful of bats in the basement, I kept saying as we took it outside with gloved hands to free them.

"Not a boxful," Sophie said. "Only three."

But three bats are not just a boxful, but a basementful, as far as I'm concerned.

I carried them out, recoiling. I wasn't sure what to make of the unerring instinct of bats, whatever had led so many right into the grill of a window fan, whatever had led all three of these bats through the same cavernous basement to trap themselves in the same small box. Some signal of air and sound had failed them, and yet, miraculously, it had failed every one of them in the same way. I knew these bats represented a cautionary tale, and yet, there was something magical to me about those instincts, about my own intuition that I'd fought so hard to trust.

But I also understood that when it came to parenthood, a little self-doubt might keep me on my toes.

Chapter Five

October 2008

When I first came to China, to adopt Sophie, the trip was a bizarre juxta-position of packaged tour and life-changing experience. Our group shivered in chilly winds through tedious lectures about emperors and dynasties at the Forbidden City and the Ming Tombs. We trudged in the hot sun up the Great Wall and around a tea plantation. Even after we added heavy, fussy babies to our loads, we continued to visit tourist attractions in order to pack in as much of China as possible to tell our children about someday.

Preoccupied first by my anticipation and then by my squirmy, noisy baby, I absorbed little. Maybe returning to the same places will help me find out what I missed. But I've been dreading another arranged tour, another scripted, sur-face view of China—the "Beijing-Xi'an-Panda thing," as film editor Andrea Williams refers to the typical China homeland tour. But since I know of no other way to introduce my child to her home country, I resign myself to a less "authentic" travel experience than those reported by people who avoid packaged tours. Unlike travel writers like J. Maarten Troost or Polly Evans, we likely won't view Mao's corpse, travel by mule, or visit a rural market fea-turing Siberian tiger paws, cobra hearts, and scorpion kabobs. Unlike Larry Herzberg, we won't hop off a stalled train with a group of new acquaintances to visit an ancient rural village with grazing water buffalo, cobblestone streets, and peasant homes made of mud bricks, a place that time forgot, where no one has seen a foreigner in over forty years.

Though these experiences make for interesting stories, I'm not convinced that they are always more inherently honest ones. Capturing the spirit of a country through a collection of quirky details can be like assembling a picture of the U. S. through, say, witnessing a snake-handling ritual at a Pentecostal church, touring the Zippo lighter museum, stopping at highway diners named only "Good Food," participating in a Civil War reenactment, and visiting Donner Memorial State Park. Certainly one might make some valid conclusions about American life while missing the point about ordinary citizens who largely don't use venomous snakes to test their faith, enjoy creating wall-sized American flags from multicolored cigarette lighters, celebrate a historical period that promoted human slavery, and dine on white bread with congealed fatty beef tips when they're not snacking on one another. Or maybe, on second thought, this is a pretty true picture of the U. S. But it's just one of many.

"We specialize in helping children fall in love with China," is the motto of our tour company. Immersing ourselves in the more bizarre details of a foreign culture would, at this stage, be counterproductive. Our position as foreigners with a deep investment in this country makes us different from many travelers and means that our objectives are easily misunderstood.

"Going to China will make Sophie grateful for what she has," people kept saying to me before we left, as if I'd saved for years and years, shopped and packed and secured visas and taken a sabbatical for the sole purpose of instilling gratitude. The comment implied that the point of visiting a birth country is to make a child feel relieved that she is no longer there. Did people think we would see abject poverty, child-prostitution rings, tanks bearing down on protestors, or sweatshops employing minors, rather than ordinary schoolchildren in sweat suits eating treats on sticks from street vendors? If anything, Sophie has been jealous of their three-hour lunch periods, though not so much the early start and late dismissal of each school day. When I chafed at well-meaning comments about the gratitude Sophie would acquire, I think now, it was the implication that one misses an impoverished rural foreign family less than a comfortable American one that most bothered me. It was the implication that money and comfort can compensate for a primal loss.

Just as we're not here to seek strangeness, we're also not here to compare China unfavorably to the U. S. We've come to forge a general, hopefully positive, understanding of my daughter's birth heritage, of Chinese history and culture and people. If that requires a somewhat generic approach to China, so be it. Although there's something about China, even for Americans in five-star hotels and private vans, that defies the generic.

By the second day, though, I'm starting to wonder if the tour hasn't been just a little too successful in helping Sophie fall in love with China. My formerly mercurial, occasionally misanthropic daughter remains a stranger, a glass-half-full humanity-loving sort of person who casts only the most benevolent eye on her surroundings. The smoke that filters into our hotel room, forcing her to use her inhaler for the first time in weeks? No problem. That's what inhalers are for. The guy at the exchange counter who tries to cheat us? She doesn't even notice.

He hands me a pile of bills but snatches them back when I start to count. "Sorry, sorry," he says, adding more to the pile. He counts out money for Sophie, sliding over another pile, then retrieving it abruptly. "Sorry, sorry," he says. He plucks a couple of bills from the stack, then passes it back as if to convey that he's not dishonest, just inept.

When Sophie was six, she announced that for her next birthday she was going to have a Helen Keller-themed party. This made total six-year-old sense: she had recently read a biography and discovered that she and Helen Keller shared a birthday. I kept trying to figure out what activities such a party would involve. I pictured the key events recounted in Keller's autobiography, events further locked into my memory by children's books based on Keller's work and the play-turned-movie *The Miracle Worker:* a feral and straggle-haired child snatching food from others' plates; words spelled into her hand: *Cat cat cold cold doll doll;* the moment at the pump that Annie Sullivan spells the word *water* and suddenly, finally, Helen understands. Sophie's plan mercifully faded before she turned seven, and we had an ordinary small party at Pizza Hut. But later, it struck me how these essential facts of Keller's life seem to be set in stone, all other experiences, all ordinary daily details, subsumed by legend while we replay endlessly the same familiar narratives.

A few years ago, I wrote a book about adopting Sophie, about how despite my doubts and anxieties, mistakes and flaws, becoming her mother turned out to be the luckiest, best thing I could have ever done. Too often, newspaper stories and reviews missed the point, portraying me as a saint rescuing a destitute orphan, a common theme in the media surrounding adoption, one that continues today; a recent review of an adoption memoir expresses amazement that though the author "saved" his daughters from "a life too terrible to contemplate," he is the one who feels lucky. I'm dubious about this firmly entrenched narrative, since no one knows what other fabulous family Sophie might have landed in instead of mine. It's a narrative that assumes that adoption is all about parental sacrifice, not fulfillment. It implies, however subtly, that an adopted child is more a burden than an amazing gift. It ignores the miracle by which a lovely, fully formed baby enters your life and becomes your own child.

I learned quickly how hard it is to fight the stories that people want to tell, the scripts that we have always followed. Maybe this is why I chafe so much at being a tourist, too, following the course set out for us.

Even factory tours follow the same basic pattern in China, something I'd forgotten. My friend Gaj later tells me that this sort of tour is also standard in India. First there's a display. Then there's a demonstration accompanied by a lecture on how the art in question is a dying one, costing its painstaking practitioners their health and eyesight, an art that is tragically no longer valued by the current generation. This segment is followed by a showroom full of stuff for sale and heavy pressure to buy.

Ten years ago, we visited jade, enamel, and silk factories. By the third tour, the format was so predictable, the machinery so loud, and Sophie so restless and fretful, I withdrew, skipping right to the last step, jiggling her up and down as I paced the aisles of the shop. I'd only known her for a couple of days, and she remained suspicious and wary of me. In that silk shop, long ago, a Chinese woman had barreled, cooing, at Sophie, lifting her out of my arms, holding and admiring the beautiful baby. Sophie's head whipped around, her eyes frantic. She held out her arms to me. And I rushed over and took her back, realizing that somehow, in the brief time we'd been together, we'd started to belong to each other.

I would not have traded that moment for another factory tour, but this time, ten years later, at another silk factory, I vow to pay attention, make up for what I missed. I ask questions and snap pictures as our guide shows us skeins of colorful threads hanging from racks. We proceed to baskets of cocoons containing dead silkworms. Next are jars of items used to make dye—henna, saffron, acorns. A worker sits on a bench before a frame, knotting threads. Sophie learns to knot while our guide explains that making silk rugs by hand is a dying art, straining the eyes and requiring great patience.

While Sophie focuses on her lesson, the tour guide and Lily comment on Sophie's beauty. "Her eyes are very pretty," Lily says. The proprietors of a local Chinese restaurant at home have said the same thing. White Americans are much more likely to comment on her silky dark hair. I'm pondering this cultural difference when the women ask if I speak any Chinese.

"Wa bu shi daifu," I say: I am not a doctor. The reason this sentence has stuck so fast is that the guy on the language tape, Gubo, sounded like he was saying "bullshit." Now, in my head, I translate the sentence, "Bullshit am I a doctor!" This is undoubtedly completely incorrect, but my translation helps me remember to unleash the words with indignation. I doubt that Gubo was really feeling irritated at having been accused of being a doctor, but if I imagine him that way, I get the tones and inflections right.

Lily and our guide nod approvingly. "That is very good," they both say, and I am inordinately proud that I can say "I am not a doctor" and be understood by native speakers.

We are whisked off to a room that is heaped with silk rugs. The stacks are as high as my waist. For a dying art with few practitioners, there sure are a lot of rugs here. The guide lifts a few to compare the backs. She explains the difference between the expensive ones with six hundred knots per inch, which take months to make, and the cheaper ones with only one hundred per inch. The Chinese are particularly suited to arts involving discipline, concentration, and delicate precision, something they learn from early childhood by using chopsticks, she tells us. The eating utensils develop focus and intellect, improve memory, increase manual dexterity, and lead to better writing and artistic skills.

"Wow," we say.

The guide maneuvers a rug around in a circle, throwing it up as she rotates it so that it lands rippling in her hands, the color seeming to deepen. This is how you identify real silk, she tells us: it subtly changes color as you move it.

"Wow," we say, admiring the shifting, shimmering gradations of rich color.

The guide holds up rugs, magnificent florals, playful pandas climbing bamboo, colorful birds on branches. "Only 4,900 yuan!" she says. "Only 14,000 yuan. And we ship!"

"Wow," we say. We take pictures from all angles. I convert prices in my head: $700, $2,000. It doesn't occur to me for the longest time that she's not just reciting facts for my entertainment or prices for my edification. She's not actually boasting about the factory's shipping policies to incite my awe at the technological modernization of China. As her growing exasperation becomes apparent, it finally dawns on me: I'm supposed to buy a rug.

Americans are regarded as rich. Although I saved for several years to afford this trip, such savings would be out of reach for many Chinese. I could go into debt and buy a rug and pay it off within a year or two, so it seems ludicrous to say that I cannot afford it. But I have no wish to go into debt to buy a rug for which I have no use.

During the last few years, our house has been overtaken by family heirlooms. My mother shipped me all of her Desert Rose Franciscanware with pink petals and green leaves, and all of her fine china rimmed with blue and gold, stars bursting around the periphery. They came in six chest-high crates, bundled in layers of bubble wrap, packed in Styrofoam peanuts. I had always kept a stash of paper plates and cups. I didn't own a dishwasher. I'd pitched Sophie's tent in the empty dining room.

But that day, the entire weight of family history and obligation had arrived, 239 heavy, breakable pieces that required a china cabinet. And then after my mother died, I brought home vases, glass bowls, Hummel figurines, framed pictures. I brought home my mother's thimble and spoon collections.

I packed away most but left out some: pictures on the piano, glassware on the mantel, thimbles along the top of the doorframe. This is all part of our family history, but to reflect the whole of our heritage, we need to display things from China, too. But it bothers me that consumerism is the only language that we all speak. Consumerism is one of the few ways we know to connect our children to their birth cultures.

Sophie and I pick out an inexpensive silk picture, a white moon in a blue sky, yellow flowers and gray reedy plants. It is so shimmery that the blues and whites and grays all look like gradations of silver.

We drive by Olympic venues, shooting obligatory photos of the Bird's Nest and the Water Cube and the Olympic village, where colorful flags hang from balcony rails. After that, I'm content to stare out the window as steel and glass give way to craggy mountains, some barren and rocky, some furred by trees.

Lily has given Sophie a notebook packed with worksheets to fill out, and now there is an assignment for me, too, a quiz—"100 Questions Adoptive Parents Should Be Able to Answer about China." I gamely tackle the first few questions, but they're all about emperors and government officials. I scan for questions about literature, art, customs, or holidays. There are none.

Briefly I feel like an inadequate parent, unable to recite which emperors lived where and when or the names of current political leaders. In my younger days I was a straight-A student who saw quizzes as exciting challenges. I no longer feel the same need to prove myself, but I'm discovering that there is nothing like being in a foreign country to make people feel dumb.

I ask Lily for the answers, but each question becomes fodder for a ten-minute lecture. I half-listen to facts and information, recited without the dramatic embellishments or thinly veiled opinions that most Americans would consider essential. Those of us raised in a democracy have been taught to value free thought, admittedly sometimes to the point of flakiness. In contrast, *China Survival Guide* reminds me, "Chinese are used to being told what to think by the Communist Party. They have not been encouraged in school or in the workplace to form their own opinions about anything."

After years as a teacher and writer emphasizing the importance of voice and original ideas to my students, I often fall at the opposite end from typical Chinese thinking. The expression "think outside the box" puzzles me, because I'm usually unaware of the box's existence or its boundaries. There's an especially exaggerated cultural divide between someone like me and someone raised in a Communist system, equating learning with the rote memorization of long strings of facts.

Still in good-student mode, trying to be a role model for Sophie, I strain to apply myself to the task of completing the questionnaire. But as Lily talks, as I jot notes in the lurching van, my head starts to throb. I try to concentrate on Lily's words. But wait, I think. In college, I didn't want to devote an entire weekend to setting up the books for my own imaginary small business, so I dropped accounting. I faced a life crisis during my first year with a full-time job, and French lessons went by the wayside. I feel no shame about putting down a book that doesn't engage me. So why am I struggling so hard to remember Chinese dynasties?

The van speeds along without regard to lanes, veering onto shoulders and mounting sidewalks, squeezing between lanes of traffic as if the van is a motorcycle. My head pounds. I'm nauseated. Quietly, I fold the paper away.

As we approach the Great Wall at Badaling, we run into a great wall of vehicles—vans and buses and cars all askew, forcing their way into the stream that has slowed to a trickle. Frequently, we come to a standstill. Pilgrims on foot flow by as we jolt forward, slam to a stop, passing *One World, One Dream* signs and a freestanding sculpture of Olympic rings. In the groups of people hoofing it to the entrance, I count four little boys to every girl. Sophie quietly takes it all in.

Finally we arrive at the wall. It appears that the entire 1.3 billion population of China—one of the few quiz questions I answered correctly—is on the Great Wall, which winds serpent-like ahead of us, up the mountain, its width packed with bobbing hats and bright jackets. The sheer number of wall-to-wall people is daunting. I think of the photo of the Man tucked into the plastic pocket of my journal and of my daughter's birth parents, who may or may not have relocated in the last ten years from a small rural area to a large urban one. Now I fully understand how unrealistic my hope is of finding a connection to my daughter's past, how much the search might feel like looking for a thin silver needle in a barnful of hay.

We bypass all of the attractions at the base, the hotels, restaurants, T-shirt vendors, films, museums, picture-taking opportunities atop camels, cable cars, and KFC, and head straight up the Great Wall. If it weren't for my Lonely Planet guidebook, I might be extremely impressed that ancient people had the foresight to install guardrails, but I have been set straight: they were part of a 1957 restoration. In fact, this whole section of the wall, the most popular and touristy one, is a reconstruction of ruins, not the original fortification built to protect the capital city against invasions of Mongols during the Ming Dynasty.

The wall is twenty feet wide here, which enabled horses to gallop five abreast, according to one tourist website, and small holes may be seen at intervals, through which archers could shoot arrows. Smoke and gunfire signals indicated the number of enemies. I know all of this because, ever the good student, I felt I should get ready for our trip by learning as much as I could. Yet it's clear that what Sophie wants is just to be here among Chinese visitors, who far outnumber Western ones today. Sophie wants to just experience China, not learn about military history.

Although it's seventy degrees, only foreigners display bare arms. While most Chinese wear long-sleeved shirts with jackets, a few women wear suits and high heels or short skirts with knee-high boots. I can't imagine how uncomfortable such dress must be on a hike that is neither pleasant nor relaxing. Sophie and I climb slowly, pausing when we can duck out of the crush of people to snap pictures of the *One World, One Dream* sign on steel girders on the mountainside above us. We document the foliage below, which is starting to change colors. We climb through damp, dank towers, narrow, cavelike passageways made of rough stone. By the fourth tower, we've reached the level of the *One World, One Dream* sign. We take another picture and reverse direction, plunging back down the scary-steep slope of worn bricks that dip unpredictably, smoothed and hollowed by many years of tramping feet. It occurs to me that Barbie feet, molded so that they can only stand in high heels, would be ideal for descending the Great Wall. I imagine Great Wall Barbie, pitched forward at a forty-five-degree angle as she makes her way down the incline of her own miniature plastic Chinese tourist attraction.

I have to hold the railing and bend my knees, either because I am unusually tall or just very clumsy. I receive amused looks from natives. I smile and shrug. The apparent friendly disbelief at my hopelessness is the only acknowledgment of my existence. No one stares as they did ten years ago, when Americans with Chinese babies were routinely mobbed by curious crowds. Now, English-speaking Chinese girls with white parents no longer seem to be an especially unusual sight.

But as I watch the passing faces, I wish it were possible to have a real conversation with someone. I wish I spoke Chinese and could ask what their lives are like. I wish I knew more about how typical Chinese citizens feel about the one-child policy, who believes that their lives have been improved and who has suffered as a result. I wonder if anyone averting eyes politely from us has had to have an abortion, give up a baby, or pay a fine for having too many children. I wonder if anyone sees my child and thinks of her own lost children. Xinran writes that very few Chinese birth mothers know that their daughters are being brought up in Western families, and that these women lead a "lonely existence, unable to share their burden with anyone."

I wish I knew whether a returning adopted child represents shame or heartbreak, inspires scorn or envy. I feel irrationally defensive toward anyone who might look down on an "unwanted" daughter or stereotype her as a lucky American princess. I know that even if I spoke fluent Chinese, I probably wouldn't be able to dig below the surface and have a real conversation, dissolve the walls that keep me from knowing the truth of anyone's thoughts or experiences, and so I've learned what I could from studies of Chinese views of adoption. For instance, that a huge part of the population, especially that of rural areas, knows nothing about adoption, either domestic or international, and is surprised to find that it exists at all—not unlike in the U. S., where few people are aware, for instance, that many African-American and biracial children are adopted internationally by citizens of countries with less racial baggage.

While typical Chinese citizens regard adoption by foreigners in a positive light, they tend to regard adoptive parents as unusually charitable and altruistic and to see adoption as "good deeds by kind persons," according to Richard Tessler, Gail Gamache, and Liming Liu in their book *West Meets East*. They basically share the misconception of adoption held by many Americans, that adoptive parents are performing a humanitarian act rather than fulfilling their own dreams of raising children. I find myself scanning faces uneasily as we descend the Great Wall, wondering if this is how those we pass see us. Beside me, Sophie nimbly navigates her way down the slope, ignoring the guardrails, silent, observing, blending in.

On the highway, we pass a complex with unusual architecture. Turrets and towers sprout from pink buildings and flags fly from ramparts. The site resembles a U. S. amusement park. "What's that?' I ask Lily, expecting to hear that it's an abandoned city from the Ming Dynasty or something.

"An old, unfinished amusement park," she says.

I've been to the Summer Palace before, a well-preserved and popular imperial garden that, like the Temple of Heaven, functions as both a recreational park for locals and a tourist destination. I'm surprised at how little I remember about this place, not the halls and palaces and gardens, pavilions and temples and bridges, not the spectacular marble ship nor all the cypress trees that have been worn smooth by so many hands that they have the texture of plastic. I'm a bit suspicious about whether they're real.

What I do recall is walking by Kunming Lake on a cool, misty day, too cold to examine the eight thousand paintings of mythical scenes along the beams of the Long Corridor, fearing a stiff neck even if I tried. When I was here before, children distracted me in their shiny, gauzy seventies-style Halloween costumes over polyester shirts and leggings, their party dresses with big bows, their lively mixes of clashing colors, fabrics, and patterns. I watched children and wondered what my baby would look like. It's hard for me to imagine the fear and trepidation of that day now that my daughter is beside me, her face so familiar and inevitable.

But though this day is sunny and warm and, paddleboats and dragon boats churn and drift across the water, though there is no miserable cold or drizzle or doubt or distraction, my eyes are still drawn to children. Boys outnumber girls, and children's dress is now far more Western—jeans and warm-up suits. And despite my increasing conviction that finding traces of my daughter's past would be a nearly impossible task, it's become second nature for me to look for her eyes or nose or chin echoed in someone else's face.

Lily's warnings about pickpockets have Sophie so worried that she slips her money into her shoe. Then she has to squat and ease some out to buy a ball like the one I got her here when she was a baby, constructed of a lattice of colorful plastic rods with joints that, pulled out, expand the ball to three times its size, then, pushed in, contract to a smaller sphere. We board a dragon boat, sitting on old brown vinyl kitchen chairs that line the periphery and bisect the middle. Other boats with snouts like dragons, scaly heads upright, slip quietly across the water. Temples tower on the hills above us. I assume they are the ones identified in guidebooks as the Precious Clouds Pavilion and the Cloud-Dispelling Hall, the Temple of Buddhist Virtue, and the Sea of Wisdom Temple, made of glazed tiles. Across from me, Sophie squishes her balldown small, then pulls it outwide till it becomes a a round globe in her hands, shrinking and enlarging, shrinking and enlarging.

At a chain restaurant with purple cloth-covered chairs, Lily orders a Peking duck dinner. A waiter brings us chrysanthemum tea, delicious and pretty, with flowers floating on the top and rock sugar melting in the bottom. Sophie drinks so much that soon she desperately has to pee.

When we go in search of a bathroom, all we find are squat toilets. Sophie can't figure out how to use one without removing her clothes altogether. She hangs on to me for leverage, giggling as she nudges off her shoes, strips her socks, shakes off one leg of her jeans and then the other, and hands me her underwear. She thinks better of standing barefoot on the toilet's edge and shuffles her shoes along into the inlay designed for feet to straddle the porcelain hole. By then she's laughing so hard she can barely keep her balance.

Lily comes to check on us just as Sophie emerges from the stall, fully dressed, still guffawing.

"There's a Western toilet upstairs," Lily says, puzzled.

Sophie's amusement abruptly drains away.

By the time we arrive at the theater for an acrobatic show, she has to pee again. Lily offers to give her "squatty potty" instructions. They go off together and soon return, triumphant. Sophie can hardly wait to have to go again. She sings the praises of the squat toilet. She's a fan now, a total convert, an evangelist. She wonders if we could install one at home.

We're wiped out but obediently take our seats, dreaming of our pajamas and beds. I find acrobatic shows mind-numbingly dull. It seems to me that every balanced umbrella, juggled ball, and human pyramid is milked for maximum audience response. Performers balance and pose and the audience applauds: balance, pose, applause, balance, pose, applause. Contortion extortion.

Recorded instrumental music plays as we wait for the show to start. I recognize "From a Distance," then a sweet, tinkling music-box version of "My Life," so subdued that all the bite has been stripped from Billy Joel's declaration of independence. "Love Me Tender" trickles out over the sound system, and a British woman below sways in her seat and sings along with apparent relief at reclaiming her own language.

As the show begins, I slump down in my seat, nodding off a little. Straightening up, I force myself to pay attention. The current act, the wall screen says, is called "contortionists with glasses." Nobody's wearing glasses, though. Maybe, I think, the contortionists are wearing contacts. I don't get what's so special about contortionists wearing corrective lenses.

Then I realize that the contortionists are placing delicate fluted wineglasses on their feet and lifting them into the air as if in a toast, and that I am very, very tired, just as I was ten years ago, so that later I tend to remember these shows as weird hallucinations.

My friend Helene is enchanted by tightrope walkers. She finds them miraculous; she exclaims about their feats as if they were high art. In their performances she finds drama, suspense, and profound commentary on human mortality. When she raves about this, I wonder if she is completely insane. Stunts involving balance do not normally compel me to lapse into prolonged reflection on the nature of risk, equilibrium, or the preciousness of life in the face of inevitable death. I yawn. I tap my foot. I stare at my watch. After a point I just don't care that a woman can balance long-stemmed glassware on her head, shoulders, hands, and feet while pretzeling her body into a human chandelier.

I'm feeling like a contortionist myself, aching legs jammed into a space big enough for your average Chinese midget. But now a man is tap-dancing while juggling and dribbling balls. And now twelve young women have managed to stack themselves so that they can all ride one bicycle. I wake up. I have to concede that this is an unusually interesting and fast-moving show, that the costumes, lighting, and choreography are dynamic and colorful.

No one writes about China without describing it as a world of opposites. Its angular ancient wooden cities stand side by side with rounded space-age architecture. Its celebration of balance, harmony, serenity, and filial piety coexist with yelling vendors, stampeding crowds, spitting men, and honking horns. Talking about China's opposites may defy cliché, may feel like a fresh observation each time because the contrasts remain so striking. Still, I think back to graduate-class discussions of binary opposition as a particularly Western concept, one regarded very differently by Easterners, who in apparently polar concepts like yin and yang emphasize that seeming dualities are actually complementary, interconnected, and interdependent.

I wonder if what seems like one thing might actually be another: wild driving punctuated by impatient honking and near misses really a ballet of skillful maneuvering, expert lightning-quick judgments of timing and space. Or what seems to Americans like lack of manners, like bared-teeth everybody-for-themselves pushing and shoving, may really be cheerful communal jostling. That would explain the wide smiles of those who heave us out of their way. Or it could just be that seeming rudeness and disregard for strangers are necessary counterbalances to the Chinese emphasis on wisdom, virtue, happiness, and deep loyalty to family and friends.

I don't know if my interpretations contain grains of truth or are total bunk. I'm just trying to see China through my daughter's eyes, with her new, positive outlook, her ability to be enthralled by a human pyramid, her decision to embrace the balancing act of squat toilets, her absolute belief in the precision and artistry required to eat with wooden sticks.

"I want to live here someday," Sophie says the next morning as we prepare for a walk.

My future flashes before me. A relationship by e-mail and phone. Twenty-four-hour plane rides to visit my Chinese-speaking grandchildren.

"Maybe after college you could come here to teach English," I say.

And then return to the U. S. to live, I think.

It turns out that she wants to live *here,* in this hotel, on this street, in Beijing. She loves walking up and down sidewalks, observing the way people start pedaling their bikes with one foot while still flinging the other leg over. Her eyes light up as she peers into shops that sell fried dough and barbershops with checked rather than striped poles. She stops to watch two fat cats in a cage. I'm not sure if they're pets or food.

When kids at school taunted her, claiming that Chinese eat dogs and cats, I wasn't sure what to tell her. I'd heard the Chinese joke that natives will eat "anything with four legs except a table and anything that flies except an airplane." My friend Sara, who'd once lived in China, quoted to me the Cantonese saying, "Anything that walks, swims, crawls, or flies with its back to heaven is edible." But, Sara said, they don't eat people's pets. They eat only dogs and cats raised specifically to be food.

We pass a butcher shop with carcasses hanging in the window, WuMart Supermarket, and a Hello Kitty shop where Sophie buys a wallet. She says nothing during the transaction. She hands over the wallet, the woman says the price in Chinese, and Sophie produces her money. She pockets the change and exits, bag swinging.

We spend the afternoon in the Hutong, the residential neighborhoods of Old Beijing formed by alleys around traditional courtyard residences. The alleys are too narrow for cars; most visitors travel by pedicab. We find a long line of them waiting for customers when we arrive in the ancient part of the modern city. Here, instead of living in high-rises, families occupy low, gated residences passed down for generations.

Outside the residence of the family we have come to visit, a cricket chirps in a small wooden cage hung from the doorway. We are admitted to a court-yard crowded with plants, pet birds and grasshoppers in cages, and grapes covered in plastic, dangling from the arbor that serves as a ceiling. Red paper lanterns have been strung up the side of a rough-hewn ladder, and gourds perch on a windowsill. This courtyard is the family's central living space, with rooms built off of it. Lily tells us that we can look around, but it feels nosy to prowl through someone's home. When Sophie wanders to one end of the courtyard, Lily calls her back.

"Don't go over there," she says. "An old grandpa lies sleeping inside."

Through the fringes of colored plastic that curtain doorways we glimpse a dining room, a bedroom, and a kitchen. The rooms are neat and austere, no crumpled clothing or dirty dishes, no television or books in sight. The kitchen table has been set with ten plates, bowls, and mugs, low red stools squatting around it. Most of the furniture has probably been here since the 1950s.

This family make their living by giving tours of their home to foreigners and by selling artwork produced by the husband in a studio, a room separated from the rest of the home. Inside, framed pictures take up every inch of wall and are piled along the floor: big black-and-white posters of the Great Wall, portraits of the woman, and carefully calligraphed traditional Chinese symbols. I buy an inexpensive drawing of the Great Wall undulating across mountains.

Outside, our pedicab driver waits to pedal us to a school also in the old city, also built on courtyards, unlike the typical city school in a high-rise. A pomegranate tree stands in front of the main office. I read signs posted along the outside wall, Chinese followed by English translations:

The talent is 1% inspiration, 99% blood and sweat.
The human body wants to work, but not when causes extremely the ear.
No chasing, beware of hurt.

We eavesdrop on an English class. Thirty-five kids take turns standing to answer a question projected onto a screen, "What does your mother do on weekend?" Their responses are all in Chinese, I assume, since I don't understand them, although the kids cut their gazes toward us as if trying to impress us. Later, I ask Sophie if they were speaking English.

"Why would they have been speaking English?" she asks.

"Because it was an English class," I say.

"It was?" she says.

We wander around a courtyard that serves as a playground and assembly area, a stage and flagpole across from Ping-Pong tables and a bike shed. Posters show step-by-step graphs of morning exercises and the fifty-six minorities of China. "Safety first," cautions a more familiar sign. Off this courtyard is a series of rooms: "Moral Education Place," "Multimedia Classroom," "Labor Room."

Fifth-graders march out for gym class, wearing red warm-ups, their school uniforms. The kids line up for calisthenics. When they begin jogging around the courtyard in a circle, I try not to stare, not to examine the faces of strangers that look so much like and yet so different from the face of the person I love best in the world. Her white American classmates are mostly taller than she is, and they have larger frames. Among Chinese fifth-graders, Sophie is an average height but still skinny. I imagine her running with them, cutting up, talking incessantly, bouncing up and down, being the vivacious person she is among her friends rather than the quiet, observant spectator she has become here in China, subdued, impassive. The other kids glance at her out of the corners of their eyes.

Later, I pepper her with too many questions: wasn't it cool that there were kids your age outside? What was most different from your school? What do you think it would be like to go to a school like that? She gazes at me, not answering, still processing, keeping her thoughts to herself.

Next we stop by the Quiling workshop, also built on a courtyard, where people with disabilities do crafts, play games, and socialize. First we are ushered into a room to make paper-cut cards and write characters on red paper with calligraphy pens and black ink. Then we join our new guide Charles in the courtyard for games. Sitting at a picnic table or spreading out across the yard, eight or nine men and women hold sticks in each of their hands while spinning two discs on a string. I sit on a stump and watch these intently focused faces, some with the flat features of Down's syndrome. As everyone moves their sticks up and down and the yo-yos accelerate, a man with slurred speech says something to a woman with cerebral palsy, who laughs. Charles shows Sophie what to do, and she joins in. All of the toys sing on their strings with a high-pitched sound. Gradually the volume increases, so much so that I first mistake for the sound for sirens in the alleyways and wonder if there is some emergency outside.

Everyone switches to a hackeysack-like game that uses a shuttlecock. They all bounce shuttlecocks off their knees. The plastic feathered objects fall to the ground and are quickly swept up again. A couple of people get into a rhythm of scissoring knees and rebounding birdies and everyone laughs and cheers. Sophie gets it, kicking up the birdie, catching it with her knee and sending it up again. Everyone applauds her. Charles goes to shuffle through a box full of toys and pulls out a small square cloth and a stick. He shows Sophie how to twirl the cloth. Soon shuttlecocks lay abandoned on the ground while everyone twirls cloths on sticks. Few words are exchanged. There is lots of laughter.

A few people drift off to practice for a concert. Everyone else forms a circle for badminton. The courtyard reverberates with drums and cymbals. A woman offers Sophie a handmade bracelet as a gift. The courtyard is so alive with goodwill, cheering and smiles and nonverbal interaction, I forget that we're in China and that we don't speak the same language as the people around us. I forget that many of them have disabilities. They're just a bunch of people having fun and absorbing Sophie into their group. This place contradicts everything I thought I knew about Chinese attitudes toward disability.

Americans, we who pride ourselves on social policies that accommodate disability and diversity, nevertheless retain the notion that only weak people get sick and that virtuous people can cure themselves. I've been told many times, for instance, that Sophie would not have allergies or asthma if she'd had pets as an infant. Since she came to me with allergies, I find it ludicrous to imagine torturing her by intentionally exposing her to anything that would have given her hives or impaired her breathing. And last summer I became unusually aware of the impatience and even rudeness with which Americans often regard the disabled. While I was trying to help my mother, who could barely walk, we were frequently ordered to hurry up, move, and get out of the way. A clerk snapped at us in a drive-through because I held up the line passing change and then food to my fragile, slow mother, who fumbled as she put the change in her purse and checked to make sure we had everything we'd ordered. An airline employee rolled his eyes and made a sarcastic comment when we didn't dart out of the way of a kiosk immediately upon printing out my mother's boarding pass. I was shocked. Public places in the U. S. are required by law to provide accommodations for the disabled, but sensitivity cannot be legislated.

My sense has been that China is even more backward when it comes to policies related to illness and disability, an impression confirmed by the fact that I have never seen even a wheelchair ramp at a museum, factory, palace, park, or temple. *China Survival Guide* talks about the architectural tradition of very high thresholds into homes and temples. "This high threshold is to prevent evil spirits from entering. It also proves a true barrier for the handicapped," write the Herzbergs. "Add to that the Chinese predilection for long stone staircases leading to the inner sanctum of ancient temples as well as up the hillsides to even reach the temples . . . . it is rare to see any handicapped Chinese people venture out to many historic sites."

Most restrooms do have handicapped stalls. They're not wider to fit wheelchairs, nor do they typically have bars along the walls. They are simply Western toilets, presumed to be necessary only for the elderly and infirm, a commentary, I cannot help but think, on the wimpiness of Westerners. I feel like I'm copping out whenever I enter one, like I'm admitting to a weakness. Just as it sometimes seems that Chinese custom creates a parallel between Western toilets and infirmity, I wonder if Chinese superstition ends up creating an unintentional association between the disabled and the evil spirits that high thresholds are designed to exclude.

Americans' lack of awareness has seemed to me exponentially increased in China. So I am heartened by the Quiling workshop, which has a warm, comfortable, and accepting atmosphere, where able-bodied volunteers and disabled regulars merge and include Sophie in their games, so she is no longer a tourist or a foreigner.

Idly, I watch a young woman with dark hair and glasses. Next to her, Charles catches the birdie on his racket and she says, "Wow." Sophie misses and the young woman says, "Oh, no!" A man barely catches it and the young woman says, "Whoa."

Gradually it dawns on me that these are English words. I ask the woman where she's from. Her name is Rachel, her mom is Chinese, and she grew up in the D. C. area. After college graduation, she came here to teach English for a year.

I call Sophie over and introduce them. "Sophie wants to live in Beijing someday," I say. "Maybe she'll come here after college and teach English, too."

Sophie's suddenly too shy to ask questions, this child who never stops talking at home, who, once when she was four, asked me forty-seven questions in a thirty-minute period. After I set a timer and made a tally, I began to understand why life with my lively child was often so exhausting. But in China, Sophie has become a watcher, a listener, so I try to ask questions that will elicit useful information and inspiration for the future.

Rachel tells us a little about her work, including her volunteer job here at Quiling, which she loves. "That's great," I say. "How interesting." I try to resist the urge to say more, to make too many comparisons between what Rachel's doing and what Sophie could do someday. I'm afraid that encouraging Sophie's dreams will sound too much like pushing her out the door. I am built on opposites, just like China, wanting my child to go experience the world, wishing she could stay close.

Tonight we're scheduled to take the soft sleeper train to Xi'an, which is why we exchanged tour guides—well-spoken, authoritative, and kind Lily for strong, thoughtful, boyish Charles. Apparently it was important to appoint a man to protect two females alone on an overnight train. But first, we head to Tiananmen Square. As we stroll past guards, Charles confesses to me that he is an adamant Obama supporter.

Sophie maintained that she was voting for Hillary Clinton long after the nomination went to Barack Obama. Gradually she has shifted her loyalties. I can't tell if she's listening as Charles says, "Chinese people like Obama. We feel a connection to him as a black man. We also have great admiration for Dr. Martin Luther King."

Don't discuss politics, tourists are cautioned about making conversation in China. *China Survival Guide* says not to talk about current leadership, Taiwan, Tibet, or military issues. I'm not sure whether there are any taboos about discussing American politics, and I'm fascinated by Charles's views and his unusual openness. But I keep reminding myself that we're in Tiananmen Square. This is the place where twenty years ago, tanks went after idealistic young people who championed democracy.

Charles wants to talk about democracy and free enterprise and the American economy even though the square swarms with uniformed guards. It must be okay, I think as we stroll toward the portrait of Chairman Mao, the one Sophie copied for her undiscovered land a few years ago. It's a relief to talk to Charles after days of pantomiming and reducing every idea to simple English sentences. But I stop asking him questions after a while. The uniformed guards make me too nervous.

After Charles helps Sophie fly a kite that soars high above the other end of the square, he leaves us to wander around a department store. And so we meander aimlessly, riding the escalators up and down through the gleaming multilevel establishment. It looks like an upscale Macy's or Dillard's or Bon Ton, except Sophie tells me later all about a display of Playboy products I somehow overlooked. I know parents who swear that their ten-year-olds know nothing about sex. They also confess to a feeling of physical illness at the thought of their children growing up. Maybe they hope that keeping their children in the dark will slow the process. I too would like to yank my child back from the threshold of adulthood, but I can't seem to withhold any information from her. She is far too observant.

We ride the escalator up and down, past shoes, jewelry, men's clothes, baby toys. Strategically placed signs urge us toward the "International Fast Food" to be found in the basement. I imagine a food court with treats from Japan and Russia and Ethiopia and France, but "International Fast Food" turns out to be a McDonald's. On the department store's top floor, there is a play area where parents can stash their children and shop in peace. I note all of this vaguely, my attention focused on my search for a handicapped bathroom stall. Sophie rolls her eyes and uses a squat toilet.

The sleeper train slides gently through the night while Sophie and I read and write in our journals on our bottom bunks. Across from me, she plugs her MP3 player into her ears and props up a *Quizfest* magazine in her hands. I look out the window and think about my mother, who four months ago boarded a sleeper train in Newton, Kansas, and rode through the dark, through sleeping towns, to Erie, Pennsylvania. She died two weeks later.

A businessman enters our compartment, heaves himself upon the bunk above Sophie's, stretches out, and immediately starts snoring softly. Above me, Charles turns and the mattress springs crackle like a tumblerful of ice breaking up under a spray of hot water.

I don't sleep well. The bunk beneath my thin mattress is hard, and I can't get used to the odd intimacy of sleeping in a compartment with strangers. I wake early and plunge under the curtain that reeks of smoke. I watch China go by, the low flat buildings, the blue mountains outlined by a pink sunrise, bok choi fields and apple orchards and shimmering silver rails. Across from me, Sophie is sacked out on her stomach, her breathing deep and regular.

Suddenly, an attendant flicks open our door, strangely urgent to collect headphones at 7:00 A.M. Sophie uncurls herself abruptly. She raises her head and glares at me as if wondering who I am. Charles and the businessman lower themselves from the bunks above, gradually descending like spiders on threads, first one leg down, then the other, then gentle bent-knee landings on the wobbly floor.

I whisk back the curtains to let in light, and the men rattle newspapers and I try to avoid any more trips to the toilet, a Western one that is by now so foul and sticky that I gag and retch and understand why squat toilets are considered more sanitary. In the corridor, a hubbub of morning voices arises. A man hawks. Lighters flick. People troop to the washroom in slippers, carrying toiletry kits. Cigarette smoke fills the car. A small child sings and chants, and we listen, smiling. I remember how I used to pick Sophie up from day care when she was three, how she'd be playing while singing an endless, tuneless song of her own invention, oblivious to the amusement of teachers and assistants. I wish I remembered the words she sang so rapidly and fluently. If she'd been a three-year-old in China instead, what words would she have sung, to what tune?

Sophie and I face each other, peeling and sharing an orange. I hand her a slice, and we exchange another amused smile at the singing and giggling that continues to waft into our compartment. With a trick of fate, Sophie could be a foreign girl I'd never met, singing a different song, and so when I look at her, I feel that the conjunction of our lives is a bizarre miracle. Thoughts flicker across her face, and she licks juice off her fingers. For just a moment she seems foreign to me, her own person, never an extension of me in any way.

I watch her, thinking about the moment when she awoke this morning, looking at me as if I were foreign to her also. I can't get out of my head the way she stared at me, squinting and puzzled, as if I were just another stranger on a train.

Chapter Six

The year before we went to China, high winds ripped a twenty-foot branch from a neighbor's maple tree and flung it toward the kitchen window just as Sophie was climbing up on the sink to close that window. As the branch cracked like a gunshot and flew toward her, she leapt backward, hitting her head against the counter. The limb crashed to the ground, shattering into a muddle of twigs and leaves. All over town, whole trees lay in yards, roots and dirt exposed, bundled at the ends of their trunks.

From then on, whenever she arrived home, Sophie latched the screens then locked all the doors, battening down the hatches. She scanned the sky anxiously, mistaking the gray of dusk for rain clouds, mistaking the rumble of trucks on the highway for thunder, noting, on sunny blue days, the one dark cloud off to the west.

I think of that moment as the inciting incident in what proved to be a difficult year, but maybe it really started sooner, around the time of a trip home to a family reunion in the summer, around the time plans solidified for us to finally go to China the next year. Suddenly, every reaction seemed exaggerated. Sophie was giddy and hyper one moment, angry and unusually fearful the next. As our trip transformed from hypothetical to certain, the sun shone brighter, but the clouds turned, more often, to monsoons of blinding rage. After the complicated undertaking of culture camp, I should have been braced for her mixed feelings toward the China trip, a thousand times more exciting and frightening.

I was the one who'd been irritable at the family reunion, though, where my cousins clustered in a frigid hotel conference room, discussing race. In recent years, one cousin had married a man from Vietnam; two of us had adopted girls from China. My cousins remarked on this favorably, on living in a time when people of different backgrounds could not only accept one another, but become families. They ripped open bags of chips left over from lunch, agreeing: they didn't get why some nonwhites were hostile in the face of our good intentions. Those people, they concluded, were the bad eggs.

And that's when I started to feel out of sorts, antsy, testy, freezing cold, wildly protective of my child, of her complex anger, so casually dismissed. And I realized how, in just a few short years, my thinking about adoption had changed radically. I still firmly believe in it, but I have more reservations. I am uncomfortable with cozy, sometimes saccharine discussions and talks about what a wonderful way adoption is to build a family, the kinds of attitudes that are prevalent at adoption events, gatherings, and culture camps. *Build* is the operative verb, and God's will is invoked frequently. There is little acknowledgment of the other side of the equation, the thing that I've had to accept as part of my foundation since I became a mother: that the addition to my life is a subtraction from someone else's, that my joy is founded on someone else's grief. Can I believe in a god who wills one person's destruction so that another one can build?

I felt completely inarticulate, sitting there in that conference room, not even sure where to begin to talk about all the assumptions that I'd come to question over the years. Like that only a minority of adoptees suffer ill effects from their sense of rejection. Or that children are usually better off with middle-class adoptive parents than with poorer birth parents, who are assumed to be unstable and ill-equipped for parenting. That attachment disorder is rare, when, in fact, it now seems to me perfectly normal that being torn from one home and placed in another might make it more difficult to trust, that even if a child doesn't remember the loss, it is still always a part of her story. That internationally adopted children have been saved from terrible lives, when, in fact, the desire of privileged Westerners for adoptable babies may be leading to child trafficking in other countries.

I had to escape from the family reunion. I couldn't participate in the conversation without putting a damper on it. My own feelings felt too tangled for words.

Out in the hotel lounge, my Chinese-American daughter and her Chinese-American cousin Josie blasted Hilary Duff CDs. Josie swayed, dreamily stretching into elegant ballet poses, a wobbly arabesque, an unsteady pirouette. Sophie squeezed her head in a drugged-out rocker way, long hair whipping around. She was all fierce power, her cousin all giggling delicacy as she scissored into a small, cautious leap. My daughter cartwheeled into splits and executed a crossover step back onto her feet. The girls giggled and fluttered and spun, for the moment far away from difficult questions and too-easy answers, layered issues and complicated emotions.

～

Though I had come to see the complications of fully grounding my child in my world, in the history of our family, it still seemed important to pass on family heirlooms. That's why I recovered my old dollhouse from my mother's garage in Kansas and moved it 1,175 miles to my own in Pennsylvania. My dad had built it almost forty years before, and I had an impulse to repair it, though no idea where to start. I wasn't good at crafts, and I'd never built anything, but it seemed to me that this dollhouse ought to be Sophie's now.

I'd been about seven when my dad had put it together, probably from a kit, in the basement after I'd gone to bed. Back then, the house stood as high as my waist. It was white with green shutters, six rooms, a widow's walk, and best of all, a balcony. Now it was so dirty that it looked brown. The pink and blue carpets, scraps from my brother's and my toddler bedrooms, were filthy and discolored. The spool chimneys had fallen off along with the railings my dad had cut from wire coat hangers. When I lifted the dollhouse, crawling with bugs, webbed by spider silk, strings of dust wafting from it, the rotted wood at the base split and separated.

In September, shortly after the storm, I took wet cloths out to the garage and wiped off the dollhouse. The white rags turned black, uncovering a rickety structure with a dull surface. I felt overwhelmed, so I closed the garage and threw the cloths in the laundry. The dollhouse became just another unfinished thing hanging over me.

It turned out that there was something more hanging over us, something besides undone projects and the looming trip to China, something literal: a tree in our backyard had cracked in the storm. It was tall enough to smash through two neighbors' roofs, said the guy from the tree-removal company who came to inspect the neighborhood. And now it was precarious enough to topple over in a good wind.

Half of the tree was dead anyway, sawed off at the top by some previous owner. The other half still thrived, producing leaves that shaded the yard in summer and filled it in fall. The tree had been molting steadily for years, bark peeling off in chunks, but I hadn't noticed the crack at the base, the sawdust on the ground. Rotten, said the service guy. Gnawed by ants. The tree service could remove it in the next month. But, the guy warned me, the roots had likely spread under the patio, had likely claimed the whole backyard and could not be evicted without damage. I imagined the murky underground tangles and tried to conceive of what it might be like to be rooted so deep.

Leave them, I said.

～

"I'm nervous about the weather," Sophie said to me once, twice, three times a day. She said it repeatedly during the month we waited for our tree to be removed. I was on edge, afraid of snow and the burden it would lay on the remaining leaves, terrified that the tree would pitch over and decimate the neighborhood. If this tree fell and no one heard it, would it make a sound? I wondered. In Sophie's mind it fell again and again, imagination fueling anxiety.

If a tree doesn't fall but you check it a million times a day to make sure it's still standing, if a tree doesn't fall but you have nightmares that it does, if a tree doesn't fall but you believe it will imminently and that's all you think about, does it matter that it's still standing?

Such anxiety was unprecedented for Sophie. Normally, like me, she got angry at what bothered her. I was used to the push and pull, the storming and name-calling, the relenting and clinging, the neediness and independence that might have had something to do with adoption and attachment or might have just been normal childhood. But the outsized fear, this was new.

Traveling sometimes worried Sophie. She had decided that she hated flying when we went to Kansas and Colorado. She was resistant about a trip to Chicago. It turned out that she had seen news footage of the KKK burning a cross and then someone in Chicago burning trash, and the two had become conflated in her mind and she was afraid of the KKK in Chicago. I expected this trip-related anxiety to rear up when we started planning to go to China. It didn't, at least not in obvious ways.

There were the inevitable intensified accusations about how I wasn't her real mom and insistence that her birth mother would understand her when I didn't. Occasional comments along these lines are typical for adopted children, so I didn't take them too personally. I felt like we were on a roller coaster, its chain pulling our car arduously up a long hill. The ride would be worth it, I was sure, reading the testimonials on listservs of other parents who'd taken their children back, who wrote about the downhill rush of absorbing China, its history and culture and people, the way smelling and tasting and hearing China firsthand led, finally, to a kind of closure. Parents sometimes used that word, *closure,* as if a car had creaked to a stop and their children had thrown off their restraints and stepped out onto steady ground, walked on it from then on.

Our rotted tree hung over us, preparing to fall, and with trees on the brain, I started noticing just how much we talked about identity, especially in relation to our family heritage, in terms of trees. Of course there were family trees; I'd been relieved that Sophie had never brought home the school assignment most dreaded by adoptive parents, the one to make her own family tree. If she had, I was prepared to show how she was grafted onto mine and to include branches for her family in China. Now, suddenly, waiting for the tree service to show up, I saw trees everywhere.

In a series of articles about homeland visits, Becca Piper uses the tree metaphor in discussing why adopted children need to know as much as possible about their pasts. "Like seeds planted in the ground, without knowing our soil and environment we don't know if we will become a palm tree or mountain pine," she writes. "And it bugs us, despite the fact that both are immensely beautiful." The Chinese journalist Xinran tells about Chinese families who say that if the first child is a girl, it will not be allowed to live. "If it did, it 'broke the family's roots,'" Xinran says. "The first surviving baby had to be a boy."

In October, when Sophie accompanied me to an adoption conference in Pittsburgh, keynote speaker Emily Prager talked about how adoption intertwines the roots of more than one tree, her own family now connected to that of her daughter's birth family. This brought on some rustling and bristling from the audience. A woman raised her hand. "Isn't that just a comforting myth?" she asked. "Isn't that something adoptive parents say to make themselves feel better?" She sounded angry. I'd expected that the atmosphere at this academic conference would be different from that of other adoption events. I hadn't expected so much active hostility about adoption, though.

Prager shrugged. "It's just a fact," she said. "Whether we like it or not, our roots have become connected."

A small woman in a black suit raised her hand. "Would you adopt your daughter again, knowing what you know now?" she asked. She made it sound like China adoption, any adoption, being a parent, could be a detached intellectual exercise.

I glanced uneasily at Sophie. She wasn't paying attention, sparing me from answering a thousand difficult questions.

But I kept wondering. What did we know now that we didn't know ten years ago? Back then I was aware of class and age differences between the profiles of many adoptive parents and birth parents, but I'm not sure that the race disparities were quite as pronounced. Karin Evans points out that most adopting parents are white while most adopted children are not and that because of this, some people regard transracial adoption as a kind of cultural genocide. But fifteen years ago, the basic needs of children seemed to me more urgent than such politics, and I maintained a naive confidence that I could address cultural issues when they arose.

Like many who later adopted from China, I was motivated to act by the 1995 BBC documentary *The Dying Rooms*. In it, reporters Brian Woods and Kate Blewett visited Chinese orphanages carrying hidden cameras and filmed what were often devastatingly inhumane conditions. Their footage showed abandoned baby girls with untreated gangrene, rashes, infections, or illnesses who were left in cribs, tied to potty chairs, neglected, starving, handled roughly by state-hired nurses with limited time and resources and too many babies to care for. Babies in especially bad shape were sometimes shut off in separate rooms to die.

Watching the film in 1996, I couldn't move or breathe. I was alone in my second-floor apartment, a newly minted English Ph.D. with enough love and at least enough earning power, I thought, to give one of those babies a better life than the desperate ones that unfolded before me. I had many Asian friends and a love of Asian-American literature. I imagined myself equipped to balance out pictures of horrifying practices like those in the documentary with knowledge of an ancient and beautiful culture. And from that moment on, I was completely focused on one goal: to go to China and adopt a baby. A year later, having landed my first tenure-track job, I started the paperwork. Two years after that, I headed to China to meet my daughter.

The Dying Rooms inspired additional media coverage and considerable fallout from the Chinese government. Critics claimed that the documentary's portrayal was exaggerated, outdated, and inaccurate. They defended welfare institutions that were operating as best they could in the midst of poverty and with limited medical or social resources.

Chinese officials denied that dying rooms existed and, for a long time afterward, prohibited foreigners from entering orphanages. That's why most of us met our babies in hotels and never saw the environment in which they'd spent the last several months of their lives. Even today, impromptu orphanage visits are not allowed; potential visitors must apply months in advance and then tour the facilities under restricted conditions.

Applications to adopt Chinese orphans poured into the China Adoption Center throughout the late 1990s and the early 2000s, particularly from prospective parents who had seen *The Dying Rooms*. The babies we adopted were generally healthy for having spent months in an institution. Information from China is tightly controlled, and reports may well have been inaccurate or sensationalized. Nevertheless, many of us had the sense, from news reports and rumors and our agencies and the few approved orphanage visits, that conditions radically improved as Westerners traveled to China to adopt and paid much-needed fees.

In 2005, when American adoptions from China peaked, China tightened its regulations. There was outrage among groups no longer allowed to adopt, including singles, people who had facial deformities or exceeded weight limits, and couples in which one or both members had ever taken antidepressants. ("So they want people with untreated mental illnesses to adopt?" my sage friend Rachel asked.) Although many of these changes were based on cultural prejudices, I could understand the logic of excluding single parents. It was based not on the American view that married parents are inherently more qualified and committed, but on the fear that with only one parent, the child could be orphaned again. I myself share this fear, although the policy strikes me as counterproductive: if my child had a sibling at least she wouldn't end up alone in the world.

The main reason for tightening regulations was the diminishing number of available Chinese orphans and an attempt by the Chinese government to encourage domestic adoptions, which doesn't limit families who adopt to only one child. But though the number of babies available for international adoption was down in most places, the continued demand for Chinese babies and the influx of Western money may have also set the stage for corrupt practices. The 2007 State Department Trafficking in Persons report calls the kidnapping and selling of children "the most significant problem in China." Some orphanages have created baby-buying programs that illegally solicit and pay for children in order to fill the applications from foreign families, who spend five to ten times more on adoption fees than do Chinese families.

Had conditions remained as they were portrayed in *The Dying Rooms,* even knowing that a vast machine of corruption might be set in motion, would I still have adopted my child? How is it possible to answer such a question? How do we imagine life without our children, and yet, how do we acknowledge that in trying to do a good thing, we may inadvertently contribute to a system that causes abuse and suffering? Who can say whether we made the wisest decision? This dilemma gives new meaning to the Buddhist description of the human condition: "One foot in suffering, the other in joy." "I've seen orphanages that have turned into business enterprises," a former orphanage worker told Xinran. "Still, even that's better than lining up the babies on the floor to be bitten to death by bugs."

A friend recently told me about a China adoption listserv controversy. Stories had surfaced about government officials who had seized babies from loving parents who already had a child and had failed to obtain permission or pay fines for a second one. The babies were sent to orphanages where foreigners would pay fees to adopt them, making the government itself a trafficker of children.

Some adoptive parents are far more disturbed by the idea of such direct and brutal third-party intervention for the sake of money than they are by the myth of less-than-human parents who didn't want their children. If foreigners really want to help Chinese orphans, we are sometimes told on listservs, we should fight corruption by donating money to the care of children in orphanages rather than by removing those children from their birth countries. But the impulse to build a family springs from a different place than the impulse to provide humanitarian aid. I certainly went to China with the desire to do some good in the world, but I also knew that I would receive far more than I gave; my motives were ultimately as selfish as those of any parent who wants to raise a child. Still, over the years, I've come to understand that something that seemed to me both simple and miraculous—a child who needs a parent is matched with a parent who needs a child—can be, like most things, far more convoluted.

At the academic adoption conference, Sophie was still young enough to be oblivious. She got her book signed. She wandered past display tables, accumulating free brochures, pencils, and buttons. Because she was with me, I was not accosted, as others were, by the birth mothers or adoptees who'd come hoping to make their voices heard, who were attempting to accomplish this through confrontations. They stopped adoptive parents, demanding that they justify their roles in their children's lives. They accused other adult adoptees of being naive. Sophie picked up a button for Bastard Nation. Fearing that she would pin it to her backpack and attract questions from other fourth-graders, I hastily explained what *bastard* meant, and that the group was radically antiadoption. When I was a few words into my awkward explanation, Sophie suddenly flung the button across the room as if it were as slimy and lethal as a poisonous snake.

It was a relief to return home to our ordinary life. Killing time before a movie by strolling around a home improvement store, we lit on a wooden railing that would be perfect for a dollhouse balcony and a drawer pull to replace the lost spool chimneys. Suddenly, we were committed. Home again, I lugged the dollhouse inside, setting it on newspapers on the dining room table. Then we stared at it, mystified. My dad had made this for me. If he were still alive, it would be him refurbishing the dollhouse for his granddaughter, rebuilding the base, repainting the walls. But now it was just us, and I had to figure out how to shore up this decaying monstrosity.

Sophie embraced this part of our family heritage, but there were others she wanted no part of. My cousin Mike had recently participated in a DNA database project that established from which of sixty-one lines of Wests we descend. A few months later, *60 Minutes* ran a segment on a woman named Vy Higginson, the director of an arts foundation in Harlem, who registered with the same database. Soon after, a cattle rancher named Marion West contacted her. "I understand we're cousins," he said.

Vy Higginson was black. She claimed to never have seen an actual cow until she was in her twenties. Marion West was white and had begun researching his ancestry in hopes of connecting his bloodline to British royalty.

The *60 Minutes* story was warm and humorous. But e-mail from viewers complained that the show had downplayed the degradation and atrocity, human slavery and violence that had led to such DNA connections. "Many female slaves were impregnated by white owners to produce a breed of slaves that brought in a higher price because of their lighter skin. Love had nothing to do with it," one viewer wrote.

Mike concluded through research that one of our sixty-four great-great-great-great-great grandfathers was an ancestor of Higginson's as well. My cousin quoted her: "It's like discovering American history through yourself."

I know that Vy Higginson was probably a descendant of this man and one of his slaves. Love probably didn't have anything to do with the place where her line and mine intersected. Another of my ancestors left property to his slaves, but I don't know whether it was out of love, or shame, or something more complicated.

Sophie was horrified to learn that our family's past—*your* family's past, she said—had involved slaves at all. I tried to explain that tracing back the lines of most white Americans would eventually yield slave owners. I like to imagine that, had I lived in an earlier time, my crusading instincts would have forced me to be an abolitionist. But my daughter saw me as tainted by my family history. She could imagine that her own unknown line was pure.

In her strong sense of kinship to Vy Higginson's ancestors, I wondered if she yet recognized that like them, she had not chosen to leave the country of her birth. She had not chosen to become part of a white family or community. Love had everything to do with it, I'd always told her. I'd assured her that of course I'd help her find her birth family, if the political climate in China changed enough, if DNA testing were advanced enough.

My promise was easy. When I made it, it cost me nothing. There were so many obstacles. And even if we overcame them, Sophie and her birth parents wouldn't speak the same language. Even if they had a million things in common, there would be no easy way to communicate. I hadn't yet thought about all the implications of finding relatives, like the sense of financial responsibility we might feel toward an impoverished birth family.

Sophie narrowed her eyes at me sometimes, blaming me for my ancestry and for the stupid comments of other kids, white kids. She understood the insignificance of good intentions. She was learning the limits of love.

In late November, a crew finally arrived to take down our tree. A woman used a hook to lift up electrical wires, allowing a bucket truck to squeeze into the driveway. A guy rode up in the bucket to lop off branches. He sawed off a three-foot piece of trunk, tied a rope around it, and raised it into the air where it swung like a wrecking ball, swaying a little too close to an upstairs window. Its range of motion tightened as it slowed. Gently, the guy lowered it to the bed of a pickup truck that transported it to the street. There, it was fed through a machine that ground it to dust. And so, little by little, the tree shrank. Its top sat on a level with the roof, then the upstairs windows, the live part now even with the dead part.

Then, late in the afternoon, the chainsaw hit concrete.

Once upon a time, it turned out, someone had poured cement into the tree to preserve it. Which is why, despite the crack, it never fell.

Eighty years ago, someone had built the house two feet from this tree, leaving a hole in the patio to accommodate it. The tree had shot up and up, towering over the house. When part of it rotted, a previous owner had shored it up with concrete and sliced it off, creating an excellent bird feeder platform outside the upstairs window.

And then I came along. I came along and destroyed what someone else had tried so hard to preserve. And the whole venture had been pointless. Though only ten feet of tree remained, not enough to smash much even if it keeled over, Sophie still latched the doors against wind and rain and snow.

"I'm nervous," she said at least five times a day.

"What about?" I'd ask.

"You know, the weather."

"What exactly are you afraid of?"

"Lightning and thunder."

"Why?"

She paused a moment. "What if a lightning fireball rolls into our yard?" she finally asked.

When it got cold, we stayed inside and worked on the dollhouse. "This is fun," Sophie kept saying as we painted and talked. Sometimes we messed up; it was tough to stay inside the lines. We dribbled orange paint onto the green floor. We slapped green paint meant for the roof onto the white siding. We touched up our mistakes, but our results were never perfect.

"Grandpa made a mistake!" Sophie crowed. She pointed to the place where his green brushstrokes had overlapped onto the white ceiling. I discovered wispy green streaks edging past the roofline, a blob of green paint spilled between shutters. I'd never noticed these imperfections. Now I found them, the evidence of the mistakes that all parents make, comforting.

With help from friends, we finished the dollhouse in time for Christmas. Harold rebuilt the base, returning it sturdy and primed, original porch railings securely reattached. Carol decorated all the windows with small home-made wreaths. Carys dropped by with little lace curtains she'd stitched.

The day we put on the final touches, snow blanketed our driveway and walk and balcony. Inside, paint erased years of dirt and brightened faded colors. For a brief time, the world spread before us, clean and new. We glued on the balcony railings and cut up new carpet remnants, pink and blue, for the bedroom.

We hoped to find a blond mom/Chinese daughter combination to move into the restored dollhouse, but our selection on the Internet and in the doll-house section of a Buffalo craft store proved limited. We did add a rolltop desk, a candy-striped couch and chair, and a tiny toothpaste rack and toilet paper dispenser.

Every day, Sophie assessed the sky. "It's overcast," she always said.
"Looks pretty blue to me," I'd reply.
"I've seen bluer," she'd answer.

By late spring, her persistent fear of our roof caving in had unnerved me. It didn't help that after all the snow finally melted, shingles hung loose off the edge of the thirty-year-old roof. I'd paid the deposit for the China trip and couldn't really afford any work on the house, but finally I took out a loan and hired a contractor. For a day, green shingles tumbled past windows and crashed to the ground. As workers removed three layers, we felt like we were caught in a combined earthquake and hailstorm. Finally, above us, the wooden roof was bare and slightly bent from holding so much weight—three tons of shingles, the roofer swore.

Even after our new roof was in place, whenever dusk fell, Sophie kept asking what time it was, and if it was a normal time for it to be dark, or was the darkness a sign of an impending storm?

One day last summer, my mother and niece arrived in Erie on the train, and leaving the Amtrak station, my mother fell. Afterward, instead of shuffling along, holding tightly to her walker, she leaned into it, those curved pieces of metal all that held her up. Her knees weren't doing the job. They wobbled and buckled.

The first day of her visit, she peered up the staircase. She placed one foot on the bottom step and tried to haul herself up, but finally she resigned herself. She couldn't do it. We made her a bed on the downstairs couch beside the small bathroom with a toilet and sink. A helpful housing director on campus gave her permission to take a shower in an unoccupied handicapped dorm room. Friends offered her their downstairs showers. Her fall had done her in; she became slower and slower. By the end of her visit, we had to get a wheelchair for the trip to the mall she'd planned so that she could buy school clothes for my niece. When we returned home that night, she could no longer climb the four porch steps. A kind neighbor came over at midnight to lift her. And so, on the last day, we packed up all of her things before I took her for dialysis. Afterward the nurses had a hard time waking her, but we finally got her to the car, and I drove her and my niece to Erie, where I checked her into a handicapped hotel room so she could rest for a few hours before catching the train.

It took her an hour to get from the car to the door of the room, only a few feet. With every step, she teetered on the brink of collapse. "Sit down, Mom, please," I'd say. If she fell, I wouldn't be able to catch her. If she fell, I wouldn't be able to pick her up. One more fall, I feared, would be the end.

Finally, she reached the hotel room. And collapsed. I called 911 while my daughter and her cousin cried at the spectacle of paramedics in blue scrubs and masks, moving with assured swiftness as they asked questions, took vital signs, transferred her onto a gurney, and loaded her into an ambulance.

Nothing was wrong with her that could be fixed. Her heart was giving out, her legs were giving out, everything was giving out, and there was nothing I could do. "Risk of falling: low," said the sign on the door to her hospital room. By then, she couldn't get up, so how could she fall?

When my mother died the next week, we drove to Kansas to plan the funeral and clean out her apartment. We stayed at my brother's new house, which was actually also our family's old house, the one to which he and I had been brought as newborns. The house had come back on the market, and so my brother had purchased what he called his ancestral home. Sophie looked around his property with a critical eye. "I'd cut down that tree," she advised him.

"Are you still going to China?" lots of people asked me in the next few weeks. Of course we were still going to China. It felt like we needed to go now more than ever. Talking about China gave us something to focus on during those days when it felt like a pall had fallen over our house. It hung like the fog that swirled low over the mountains, turning my car, turning us, into solitary cells. We felt our way ahead by inches, past and future obscured. We needed to make plans.

During the weeks we'd spent in Kansas, I longed for our ordinary routine again. I imagined returning home, relaxing, cooking meals, vegging out in front of the TV and watching the Beijing Olympics. I pictured us secure under our new roof while right outside the window, birds paused to eat from a feeder on our tall stump. I envisioned us taking off for Buffalo on a Saturday—shopping for Sophie's school clothes, browsing in a bookstore, having a nice meal.

Nothing worked out the way I'd planned. During the Olympics, Sophie was prickly, irritated at my interest in Michael Phelps's races, mad when I called the Chinese divers *cute,* affecting indifference toward the blond U. S. gymnastics team. She didn't want to talk about the fact that most American teams contained members of European, Asian, and African descent, people of hybrid backgrounds, children of immigrants. She bristled when I pointed out that the American gymnasts were coached by a Romanian, or that Shawn Johnson's coach had been born in Beijing. She was defensive at any suggestion that the Chinese government might have lied about the ages of their gymnasts.

The next week, Sophie refused to talk to me at the restaurant in Buffalo where we stopped for lunch. We went on to the mall where we'd pushed my mom in a wheelchair only a month before. I hadn't anticipated the sneakiness of grief, the dizzy sickness of walking back into that mall, as if its brightly lit walkways swarming with people were dark, close tunnels of memory. I'd had no idea that time would suddenly seem all confused, that being in this place where I'd been with my mother a month before would momentarily lure me into imagining that I had a second chance, that I could do all the right things and my mother wouldn't fall and she would survive her visit and the events of a month ago had just been a nightmare. Then I passed a kiosk of strollers and wheelchairs and returned to the helpless present.

"So where do you want to go?" I asked Sophie, pretending that things were normal, that this was just another shopping trip, that I wasn't going to fall apart in a mall of all places.

"Aeropostle, but I don't know where it is," she said.

"Are you sure they have one?"

"That girl has a bag from there," Sophie said.

I stopped the teenager and asked for directions to the store. She was African-American, and she and all of her friends looked at me suspiciously before guardedly pointing the way. Sophie folded her arms and glared at me. "What?" I asked.

"Why did you ask her?" Sophie hissed. "She isn't your servant."

It had never occurred to me that there was some social code that prevented a white woman from asking black teenagers for directions. But the teenagers had looked uncomfortable, and Sophie was mortified. What had happened to my judgment? It hadn't helped me save my mother. It had failed me again in this situation. And I wasn't even sure what I'd done wrong.

The shopping trip, it was suddenly clear, had been a big mistake. I wasn't going to make it. I was overwhelmed by grief, with no resources to process in any cool, rational, properly parental way this yawning divide between my child and me. "We have to go," I said. "Now." And I turned and walked away without checking to see if my daughter was following, desperate to just get out of that mall. Maybe I'd been rushing things too much, pushing too hard to get back to normal. Maybe we needed some time. Maybe it was too soon to go to China. Maybe it was too soon for me to deal with a trip that might close the gap between us or might, instead, just widen it.

Before the shopping trip had fallen apart, we'd bought a few items. I had never taken Sophie school shopping before because it took her forever to outgrow things. I waited to buy practical clothes like jeans and T-shirts when the ones she had were worn-out or too small, and that rarely happened at the end of the summer. But when my mom had given my niece money, Sophie had been jealous. I'd never just given her money and allowed her to pick out anything she wished.

So, as if I could make up for the loss of her grandma, I told Sophie to choose what she wanted. What she wanted, it turned out, was stuff with skulls, the sort of clothing and accessories her cousin liked—a stocking cap, a bracelet, a shirt, and a backpack, all with skulls. Sophie was a little bummed that she was too small to wear her cousin's favorite pants, the kind with hems that drooped against the floor and chains that rattled wherever she went. I saw all of this black, all of these skulls, as her way of mourning.

"It's not Halloween," said one of Sophie's friends when she saw Sophie all decked out in skulls. The friend was wearing a T-shirt featuring a Disney tween sex symbol. "It's not Halloween?" I blurted out. "Then why are you wearing your Zac Efron costume?"

That evening, our friend Gaj told Sophie, "If anyone tells you it's not Halloween, say, 'What's the difference? You all look like ghosts to me.'"

Sophie loved that comeback. Gaj later protested that he was just being goofy, not ribbing pale-skinned people. But that's how Sophie took it, and we laughed, me the palest ghost of them all.

Soon we started packing. First we covered the dining room table with everything we thought we needed. Then we changed our minds and weeded through the stuff, added more, weeded again to keep Lysol wipes and medications, laundry soap in plastic bags, paperwork and luggage locks, underwear, socks, and jackets, money belts and neck pouches and daypacks.

I thought about the last project we'd completed on this table, which had been covered with newspapers as we'd spent hours turning the dollhouse, painting and gluing. We'd taken pictures of each step to show to my mother. In them, shot from the living room doorway, you can see the tree through the back window, extending up past it, its old and new selves side by side, intact, reinforced, unbeknownst to us, by concrete. Under the ground the roots had crawled all through our backyard, claiming it irrevocably.

Before my mom's visit, we'd put all the pictures together in a blank book and written some text, telling the story of the dollhouse. Two weeks before she died, she'd turned through it, over and over, thoughtful, studying each photograph. The one of me as a little girl, front teeth missing, crouched in front of it. The ones of the dirty, rotted house sitting in my garage. The ones of Sophie and me united, putting the past back together, building something new on the foundation of something old, painting away flaws. One of me, rinsing the brushes afterward. You can see how the water runs orange and green, turquoise and yellow, but not the way, outside, tranquil snow had whitened our yard, making the world new.

There's a final picture of Sophie crouched beside the dollhouse in the same position I was in almost forty years before in the first photograph. But there is no photo of the way, finally, after rinsing and turning, rinsing and turning the brushes, the globs of paint had fallen off, the traces of color had begun to fade, and the water had finally begun to run clear.

Chapter Seven

October 2008

Our Xi'an guide, Ivy, meets us at the train station and then sets off at a brisk pace, empty-handed, without glancing back to make sure that we're keeping up. We're not. One of our duffle bags has a good metal handle and rolls easily. The other has turned out to be a mistake. With only a strap, the bag is impossible to maneuver up and down curbs and around cars, parked bikes, and squares cut out of sidewalks to accommodate trees.

Sophie has the good one. I am left to wrestle and heave the uncooperative bag along on this long, fast-paced walk. I didn't sleep well last night, and am starting to have a feeling of déjà vu: this experience is more like my memory of China than any previous part of this trip. I'm recalling the soul-deep exhaustion and despair of lugging around a screaming baby while trying to manage luggage. Efficient tour guides, all business, rushed us from one place to the next, lobbing facts at us. I felt bruised by facts, weighed down by the responsibility of not just a baby, but of the whole history of an ancient culture to convey to her.

My bag flops over, wheels on top spinning with the frantic energy of the legs of a bug flipped onto its back. I remember that baby with nostalgia, the kind of nostalgia that comes from the knowledge that it all worked out. Look at this lovely child next to me, so proficient at hauling her own luggage. She has to be dead tired, but she's looking around with bright eyes, my walk down memory lane her return home. I can feel the tension between us rising as we become more and more exhausted. We were both born in years of the tiger and can be fierce and strong-willed and stubborn. And especially now, worn out after a night on the train, I suspect that we are like two trains hurtling toward each other, bound, eventually, to clash.

I resolve to be patient and careful. In only six days we will visit the orphanage, see my daughter's finding spot, and ask about the Man. Whatever happens, I want this trip to be a good memory for Sophie, something she can carry with her for her whole life. So I struggle to keep my thoughts to myself.

I will not scold or nag. I will not get angry or frustrated at how out of sync with each other we sometimes are. I will not negate any of her positive impressions.

On homeland tours, many adults wax sentimental about their adoption journeys and relive the joys of their first days as parents. This is far from my own reaction. I am mostly relieved and grateful that those days are over. Though I never for one second regretted the step I was taking, though I found myself quickly attached to my fussy, beautiful baby, those days were unremittingly difficult. When I think of the acquaintances who said, "This trip will make Sophie grateful for what she has," I see that they had it backward, that it is I who am renewing my own gratitude.

When I look back, it's as if I stumbled across buried treasure—a chest that at first seemed heavy and unwieldy, which I have spent the last few years unpacking, little by little, marveling at the riches that are too much to take in all at once. This trip isn't for me about reliving joy so much as about celebrating the survival of hardship, but I'm still like other parents who ultimately see homeland journeys as confirmations of the families they've formed. I know this is quite different from the experience of many children for whom homeland journeys confirm the reality of the families they lost.

Also I will learn from later reading that other adoptive parents feel, as I do, in the absence of the ability to meet my child's birth parents, a "sense of kinship" with the country of China. Perhaps children develop similar senses of kinship; maybe this is why Sophie, instead of vocally idealizing unknown birth parents, romanticizes the place of her birth. While for me, China is like a distant relative, for Sophie, it's a parent. I tend to be analytical, which can sound like criticism. Sophie just wants to experience things, take them in to process later. She is quietly taking ownership.

I have read many studies and stories and interviews. I know that during homeland trips, many children wonder what their lives were like before they met their adoptive parents. Some harbor fantasies of miraculously discovering a birth parent or sibling. Others don't think consciously about their own pasts but instead worry about beggars on the street or children still living in orphanages. I can't say whether any of these thoughts have occurred to my own daughter. Despite all my reading, I'm still not sure about the best way to support her through this emotionally loaded journey. That's why I sometimes wish we had a tour group, other parents and children struggling with similar differences in vision and experience.

I will be startled, later, when people ask about our vacation. I have never thought of this trip as a vacation like a trip to a beach or an amusement park. The exhaustion, tension, and emotional baggage of this trip have often made it feel more like work. It certainly feels like that on our arrival in Xi'an, but maybe that's just because we've been on a train all night.

The hotel upgrades us to a luxury suite with four rooms overlooking a park. It's a concrete rectangle with fenced-off squares for trees and gardens and cutouts for shrubs, nature carefully contained. Ducks waddle in the grassy areas while spectators look on from brick walks. We'd like to sit in our window and watch, or go for a stroll, or take a nap. But we have an hour to unpack and eat breakfast before meeting Ivy again.

She is right on time to accompany us to the Big Wild Goose Pagoda, a Buddhist temple built by the first dynasty, the Qin. The pagoda was named to commemorate a big wild goose that fell from the sky before a group of hungry monks, a fact that Ivy imparts with evident pleasure. Later I will find out that I have somewhat misinterpreted this story by viewing it through the lens of my own Judeo-Christian tradition. If a Westerner prayed for food, and a goose instantly broke its wings and thudded to the ground, we'd believe that the Lord was providing for us. In fact, we'd be convinced that through this act, God was expressing approval of all of our moral and ethical stances as well as reaffirming our dominion over other living creatures. The hungry Buddhists who witnessed the falling of the bird were instead humbled by it, built a pagoda to honor it, and stopped eating meat.

I sleepily listen to Ivy's story and think how cool it would be to name things in this way, choosing titles that evoke memories rather than honoring donors, denoting locations, or defining functions. Swaying in the backseat of the van, I drift into sleep-deprived musings. I remember searching for dinner for my mother and niece the first night of their July visit and discovering bacon-wrapped steaks in the Walmart meat cooler. They proved to be hits. Our van hits a bump and I start awake, having drifted briefly into dream logic, imagining renaming Wal-mart the Yummy Bacon-wrapped Steak Store and having an emperor's power to make everyone refer to it that way.

Coming back from my mother's funeral a few weeks later, we found a pot of chrysanthemums blooming on the back patio. They'd been limp and wilted when we left, dead I would have sworn, but in our absence had mysteriously sprung back to life. Somehow, brown bent flowers had turned colorful and straight, a profusion of yellow flowers with their big heads crowded close together. At first when I glimpsed them through the fence I wondered if a passing cheerleader had inadvertently dropped her yellow pom-poms in our yard. Maybe I will call our patio the Yellow Chrysanthemums Blooming Patio.

I open my eyes as Ivy begins speaking, twisting around in her seat. She casts a bemused smirk toward Sophie, who is nodding off, as if it's a weakness to need to sleep. But Sophie is a child and can be forgiven. Me, I have to stay awake.

Ivy, young and slim with hair past her waist, skinny jeans, and jacket with a cinched waist, is well-prepared with long strings of facts, and I hold my eyes wide open as she recites them. She really sparks to life when she explains Chinese symbolism. "In China, a circle is not just a circle, but a symbol for something that continues on and on," she says.

"Yes, in the U. S., too," I say, and she looks confused.

"That's why married couples wear rings," I say.

She looks uncertain for a second, thoughtful. Then she suddenly perks up. "It is traditional to give pomegranates to married couples to wish them many children," she replies. "But the pomegranate has many seeds. Now, with the one child policy, it should be a peach."

I laugh, and she looks pleased. My eyes start to close again and images drift through my mind: pomegranate seeds like ruby red teeth, the wooden stones of peaches, the wedding ring my mother gave me the week before she died, a circle that went on and on. "I want you to take it now," my mother said. "I don't want it to get lost." I tried to refuse it. "Your dad died nine years ago," she pointed out, insisting that I take it. "I don't need to wear it anymore."

Ivy is talking again. "We say, to understand the future, go to Shanghai; to understand the present, go to Beijing; and to understand the past, come to Xi'an." The van driver pulls against the curb.

"We're going to all of those places," I answer as Sophie sits up, blinking again.

We enter the gates of the Big Wild Goose Pagoda complex, and Ivy patiently points out to Sophie characters on metal tablets and explains the meaning of each. Then she ushers us past statues, men in white sailor caps sitting in a doorway, and rows of brass candleholders, long red candles dribbling and drooling strings and braids of wax. The pagoda itself, a tall tan building, is wider at the bottom than the top, each of its seven stories a little narrower than the one below it, so that it looks like an ancient square cone tapering off into the sky. I'm not sure how much of the structure is original. Constructed between 589 and 652 AD, it has been destroyed by war and earthquake and rebuilt and renovated many times. Now it leans a little toward the west.

"I have to pee," Sophie hisses.

"Sophie needs to go to the bathroom," I say. Ivy looks confused and zips on. I want to slow down and take pictures. Instead I quickly snap the colorful rows of candles and incense through the window of a small shop, workmen repairing wooden latticework behind a building covered with plastic sheets and enclosed in scaffolding, and the small narrow room of a monk, containing only a flat bed.

Sophie throws me a desperate look.

"Bathroom?" I call to Ivy.

She seems to understand this time and leads us down a sidewalk to a restroom, bending down to pick up a five-leaf clover and present it to Sophie.

"This is very good luck," she says.

"Like four-leaf clovers in the U. S.," I say.

"Five leaves are even better," she replies.

There is too much to absorb in an hour. We observe the quiet reverence of the temple area and then pile back into the van, whisked on to our dumpling banquet. Ivy drops us off, promising to come back for us in an hour. We've been looking forward to the seventeen courses of different kinds of dumplings, a Xi'an specialty. Our tour materials warned us to pace ourselves and eat sparingly because the courses would keep on coming.

However, since there are only two of us, the word *banquet* proves to be a pathetic misnomer. There is no long table, formal meal, lavish amount of food, background music, conversation, speech, or entertainment. It's just us at a dinky table where a server brings us bamboo containers, each with two dumplings.

At home, Sophie is regularly asked questions about Chinese language and culture by her classmates. She gamely tries to answer even though she remembers nothing about her life here. She often finds herself in the position of spokesperson for a country she doesn't know well, forced to defend a government about which she knows even less. Most recently, she has been accused of being from a country that misreported the age of its Olympic gymnasts. Children who are unaware of most of the actions of their own government hold her accountable for China's, and she feels a duty to respond to these charges. In China she is once again the single representative of her people, the only Chinese-American child anywhere we go, handling questions about the U. S. with aplomb. There would probably be less pressure if we were part of a large group.

Now, as we sit waiting for our dumplings, this wish to be part of a group magnifies. Now, on our sixth day in China, a powerful loneliness sweeps over me, an intense yearning for adults for me to talk to, children to share with Sophie the experience of discovering China, extra servings of the dumplings that I like, quiet avoidance of less-appealing ones.

Sophie doesn't relate to my wistfulness. She jumps right in to boost my sagging spirits, very grown-up about holding up her end of the conversation. She chatters about the dumplings: the ones filled with duck meat, shaped like little ducks complete with small beaks, the walnut ones all wrinkled and pinched to resemble the nuts that were crushed to make their filling, celery ones formed into leaves. We like the pork and shrimp, fish, beef, and chicken dumplings, but are less enthusiastic about the mixed-nut variety. The dumpling soup is good, but by then I'm full, so I nod when the waitress gestures at my bowl, asking if she can take it, I think. She refills it to the brim. Sophie laughs at me.

We're swallowing our last bite when Ivy reappears to hurry us to our appointment at the art institute. It's another tour-demonstration-activity-sales pitch, though more muted and with minor variations. A young man guides us through a gallery of contemporary peasant paintings all portraying happy scenes from daily life, including lucky symbols like ducks and roosters and rabbits. We admire traditional-style paintings on rice paper or silk, mountain and flower landscapes, the titles and artists' names in calligraphy down the side, seals stamped on the bottom to show who has owned the paintings. The young man gives Sophie a calligraphy lesson and mentions that the paintings are for sale. I nod vaguely.

Ivy arrives again to hustle us to the Great Mosque and Muslim Quarter past bustling, colorful rows of stalls to the prayer hall built in a Chinese style. Art students are strategically perched on steps or sitting on grass, sketching. Muslims, Ivy informs us, are the largest Chinese minority. She tiptoes through the courtyard, hushed, because a religious service is going on in the building that only Muslims are allowed to enter.

She quickly herds us past the stalls again, tables of Chinese slippers and jewelry and jade carvings, the usual tourist fare, back to the van. I still need to buy gifts, but Ivy regards the market as a necessary evil to be dashed through. In fact, her speed has increased steadily as the day has passed, but I don't object. I'm ready to go back to the hotel and crash.

Sophie has other ideas. Remembering the lights and noise, crowds and shops on the streets of Beijing, she's pumped to go out walking. We venture out, one block, two, three. We find nothing but hotels, banks, and cell phone shops, Samsung, Motorola, China Mobile. We try the opposite direction. Still nothing. Disappointed, we return to our room where Sophie switches channels until she locates a movie in English—a late, obscure entry in the *Home Alone* series, I finally figure out.

Sophie tries on the white bathrobe in the closet and channel surfs through Chinese soap operas. In them, weeping hysterical women helplessly beat small ineffectual fists against the chests of hunky men. The men are solid and wise, straining gently to comfort the women, who strike their brows and wring their hands attractively. They cower and whimper, inconsolable but ever-decorative.

"Why are the women such wimps?" Sophie asks. I am puzzled, too. The Chinese women I have known are smart, outspoken, and no-nonsense.

Since we found no restaurants on our street, we're limited to the choices in our hotel: a Chinese restaurant on the second floor or a Western restaurant in the basement. Sophie and I agree easily: we want Chinese food. So we stroll into the Chinese restaurant and I request a table for two.

The concierge looks worried. He urges us through gestures to take a seat on a couch in a little alcove and peruse the menu before we commit to a table. I am brashly confident that we'll find something, but I humor him. We flip through laminated pages, looking at pictures, reading English translations and descriptions. We slow down. Retrace our steps.

I have heard many people say that Chinese food in China is very different from that in the U. S., but generally our meals have seemed relatively familiar. The main difference is that there's usually just one kind of meat and one veg-etable at a time rather than the hodgepodge of them that Americans associate with Chinese food. I'm pretty sure that our guides are carefully selecting food that seems to them safest, the closest to American food they can find; in fact, we almost always have one chicken dish and one beef dish, rarely even fish or seafood, to my disappointment. We certainly haven't tried anything radically unfamiliar.

China Survival Guide advises finding out if names of dishes are poetic or literal. "Braised lion heads," it says, are pork meatballs. "Ants climbing a tree" are noodles and bits of ground beef that merely resemble ants. This makes sense to me—after all, English-speakers have comparable dishes whose names can't be interpreted literally, like toad in a hole, a breakfast treat that a student once cooked for me involving a piece of toast with an egg in the middle. Then there are those disgusting recipes for chocolate cakes decorated with crumbled oreos and gummy worms, meant to resemble earthworms poking their heads out of soil. Or what about the popular healthy kids' treat bugs on a log, celery sprinkled with raisins?

But in China some things are exactly what they seem or worse, says *China Survival Guide*. "Bee Babies" really are roasted bee larvae, "cow braid" is the stewed penis of a bull, "bamboo worms" are maggots, and "lips of deer" and "monkey brain" are just that. I expected to simply bypass these particular delicacies, but even the more mainstream choices on the hotel menu aren't familiar: they include donkey tendon, spicy and sour ox feet tendon, and fish jelly head with cabbage heart.

"Should we go to the Western restaurant?" I finally ask.

Sophie leaps up, peering furtively around, checking that the coast is clear. We make a break for it, feeling like criminals sneaking away.

Downstairs, I wish we'd tried harder. The buffet includes lasagna, pizza without tomato sauce, and colorless ham and apples and sausage. I wonder just how much dye we Americans inject into our food to make it so bright and appetizing, not to mention sugar: the flourless chocolate cake decorated with Cheerios is barely sweet.

Sophie digs in happily. At home, half-asleep and ravenous, she would be snapping at me and complaining about the food. She would be gazing out the window and worrying about the weather. I am heartened that despite my low spirits this morning and the occasional tension, we're having fun, getting along well, as if I've discovered some new store of patience, as if she left all edginess, sullenness, and panic back in the U. S.

But then, just like that, we fall out of sync. I am skeptical about the buffet. She's defensive. I try not to make my criticism of the food sound like a condemnation of a whole culture. If I even notice the constant smoke in the air, if the ubiquitous hawking and spitting gross me out, if I find a dish unappealing, she takes it personally.

She loved hearing from the Beijing silk factory guide about the benefits of chopsticks to concentration and artistic skill. She likes arguments about how they improve the taste of food, unlike forks and knives which give it a metallic flavor. She is less willing to hear about the drawbacks of chopsticks: that the Chinese throw away forty-five billion pairs of disposable chopsticks annually, the equivalent of twenty-five million fully grown trees; that chopstick use increases the risk of osteoarthritis in the hand. I reassure her that the PRC now imposes a sales tax on disposable chopsticks to encourage the use of reusable ceramic or metal ones, though I wonder aloud if metal doesn't defeat the purpose; won't those chopsticks impart the same metallic flavor as knives and forks? I'm not sure if I'm just reporting fun facts about chopsticks, or defending my greater comfort with forks. I lapse into silence, again wishing for another adult to converse with, someone who won't take everything I say as my evaluation of the worth of a whole country. The evening started out so well, us laughing as we sneaked out of the Chinese restaurant, curious as we walked up and down the aisles of the Western buffet. But now I'm back to the feeling I've had more and more often that I should tiptoe, guard my speech, keep my observations as neutral as possible. I take bites of flavorless food, observing aloud how much is lost in translation when one culture tries to imitate another. I wonder if Chinese people find American Chinese restaurants as bewildering and colorless.

I'm becoming so anxious about offending my child, I'm kind of relieved that she's not really listening. "I really feel at home here," she says dreamily.

Sophie needs her inhaler more often with all the smoke and pollution in the air, but though she wakes coughing and uses it twice in the wee hours, we get a good night's sleep. We still wake in the morning with the bone weariness, the dragging sagging slowness, that sets in after too much rushing, too much activity. A smoky fog hangs over everything, the sky grayish and hazy. Faint strains of music reach us from the park below. We watch an exercise class of about fifteen people that quickly grows to include thirty or forty. They move in unison as if performing a Chinese line dance, a tai-chi Boot Scootin' Boogie.

A truck periodically comes around the block, playing music that temporarily drowns out the fainter exercise music. The truck blasts "Simple Gifts," then "Edelweiss," then "Simple Gifts" again. Back and forth, back and forth between these tunes that I find poignantly familiar and that remind me of the music boxes blaring "Camptown Races" and "Pop Goes the Weasel" from the ice cream trucks of my childhood. Only later do I learn that these tunes do not signal a colossal demand for ice cream in Xi'an. Rather, what I heard were garbage trucks. There are no dumpsters in China. Instead, garbage trucks alert customers to their approach with loud, repetitive tunes so that business owners can rush out with their trash.

But each time the strains of music reach my ears, I find myself craving a Dilly Bar and the simplicity of my early childhood, when my dad pulled me down sidewalks in a red wagon and the milkman delivered bottles to our tin box on the porch. My heritage surrounded me. I didn't have to go to another country and hurry madly around for hours at a time to understand something about my past. Right now, I wish we could just go down to the park and join the exercise group. I wish we could lie on the couch and read. I wish I could step into the calm of the scene on a Blue Willow plate.

Instead we board the van for another whirlwind day, bumping away from Xi'an's city walls and down the highway to a workshop that makes terracotta warriors and other pottery souvenirs. Ivy advises us to buy our gifts and mementos there, because they are of better quality than those in the street markets. I just want fun souvenirs, nothing fancy, and would rather buy at street markets, but I nod.

Yesterday's bleakness returns as Ivy hammers us with facts about the terra-cotta soldiers. Sophie stares out the window. Her combined activity book/scrapbook has gone by the wayside along with my half-completed list of one hundred things parents should know about China. It might have been fun to work on these with the rest of a group, but for the two of us alone, they just feel like more assignments. Sophie is keeping a journal for school, and I have my journal, and we often forget to check her workbook to see what information we're supposed to be gathering.

I wish Ivy would quit making speeches and just chat. It's been days since I've had a spontaneous conversation with another adult without the language barrier that reduces us to childlike exchanges. I've always found myself tense and antsy around people who talk at me, guys who lapse into lecture mode or my mother whose conversational habits long ago began to feel as programmed as a church's calls and responses, a loop that formed an ever-tightening noose. Often as a grown up I felt irrationally crazed, trapped in my mother's house, trapped in the same old conversations. I quickly became a small protesting fly, all tangled up in a sticky web of irritation and frustration and guilt that bound me so firmly, I was afraid I'd never break free.

I'm feeling a glimmer of that now: I want to escape the barrage of historical information, but I can't zone out the way Sophie does. I'm an adult, I have to be polite, say, "Wow" and "Hmm," nod and smile. A headache is starting.

Then we enter the workshop and follow the usual script. A demonstration: at different stations, workers mold and dry warriors, throw pots, and paint elaborate designs. An activity: Sophie fills a mold with clay to produce her own warrior head. A display: rows and rows of life-size fiercely smiling warriors and one with the head missing so we can stand behind it and have our pictures taken. A store: a warehouse the size of a football field, full of vases and jewelry and miniature and full-size warriors. I imagine shipping a crew of these home, lining them up in my front yard to stand guard. I wonder whether the neighbors would mind.

I pick out a vase and then some necklaces and bracelets for gifts. I'd like to buy a nice tea set but am overwhelmed by the tables spread with too many choices. "Do you want to pick one out?" I ask Sophie.

"Look at this." She shows me a blue one with dragons, a rare departure from the floral patterns. I decide on that one.

Shopping has given me an adrenaline rush. I feel more patient and benevolent as we set out to see the actual terra-cotta warriors. I'm much more attentive to Ivy's speech about the discovery and excavation process, how farmers found a pit entrance while digging a well. It gives me a thrill to imagine what it must have been like, unearthing seven thousand life-sized clay figures, all different, this army commissioned by the first emperor of China 2,200 years ago to guard his grave.

Ivy points out willow trees along the way. They represent continuity, she says. You give someone a willow when you want them to stay.

Today Ivy's wearing another little jacket with jeans and shiny black pumps that click authoritatively against the long walkway. Crowds press toward the entrance of the park, past a field of saplings wrapped with thick white string.

"Why?" I ask Ivy.

"To protect them from the biting wind," she says, although it is at least seventy-five degrees. She hails a golf cart to drive us through the park to the terra-cotta warrior complex. It's been dawning on me that Ivy's flawless command of all her tour guide lines has led me to assume that her English is more fluent than it is. When I speak more simply, she tends to understand me better. Sophie disapproves. She thinks that slowing down and simplifying my language is patronizing.

Sophie and I squeeze into a small round theater where we stand in a jostling, jam-packed audience to watch an Imax movie. Then, on Ivy's advice, we buy a book and have it signed by an aged farmer sitting at a table. Ivy tells us that he is the 82-year-old man who discovered the terra-cotta warriors. I don't know if this is true, but I smile at him, and he bows his head low as if humbled by a compliment.

Then we gaze across each of three pits, acres of warriors lined up in rows. A few are headless or armless, but all of them smile, and the right hands are raised on those with intact arms, so that the eerie rows of men appear on the brink of a handshake. Occasional rows of horses break up the ranks of men that stretch as far as the eye can see. There's something breathtaking about this whole underground world of men and horses, frozen for all time. I imagine the centuries of people who walked over this earth with no idea of what was beneath their feet.

I'm not sure why I feel compelled to keep snapping photos; my pictures will never capture the details as distinctly as do the professional photos in books or on postcards. I click away anyway, as if photos could preserve my feeling of amazement. As Ivy's steady stream of information flows over me, I nod absently and puzzle at my camera's tendency to randomly turn itself off. Then I stop listening and rustle around for batteries. Ivy goes on talking.

At the cafeteria, she tells us to help ourselves to the buffet, which is sparse compared to the typical feast. We carry our plates past a few mysterious salads, condiments, pale cold cuts, noodles, rice, and fried bread. I attempt, not very successfully, to assemble a lunch. Returning to the table, we find it crowded with steaming dishes: shrimp chips, noodles, celery, pork with peppers. I'm embarrassed to have taken so much random food from the buffet, especially when Ivy examines my plate with a wrinkled brow. I realize that what I've done is the equivalent of filling a plate at an American restaurant with ketchup, mustard, salad dressing, relish, pickles, and crackers. Sophie trains her scorn on me as if she knew all along that the real meal was being ordered, but I'm pretty sure that her plate is empty only because nothing looked appetizing to her.

Ivy points out the noodles in the soup. Chinese eat long noodles, she says, to ensure longevity.

I'm not sure how to eat the soup, because there are no spoons, not even the usual ceramic ones. It seems that I am always stymied by the logistics of how to eat. I ask Ivy, who waves over a waitress and gestures at our food, making a request in Chinese. The waitress soon returns with a handful of serving spoons, depositing one of them in each dish. I have read that since the 2006 SARS outbreak, serving utensils are more common, and Ivy and the waitress look pleased to have understood me. Now I can't ask how to eat my soup, or they will feel that they have failed me. But unless I take possession of one of the serving utensils, I'm still not sure what to do.

I watch Ivy. She fishes out the noodles with chopsticks and drinks the broth. I feel foolish that my cultural block prevented me from figuring out what now seems a perfectly logical process.

Ivy orders us to "march" out of the terra-cotta warrior complex, along the "one dollar walk" that leads to the parking lot. "They will try to sell you a box of warriors for a dollar, but then tell you that the box is ten dollars," she says. That sounds okay to me. The same box was $40 at the souvenir factory. "These are poorer quality," Ivy insists. I want to buy a set for a friend who uses miniatures to shoot videos and would be embarrassed for me to spend $40. But I obey Ivy and march.

At the jade carving factory, I hope to buy some gifts. We file past the demonstration, men and women bent over tables, machinery whirring as workers carve and polish stones. There is no activity or display. We skip right to the showroom. Our factory guide waves toward a square of counters in the corner. "Those are for gifts," he says. He then makes a sweeping gesture that encompasses the rest of the sprawling showroom. "This is for you."

The gifts start at about $40. The merchandise especially meant for us to purchase for ourselves starts at $100 and escalates rapidly to include jewelry and sculptures that cost thousands of dollars. I'm not sure what to think of the notion that I should spend more on myself than my friends. Is this a Chinese custom, or a Chinese conception of the selfishness of foreign tourists?

Sophie wants a tiger necklace to commemorate that we were born in years of the tiger. The cheapest is $159. I say no. She pouts. Maybe someday, I say, but not now, not when she's ten. She sulks. I steer her over to the gift counter, pointing to the less expensive options she must choose from if she wants a necklace. She declares that she doesn't want any of that cheap stuff. I say fine. I pick out pendants for a couple of friends.

"Let's go," I say, but Sophie won't budge. She's mad that she can't have the tiger, but now that she's about to lose her chance at anything, she reconsiders. She spends forever examining the pendants with evident dissatisfaction.

"Don't buy something just for the sake of buying," I say.

She lingers stubbornly over the glass case. I'm getting irritated, worried that people will think she's a spoiled American child, even if being spoiled is not just an American phenomenon. Chinese newspapers sometimes have headlines like, "Is China's one-child policy creating a society of brats?"

 Knowing that doesn't make me feel any better. I insist that we have to go. She gives in and picks out a pendant, a jade circle, like a doughnut.

But a total meltdown is brewing. When we arrive in our hotel room, Sophie announces that the tea set is hideous. She was just pointing it out in the store, not suggesting that I buy it. "If you really knew me, you'd have known what I meant," she says.

And that is the crucial problem here. I don't know her. Don't know what she's thinking, feeling, how she's experiencing all of this, don't know what I can do to support her. Since I keep saying the wrong things, it's really pretty miraculous that we have both held together so well with our fast-paced itinerary—too much activity, too many choices, and not enough rest, all while dealing with so much emotional baggage.

In adoption and parenting memoirs and listservs and blogs, other parents seem so calm, rational, and in control. They rise above difficulties, never get sucked into their children's emotional whirlpools, never let their children provoke them to frustration, never raise their voices, and always find the right wise, thoughtful responses to their children's anger. Suffice it to say that I am not one of those parents, that I have finally reached the end of my patience, and that I fail massively at a calm, measured response. Suffice it to say that there is scolding, yelling, and tears, accusations and inadequate responses, clashes of opinions and wills. Eventually, Sophie slams into the bathroom, refusing to speak to me.

I move around the room, packing our gifts and souvenirs. I hold the jade pendant she didn't really want in the palm of my hand, thinking of another necklace, one I talked Sophie out of wearing to China. When she was in the hospital, my mother overheard Sophie say that she wanted a Star of David necklace. My devoutly Christian mother didn't know why. She didn't know that Sophie had become interested in the traditions of our Jewish friends. She didn't understand that in our lives that had so often felt like a chain of broken links, of disconnections, deaths, and places left behind, Sophie liked the idea of being connected to the long history of our friends' faith. Without asking any questions, my mother said, "I bought a Star of David necklace in Israel. I want her to have it."

Propped up against pillows, Mom explained to me where to find the necklace, but I wasn't really paying attention. I figured that when she got better, she could just give Sophie the necklace herself.

And then my mother died. It's the body that grieves when the rest of you is too busy, the muscles that cramp, the stomach that feels knotted like a fine gold chain snarled so tight there is no loosening it. I rushed around, planning, writing a eulogy, calling friends and relatives, sorting through my mother's things. One afternoon, Sophie and I searched all the little compartments in her jewelry boxes, but we couldn't find the necklace. Finally my niece Sidney arrived in her pants with chains, hems drooping against the floor. She rattled back to my mother's closet and returned, chains clanking, jewelry jingling, pendants and charms and long plain chains clipped to a hanger, swaying and tangling.

And there it was. It had bits of amethyst and garnet on the outer triangles. It was much too fancy for a ten-year-old. Sophie put it on and refused to take it off again. Except to sleep. Except to come to China. I was afraid she would lose it here.

I wrap this other necklace, the jade pendant, in tissue paper and tuck it into a pocket of my suitcase. I feel utterly wiped out. I would give anything to turn out the light and sleep for a whole day. But I can't, so I stack up the pillows and lean back against them, a book in my hand, watching the light wane and waiting for Sophie to venture out. I try to think what I will say to her, how I can remedy things, to let her know that mixed feelings and confusion and anger are normal even if there might be more productive ways to express them. To let her know that I want to support her, but I am going to make mistakes, too.

The last thing I want to do is become my mother. Whenever we clashed, she used to lament that she'd failed at her job, as if motherhood were a sport at which you could win or lose, take home the trophy that would memorialize you forever in your static, shiny glory, or come up empty-handed, ashamed of your poor performance.

"I sometimes wonder if I was a failure as a mother," Mom used to say, and I used to take this personally, as if she considered her children such poor reflections on her, such miserable excuses for human beings, that others couldn't help but notice and cluck their tongues. She had a repertoire of questions I didn't know how to answer. "Was your childhood really so unhappy?" she'd ask, apropos of nothing. It felt like a trap, since answering required first acknowledging that I thought of my childhood as unhappy. In reality, I considered it the mixed bag of joy and sorrow, pleasure and pain, loneliness and discovery that constitutes most childhoods, most lives.

As my mother got older, her thinking less flexible, she began to cycle through the same script during every visit. "Aren't you grateful for everything we've done for you?" she'd ask, fixing watery eyes on me, the tears suggesting vulnerability but also, like a microscope lens, magnifying the foreboding insistence of her gaze. Sometimes it felt that no appreciation would ever be enough, that every conflict demanded renewed thanks. "I try to please you," my mother always said, implying that I simply could not be pleased, and sometimes those words rise to my own lips when my child won't be pleased, either.

It is late afternoon, the light flattening against our window. When I had to pee, Sophie relocated to the closet, lashing out at my attempts at consolation. We are both still grieving, I know; my mother's death is still fresh for both of us. It will take me a year, ten, maybe a lifetime to sort out my relationship with my mother. Why did I get so angry and frustrated with her sometimes? We all overreact to our parents, I know, but so often, my reactions felt way out of proportion to her actions.

After her death I found letters she'd written to friends. She'd updated them on my brothers' activities, often not mentioning that she had a daughter. Sometimes when I went home to visit, my brothers' friends were surprised to discover there was a sister. Wasn't this, this lifelong feeling of being somehow erased, why I was drawn to adopt a Chinese daughter? Wasn't my own sense of being lesser than my brothers the reason that it seemed so important to value a girl from a culture that devalued females? And yet, my mother could surprise me. The same person who often made me feel diminished and whose strict religious views often felt to me oppressive didn't bat an eyelash when I decided to go off to China and become a single mother. She welcomed my daughter completely and regarded her with great pride. Without questions, without judgment, she handed Sophie that necklace, and with it, symbolically it seemed, acceptance and support for my daughter's own questions.

Maybe this trip was a mistake, I think in the melancholy of oncoming dusk. Maybe we came too soon on a journey bound to stir up too much and magnify our losses. I have the same hollow feeling I did a few weeks ago while I dismantled my mother's apartment. I sorted towels and necklaces, blankets and clocks, weeded through books, piled up recipes, boxed financial records, and distributed toilet paper to relatives. I reread a letter here, a letter there, the ones from which I was often missing, and boxed up the rest. It felt like I was looting my mother's house. A neighbor, uneasy about an open blind at night, a room in disarray, odd comings and goings, called the police. I felt even more as if I were engaging in criminal activity.

Sophie was there with me the whole time. Even if I'd had anywhere to send her, another adult to help me during those first couple of days before my brothers and aunts and uncles and cousins came, she wanted to be with me. And she helped, too, sorting and packing or, when I needed her to stay out of the way, quietly reading her book. After two days of this, we escaped to a sandwich shop for dinner. One moment we were sitting at a table eating calmly, planning for the next day, the next I was overwhelmed by the quantity of all of my mother's possessions and the dusk falling outside the big plate glass windows and the knowledge that my mother was gone and I was on my own to deal with it, all of it. Tears spilled out so suddenly I had no idea where they'd come from. My child patted my hand, so grown up, troubled and concerned.

Many of my friends shield their children from death and grief and sex and cursing and money worries and adult conversations. Those friends tend to have spouses and extended families and time to themselves. I am rarely able to have a private conversation; I have been known to turn on a movie and only realize after a few minutes that it's rated R and that the material is too mature for a child; when I frown as I balance the checkbook my daughter says, "What? What?" and I have to reassure her that we're not poor, not destitute, I just made a little mistake. Hypervigilant as a baby, she would not sleep until the whole house was quiet, and bedtimes went by the wayside long ago. My friends assume that all adults have grown-up time after their children are in bed, but I don't. We both go to bed early. If I stay up to make a phone call or read another chapter, she's in my room instantly, wanting to know what's wrong. Every glimpse of the adult world provokes a thousand questions. The children of my friends seem largely to be wound in layers of translucent bubble wrap while the small pieces I offer my daughter are transparent and never quite thick enough.

When I was a child, when my grandfather died, I don't know who cleaned and sold his house and divvied up his possessions. I don't know who planned the funeral. Unlike me, my daughter rode in a car for sixteen hours straight to arrive at a funeral home and pick out the flowers for her grandmother's casket because my older brother and I simply could not make another decision. "These," she said coolly, pointing at an arrangement in a catalog. And now she had spent days skating along the surface of grief right alongside me rather than obliviously going off to play with cousins. I felt bad. I needed to be the adult and let her get to be a kid. But that day in the sandwich shop, I didn't know how.

When all of this was over, I promised her, we'd do something fun. That's when I decided that we'd have a special day, drive to Buffalo, go out to eat, do some school shopping, browse in bookstores, play One-Two-Three in the food court. This was a game she'd picked up from one of our favorite TV shows, *Gilmore Girls*. First she picked out men for me, and if I said no to marrying the first and the second, I was, according to the rules of the game, supposed to take the third as my lifelong partner. She liked to choose men who were really, really elderly or inappropriately young so that I turned them all down, and then she'd laugh and laugh when, according to the game, I was now obligated to marry the one with seven kids or a naked woman on his Harley-Davidson T-shirt. After this, I was supposed to pick out a future husband for her. I tried to focus on teenage boys, not too old, who looked stable, responsible, clean, and kind. She tended to roll her eyes at my choices.

When the funeral was over and we'd sorted and packed most of my mother's apartment, when we finally got home and settled in and stored boxes of my mother's stuff in the attic, we took off one Saturday for our fun day. But we didn't get around to bookstore browsing or playing games of One-Two-Three. Instead, that was the day that turned into a disaster. It got off to a rocky start when we stopped for breakfast at an IHOP where most of the staff and other customers were African-American. Sophie glared at me if I smiled at the waitress or said, "Thank you." She retreated into silence. Minutes crawled by as I rearranged the salt and pepper shakers and ketchup and mustard bottles and syrup pitchers. I asked lame questions and got one-word answers. She stared fixedly at the tablecloth and didn't blow her straw wrapper at me like she usually did. I was stacking packets of sugar and artificial sweeteners when our food finally came. We dug in, still silent.

"Are you all right?" I looked up to find an elderly black man standing next to our table, eyes fixed on Sophie.

She smiled a little. "Yes," she said.

"You looked sad," he said. "I wanted to be sure you were all right." I was weirdly touched by this, by this man whose heart had gone out to a withdrawn child whose mother didn't look like her. I was touched that the man had braved talking to a strange child, maybe to make sure I wasn't a kidnapper. Or maybe he instinctively understood something about my child that I didn't. At any rate, his concern seemed to calm her. She seemed to get over whatever had upset her and resumed talking to me. It took me a long time to understand that my child, who'd once referred to a peach-colored crayon as *skin-colored,* who'd moved on to identify with African-Americans, had come to understand that she was neither peach-colored nor black, that she might not be entirely welcome in either a black world or a white one.

Maybe that's why, at the mall, she snapped at me for asking a black teenager a question, a question that to my daughter represented intrusion where I didn't belong. I didn't get that, only that she was rude to me, and I insisted on leaving. We sat in the parking lot for an hour, talking. She didn't know why she was upset. I knew why I was. My mother was gone, and my child was walking on the other side of an invisible barrier, as if she could never fit into any world completely. If she chose to leave my world and enter a different one, I could not go with her.

That day in the IHOP, I'd been acting like I belonged, but I didn't. Neither of us did. We were outsiders, me acting entitled to be in a place where we were both suddenly conspicuously in the minority. There was no active hostility, just a vague feeling that we had invaded someone else's space. Maybe, by virtue of our races, there would be times when we were outsiders to each others' worlds as well. That thought comes back to me, and I feel the loss keenly right now in our hotel suite in Xi'an. I am an outsider in my daughter's world.

I almost wish we hadn't made this trip. All our souvenirs packed away, my mother gone, my daughter ready to move to this place, dusk starting to fall, that old hopelessness washes over me again. Outside, the trash truck circulates, playing "Simple Gifts." I'd sung along this morning:

> Tis the gift to be simple
> Tis the gift to be free. . .

This morning, Sophie had said, "They must like that song because they want to be free."

In the early evening, Sophie emerges for some chocolate. She consents to sit next to me on the bed. Another storm has blown over, leaving wreckage behind. I scramble to find the right words, to salvage broken things. I remember how my dad used to say to me, "Why can't you be happy about anything?" I was often surprised by this. I wasn't unhappy, just quiet and introspective. Maybe when adults look at children and think they see unhappiness, it has more to do with adult expectations than with children's real feelings and nothing to do with adoption issues. I cringe at the echo of my dad's words even as I say to Sophie, "I want you to be happy, you know."

"I feel happy in China," she says. "I wish I never had to leave."

I don't want to be the kind of parent who won't let her child go. I don't want to be the kind that pushes her child out the door, either. "Those are normal feelings," I say, trying to keep my voice steady, trying to be one of those calm, rational parents in books. "I don't know what I'd do without you, though."

Outside, the truck goes by, now playing "Edelweiss."

"A lot of adopted kids wish that they'd been able to grow up with their birth families," I say. I try to sound neutral. I do not want her to feel guilty if she has these kinds of thoughts. "That's a really normal feeling."

"I don't mean that I wouldn't have wanted to be your child," she says. "Just that I wish I could be your child here."

"You don't have to worry about hurting my feelings," I say. "Even when you push me away, you know I'm not going anywhere. You shouldn't be afraid to tell me how you feel." I mean this, but I wonder if there is any way to say it that sounds sincere, free of my own need, free of manipulation. I'm afraid there isn't when she responds, "No, Mom, I want to be your child."

Just then, the garbage truck swings by and floods the street with another repetition of "Simple Gifts." I wonder if the Chinese like this song because they yearn for more freedom or because, like me, they yearn for simplicity.

"This is my home, though," Sophie says again as the words of the song play through my head:

> And when we find ourselves in the place just right
> 'Twill be in the valley of love and delight.

And then the song switches again:

> Edelweiss, edelweiss, bless my homeland forever. . .

We ride past all the busy flashing lights of evening in Xi'an and the endless stream of people. I can't swallow past the ache in my throat, and I again find myself thinking: my mother is really gone. We're in China, I think, and my mother is gone, and someday my daughter may spend her life missing all the things she's left behind.

I hugged my mother for the last time two months ago as I put her on a plane to Kansas. She had been released from the hospital in Erie that day, and I hoped back at home, in her own environment, among her own doctors, she would rally. My brothers and I would get her a wheelchair and home health care. All we had to do was get her home, and then everything would be all right.

Sophie hugged her, too. And as passengers boarded and we walked away, we were awed by the memory of the the impossible softness of the skin of my mother's arms, all elasticity broken down, so it felt like baby powder.

Now we cruise along between the lights, blue and green and yellow, blinking, pulsating, shining steadily, and I think how easily a death happens, like a pebble falling into water. There's a momentary pock, a ripple the size of my mother's wedding ring, a dinner plate, a wheel. It expands beyond sight. Maybe it spreads to be as big as the moon, a circle that goes on forever. But the water closes over quickly and soon the surface of the world looks the same.

Except often, at home, Sophie fingers the Star of David necklace I wouldn't let her wear here. Often her fingers wander up to trace the chain that reminds her of her grandmother, that reminds me of how my mother, who prayed often for my soul, handed over to my daughter this affirmation of her questions about faith, bequeathed her, knowingly or not, this assurance that it was okay for her to choose her own way. So often I have watched Sophie close the clasp and let the star drop, her fingers worrying her way round and round as if memorizing how one link could follow another without coming to an end, how it could circle right back to the beginning again.

The Tang Dynasty Restaurant is a huge banquet hall facing a stage where a row of traditional musicians play ehrus and bronze chime bells and other stringed and percussion instruments whose names I don't know. There, we're seated with a Canadian couple. Our dinner begins with "Pearls of Cathay," a series of appetizers—black mushroom consommé, king prawns, and tenderloin of beef. It ends with "The Widow's Medley" and "After Dinner Delight." "The Widow's Medley" is a plate of ancient imperial dim sum. "After Dinner Delight" is something called "orange surprise." Listening to the musical ensemble, talking to the couple, eating beef, I am lulled into a sense of familiarity. I forget that I'm in China until I arrive at the desserts, which are far less sweet than their American counterparts. The orange surprise resembles Jell-O that hasn't set. The dim sum looks like chocolate but tastes like bean paste.

Sophie's wearing a traditional red dress given her by the tour company, manipulating her chopsticks expertly.

"How do you like China?" the woman asks her.

"I love it," Sophie says.

"She wants to live here someday." I try to strike a breezy tone.

The woman, mother of several older children, laughs. "She's ten," she says. "Things change."

In the back of my mind, I've been turning over this problem: could I give up everything I've worked for—my job, our house—to bring Sophie to live in China? This is not so absurd. Other families have done just that. Could we at least come for a summer?

Now, this other mother's sane answer restores my sense of perspective. If I can find a way for us to come back, even live here for a couple of months, I will. But I'm giving her what I can right now, some familiarity with her birthplace. I can ask that the school keep her in Chinese classes, and I can introduce her to resources, and I can hope that she will someday figure out what she wants to do with all of this. She is ten, and things change. And as much as I hate the idea of her living halfway across the world, I hope that she never loses her fascination with China, her curiosity, her sense of connection.

I cling to the woman's offhanded reassurance as the show begins. Female dancers in midriff-baring costumes take the stage, their magnificent head-dresses upstaging them: beads and spangles, elaborate black coils like spiders, fringes and feathers. "She's ten," I think, watching the White Ramie Cloth Costume Dance. It was "choreographed as a demonstration of the flowing quality of Ramie cloth," the program says. The dance involves many floating, swirling, twirling ribbons. So, basically, it's an ancient commercial, followed by men dancing in masks like the beasts' wild rumpus in *Where the Wild Things Are*.

"Things change," I think during the Rainbow Costume Dance, choreographed by the emperor's concubine. According to the program, it's based on his dream that "he traveled to the palace of the Moon, where he saw celestial women, clothed in feathers, and rosy clouds dancing in the sky."

By the time we get to the instrument musical called "Happy Spring Outing, Highlighted by Spring Orioles Song," I have to admit that I've had it with all this happiness, especially in a country where, as one of our former guides said, less than 20 percent of the population reports being happy. Give me a little drama and tragedy, please, minus beautiful Chinese women sinking to the ground/floor/patio, shrieking lamentations at strong, patient Chinese men. That, so far, has been our only visible alternative to the happiness pervasive in Chinese art and the other TV shows Sophie reports watching.

During "Happy Spring Outing," I could swear that the chorus is singing, "Feng shui, feng shui," but now I'm getting really cranky. The string instruments celebrating the oriole accurately imitate the high-pitched, annoying persistence of a bird outside the window too early in the morning. The piece was written because a flock of orioles flew overhead during the emperor's accession to the throne, and the emperor ordered his court musicians to compose music in honor of the "majestic birds." The emperor sounds irritating to me, prancing and posturing, ordering dances based on his boring dreams and music based on his self-involved whims.

Sophie watches dreamily. She's not so fond of all the happy talk, either, but still, she's found something here to relate to. Independence, I know, happens so gradually, so incrementally, that we'll both be ready for it. In the meantime I want to help her figure out what she's passionate about, what makes her happy. I want to see who she'll become. And when my nest is empty, there are a million things I want to do, too. So why this gnawing fear?

"I want to really know you," my mother once wrote to me. "Your hopes, your dreams." I was a new mother then, and after years of wishing, I wasn't sure I wanted anymore to be known. My desires felt diminished, hopes and dreams shrunk down to get me through each tedious and miraculous day. I wrote to her instead about Sophie's lost teeth, her funny and startlingly savvy comments, our adventures with fruit, sampling whatever unfamiliar varieties we could find: Saturn peaches, tiny champagne grapes, pluots, mangoes, plantains, and pomegranate seeds. It was comforting to write about fruit instead of romantic disappointments or work struggles or Sophie's difficult moods. Those things just repeated themselves in endless cycles, whereas fruit, the details of moments, were the real intimacy, I thought.

The last few months of her life, on dialysis every other day, my mother quit recycling the same old stories, comments, and accusations disguised as questions. She wrote to me regularly with lists of things that she wanted to eat, foods her doctor had prohibited: clam chowder, biscuits and gravy, eggs over easy, bacon and hash browns, chocolate-covered cherries. And so our agendas uneasily merged: I heard daily details in her expressions of her hopes and dreams.

The dance before us celebrates beauty, grace, loveliness, the "powerful, sonorous, and forceful spirit" of warriors. Sophie half-dozes. And I understand that I can do battle, weather her struggles, anything not to lock ourselves into old habits. I want my daughter to feel free to be honest about her mixed feelings. I want us to stay dynamic, not stall in old patterns the way my mother and I did.

The show is ending with a clog dance to celebrate the moon festival, the emperor arriving to parade with noblemen and give blessings to the people of the kingdom, according to the program. Soon we will go backstage so Sophie can get her picture taken with a tired cast who clearly want to get this over with as much as we do. We will return to our van and ride back to our hotel, where we will sleep after what seems like an endless day. The cast bows, and I think of something Ivy said, that when you want someone to stay, you give them a willow. I imagine pulling off a willow branch to give to my child and realize that this is something I would never do, no matter how badly I want to hold on. Wherever she needs to go, I will encourage her.

But she's ten. Things change.

Chapter Eight
October 2008

"I have a problem," I greet our Chengdu guide, Mr. Su. "I left all of my pants in Xi'an."

This horrible revelation struck me on the plane only minutes ago. Yesterday, I sent two pairs of pants out to be washed, and, scrambling to get ready during an early morning after a late night, I didn't notice that they had not been returned with the rest of the laundry. The only pants I have with me is the pair I'm wearing.

Mr. Su promises to track the others down and have them mailed ahead to Hangzhou. He is a small, hardy guy in his early twenties used to leading Australian and New Zealander backpackers on ten-day tours involving six hard sleeper trains and miles of hiking to track wild pandas in the jungle. And now he is in charge of a ten-year-old girl and a middle-aged woman who can't even keep track of her own pants. I don't know if his expression of friendly skepticism is a characteristic one or if he's truly in disbelief at this assignment.

Mr. Huang, our driver, is equally young and very friendly, a scrawny guy with acne and a perpetual smile. Unlike our previous guides, who introduced themselves using Western first names, these young guys both wish to be called by their titles and surnames.

"Our native cuisine is very spicy," Mr. Su says as we head off toward our hotel. "I hear you don't like spicy food."

Word has traveled fast from our guides in Beijing and Xi'an. I do like the taste of some spicy food, but the upset stomach and severe heartburn aren't worth it. After my bout of nausea in Beijing, I asked our previous guides to warn me away from anything hot. The general reaction seems to be that if I'd just try it, I'd like it, and so I live in fear of being slipped spicy food anyway.

"I can't eat anything hot," I try to explain to Mr. Su.

"You will like it here," he says confidently.

"No, I can't eat it," I try again. "It bothers my stomach."

"Maybe not here," he says cheerfully.

Desperate to make him understand, I blurt out, "My dad died of digestive problems, and I have them, too. I can't eat it." I'm not sure whether he knows the words *acid reflux* or *esophageal cancer.* I've made my point, though, judging by the silence. In any culture, even one that didn't put so much emphasis on happiness, this would be vastly inappropriate information to deliver to a new acquaintance. "Hi," I might as well have greeted Mr. Su. "I have no pants, and my father is dead."

Our original plan was to visit a panda reserve in Wolong, but it was destroyed by the earthquake in May that also killed 80,000 people and leveled 400,000 homes. The pandas survived, according to an article in an online publication, "Treehugger," though the earthquake interrupted their usual mating cycle, causing them "to freeze in the trees and stare at the sky." Our trip has taken us nowhere near any of the earthquake devastation. We have been rerouted to Chengdu, where there is another reserve.

"This is the highlight of your trip," Mr. Su says, since we are, after all, on the Panda Hugs Tour. We smile and nod and don't mention that for us the real culmination will be visiting Sophie's province and orphanage. Visiting ancient cities, standing amid armies of terra-cotta warriors, and petting real pandas all pale in comparison to my seemingly modest goals that loom larger all the time: seeing where my daughter was found and where she slept, trying to find someone who knew her as a baby, identifying the Man.

Our hotel room isn't ready. Maybe, says Mr. Su, we would like to go get lunch first. We can just leave our stuff in the lobby.

Our tour group materials instructed us to carry our valuables or leave them locked up in the tour vans. So I'm uneasy as I dump our duffles on a luggage rack, but Sophie and I hang onto the backpacks that contain money, passports, and medications along with things we packed for the plane: sweatshirts, books, snacks, journals, and her stuffed dog, once named Ozzie Osborne, now renamed Zeke.

"Is it far?" I ask.

"Oh, no," says Mr. Su. "We can walk. The restaurant is right over there." He gestures vaguely.

So we hoist our backpacks and set off at a brisk pace, but we don't exit the hotel and pop right into a restaurant behind it as I expected. We march down the sidewalk alongside an angled street, risk our lives crossing a six-lane intersection, and find ourselves at the foot of a long staircase. I crane my neck in dismay. My backpack feels it has been poured full of cement. To my relief, we swerve around the steps. But that relief is short-lived as we keep going. And going. And going.

"I can't carry this." Sophie shrugs off her backpack and thrusts it at me. I dodge away. I can barely manage my own bag. She sends me fierce glares.

"It shouldn't be much further," I mutter. She whines under her breath, no actual words, just a drawn-out, grating, peevish sound.

"This is the heart of Chengdu," Mr. Su announces as we emerge into a long, busy square, more of a rectangle, actually. "The restaurant is right across."

But he doesn't mean on the other side of the square lined with department stores and boutiques, places selling bamboo woven crafts, Shu brocade, and preserved ham, cell phone stores and restaurants. He means down at the other end. Way down. At least another ten minutes away. No doubt a hop, skip, and jump to your average wilderness hiker.

People are everywhere, young women in short skirts and tall boots chattering into their cell phones, men smoking and spitting. Smells from KFC and McDonalds mingle with Chinese food, Sichuan specialties, I imagine, things I've read about, fish-flavored shredded pork and Ma Po's bean curd and spicy diced chicken with peanuts. I wonder why we don't just stop at one of those. There must be something mild that I can eat. I'm sweating and shaking from low blood sugar. Sophie sags, not looking so good either.

Twenty-five minutes after leaving the hotel, we arrive at a brightly lit restaurant with plastic seats and a menu posted on the wall behind the counter, sort of like a McDonalds that serves Chinese fast food. Soon Mr. Su and Mr. Huang deliver plates of noodles and vegetables and beef and bowls of soup.

But wait. In Beijing, our soup was served with ceramic utensils, so eating it was easy enough. In Xi'an, we fished out noodles with chopsticks, then drank the broth. Each time I think I've mastered the logistics of Chinese dining, I find myself once again stumped. Here we have a huge bowl of soup that we're all supposed to share, and no serving utensil. How do we transfer soup to our small bowls? I pull out my handy wimp-out plastic fork, which confers a fleeting feeling of control, but then I set it down. It's a weird form of helplessness to be shaky with hunger but bewildered as to the correct procedure for dishing up individual portions of food.

"How do we eat this?" I finally blurt, way too blunt, too desperate to care much. It turns out that we are supposed to just use our utensils to nibble off common plates, then transfer some broth to our own bowls. These guys are not the least phobic about germs. Later I will read that it is customary to use one end of chopsticks for serving, the other for eating, and wonder why I didn't figure it out myself.

For the walk back, Mr. Su and Mr. Huang kindly shoulder our backpacks.

Mr. Su suggests that we "rest" in our hotel room for fifteen minutes. Then we are off to a park with a teahouse. Bonsai lions guard the entrance, and a profusion of colorful flowers, chrysanthemums and cotton rose hibiscus, spill everywhere, proliferating so casually, like hundreds of Chrysanthemums Blooming Patios. Even on a weekday, people have gathered to sing, dance, do tai chi, play badminton, and drink tea. At tables they play mah-jongg and knit and read and chat.

"When the sun is shining, people leave their work and get outside," Mr. Su explains.

I can't see the sun. Through the ever-present haze, light faintly glimmers like a twenty-watt bulb behind a heavily frosted globe.

Our itinerary promises that we will enjoy a relaxing afternoon at the teahouse. We settle into bamboo chairs at a small marble table. The terrace overlooks a lake, weeping willows drooping almost low enough to dust the water. Couples paddle canoes, and a man poles by on a raft. Mr. Su orders us tall glasses of chrysanthemum tea with flowers floating on top and rock sugar melting on the bottom. He deposits a tall Pooh thermos of fresh water beside the table and we embark on a pleasant discussion of Chinese dynasties, Mr. Su's girlfriend, who travels a lot, and the length of the school day in different parts of the world. Sophie zones out. Our division of labor has become solidified. I chat with tour guides, she absorbs the atmosphere.

Suddenly men flank our tables, ringing bells. They offer to irrigate my ears or give me a massage. Six men, one after another, stand their ground, waving around metal tools that look like long-handled candlelighters as well as tweezers, tongs, and bamboo scoopers. The men are reluctant to take no for an answer.

Each finally moves on only to be replaced by the next, and then, eventually, a fortune-teller comes along. She argues with Mr. Su for ten minutes. Occasionally he turns to me to translate. She feels that it's imperative that she tell our fortunes. Mr. Su's earlobes clearly reveal luck, and his association with a pale American woman also bodes well.

Mr. Su does not curtly dismiss anyone who approaches us. He does not seem to feel uneasy or pressured or resentful at having his space violated. He engages with each person, appearing to enjoy the exchange. After a long dialogue, the fortune-teller retreats and an old man bows low before us. He is toothless, his face leathery, his eye deformed, part of his head burned. He carries a carved cane and clutches piles of money in fists that tremble with age.

Sophie and I talked about beggars before we came to China. She'd once been distressed by a homeless woman on a Pittsburgh street. Other people dropped coins into her cup, but I walked on by the way I was taught as a child. "If you give money they'll just buy alcohol and drugs," my parents used to say. "It's better to give donations to support social services."

But Sophie didn't like the idea of turning her back on needy people, making assumptions about their characters, or treating other human beings as if they were invisible. She worried about beggars in China. "I don't want to ignore them," she said.

I suggested that we save coins or follow the tour materials' recommendation to carry juice boxes or snacks to offer to children. Sophie liked that idea but now, confronted by our first beggar, we are both paralyzed. Giving this old man juice or snacks would be all wrong, inadequate, inappropriate, condescending.

Mr. Su pulls out some bills. The man bows so low I'm afraid the top of his head will hit the floor. Then he moves on. Mr. Su tells us that there are few social programs to take care of the elderly and the disabled. He looks worried about whether the old man will be able to keep the money or forced to turn it over to someone else.

Afterward, we stroll through the streets, past teahouses, restaurants, and market stalls on our way to an embroidery factory. Two people work together on each enormous loom, one in charge of the warp, the other the weft. We hear the usual speech about the dying art of embroidery, but there is no activity and no pressure to buy. We wander around looking at quilt covers and handkerchiefs, pillowcases and slippers, and then go on to dinner at a medicinal university that smells vaguely like marijuana.

The restaurant specializes in dishes with herbs to treat the lungs, blood, or heart, lower blood pressure or ease a cough. While we eat, Mr. Su tells us about the American TV shows he downloads from the Internet. He translates for Mr. Huang, who laughs and nods vigorously. They both, Mr. Su tells us, also like YouTube.

The next morning, Sophie is queasy and feverish. My throat is scratchy, I have started to wake coughing every night, and my sneezes have progressed from off-handed to body-wracking. I usually get Sophie's illnesses, lagging behind by a couple of days, so it's hard for me to gauge until after the fact how bad she's feeling. Usually, two days later, when I'm struck, I tend to apologize profusely.

This morning Sophie eats a few bites of the fruit and bread I bring her from the breakfast buffet, and then we go out into the rain to meet Mr. Su. Sophie clutches her stomach as we brace ourselves in the backseat, darting through traffic past busy morning crowds, dodging the businesspeople streaming by on foot or pedaling bikes stacked with boxes and bags. Beside us, bacon dangles inside a small truck, like a portable butcher shop. Sophie watches, briefly forgetting her misery.

My grief, two days ago carved into sharp edges and polished to a high gloss by our visit to the jade factory, has now dulled. I'm feeling much more philosophical. All parents lose their children; it's part of the job. Babies vanish into toddlers who disappear into small children who become teenagers who turn into adults who leave to forge their way in the world. In the adult, traces of the child remain, but part is lost forever. Is this why some people have huge families, I wonder, to stave off the dread of inevitable loss?

When I first applied to adopt, media reports were filled with comments and jokes about Chinese girls being trendy accessories, like fashions to be replaced next season. "Glossy media coverage has treated the adoptions of Chinese babies as a chic and upper class fad on a par with owning a Mercedes or a Porsche," write the authors of *West Meets East,* citing, among other examples, a *New Yorker* cartoon "equating interracial adoption to choosing between an Oriental or a Navaho rug." I thought the tendency to objectify Chinese children had faded, but I was mistaken. While Sophie and I loved the movie *Juno* and its soundtrack, I was surprised at the way one line of dialogue was quoted over and over by reviewers and shown repeatedly in clips as if it were the height of hilarity: "You should've gone to China, you know. 'Cause I hear they give away babies like free iPods. You know, they pretty much just put them in those T-shirt guns and shoot them out at sporting events," Juno says. She is a teenager who has never witnessed or experienced China's adoption process, so I'm not sure why her naive statement has been regarded as so witty and prescient.

Comparing our children to purses or lollipops or iPods trivializes them, this group of children called by Penny Callan Partridge "the world's first international female disapora." Karin Evans describes them as "a substantial subculture of small immigrants, a kind of nationwide sisterhood," these American girls who bridge two major cultures, two leading world powers, representing "a tale of twenty-first century cultures mixing with each other in an unprecedented way." Chinese scholars and government officials see American adoptions as a way to foster greater understanding between the U.S. and PRC; Evans calls our children "little ambassadors putting a human face on a political relationship that is sometimes fraught with tension."

Interracial and multicultural families, including those with transplanted Chinese children, continue to shrink the world. I don't know that international adoption is always in the child's best interests. I don't know if it's ever the perfect solution. But the fact is, not only does it intertwine family trees, it

knits connections between cultures, making other people less easy to catego-
rize or dismiss. All over the world, smart, privileged girls with opportunities
are growing up rooted in more than one heritage and country.

Mild exhaustion and oncoming illness tend to make me idealistic, and
on this rainy morning, as windshield wipers squeak and Mr. Su passes back
our ration of bottled water for the day, I think about how these children are
already changing the world by their mere presence. Imagine, I think, what
they might accomplish someday. My job suddenly seems clear-cut: to make
sure, as best I can, that this country with all its complexity is not merely
strange or mysterious, foreign or exotic, but familiar enough for my daughter
to negotiate, familiar enough so that she never feels alienated from an important part of herself.

At the panda reserve, we follow wet, slippery pavement between bamboo
shoots. Sophie feels so awful, she just wants to get this outing over with. She
walks briskly, staring straight ahead, glancing briefly and politely at whatever
Mr. Su points out. He is anxious to show us all the recommended sights; he
takes pride in doing his job right. I pause to read a sign explaining how "panda
friendlies" became an "Olympical mascot." Sophie yells at me to hurry up.
Mr. Su looks nervous. We have too much to see to dawdle.

But the signs keep distracting me. I pause to absorb a quote attributed to
Indira Gandhi: "the greatness of a nation and moral progress can be judged
by the animal are treated."

And then there's a verse:

> All things bright and beautiful
> All creatures great and small.
> All things wise and wonderful.

I automatically fill in the missing final line, the completion of the thought,
the punch line, the words that tie together the stanza so it makes sense: "the
Lord God made them all." It seems odd to me to run across this verse, part
of a hymn written by a minor Victorian poet to help children understand the
Christian faith, in China. I wonder if the last line has been omitted because
the Lord God was an outlawed concept under Communism or because the
reserve hesitates to alienate Buddhists and Taoists with a reference to a Judeo-
Christian god.

"Cautious falling in water," warns a sign alongside a stream.

"Wild life is not food," proclaims another.

"Come *on*, Mom," Sophie calls.

We pause to watch a panda strut like a runway model, rambling to the left, striking a pose, turning to the right, ambling a few more steps, posing again. Shutters click and flashes pop. We move on to peer through a window at baby pandas in cribs. We view giant pandas and red pandas, all wallowing in beds of bamboo, munching at yet more sticks. I first assume that we've caught them breakfasting, but it turns out that bamboo has so little nutritional value, they have to eat all the time to survive.

I don't know if we're going to make it to the panda-hugging part of the Panda Hugs tour. Sophie repeatedly gags and claps her hand over her mouth, perilously close to throwing up. I have visions of her puking on the giant panda that gnaws its bamboo while tourists pose with it. What does it take to distract a panda from its intense concentration on its food? Could sudden vomit startle, distract, or anger it? Do pandas ever attack?

"She's not feeling that well," I tell Mr. Su. "Are you sure she should do this?"

"Hurry, hurry, you're next in line," Mr. Su tells Sophie. A blond family ahead of us slips on plastic gloves and ties plastic covers over their shoes. They cross a bridge to swarm around the preoccupied bear while a woman issues gloves and shoe covers to Sophie, who obediently puts them on. She gags again. No one seems to notice. A woman collects our cameras and ushers Sophie across the bridge. I follow, willing Sophie not to throw up.

I mean to wait on the bridge, as close to my sick child as possible without crossing into the panda's space. But apparently this is not acceptable. A woman keeps yelling at me, pointing. The message is clear. She wants me off the bridge, back several feet on the pavement.

"That is my child," I say, refusing to budge, as if I could do anything to save her in the event of a panda attack. But I think of the blond family, who crossed the bridge together, unquestioned. Probably they paid extra to be allowed to do so. Still, if Sophie and I looked alike, if I could communicate that she is sick and I am worried, there might not be so much fuss.

Tensions escalate. Employees yell and continue to frantically wave me back, as if fearing that I will try to rush forward and sneak in my own illicit panda hug. "I will stay right here," I say, pointing at the bridge. "That is my child." And then I blank out my expression, playing the foreigner who doesn't get it, and hold my ground as long as my queasy-looking daughter is in close proximity to a wild animal six times her size.

Sophie touches the panda's back. The fur is bristly, she'll report later. Cameras flash as employees shoot photos from all angles, horizontal, then vertical. Somehow, the cameras end up back in my hands and Sophie is stumbling to lean against me. I lead her to a bench. I can breathe now that the Panda Hugs tour did not turn into the Panda Puke or, worse, the Panda Attack tour.

Sophie promptly falls asleep in my lap.

"She is sick," I say. "We should go."

Mr. Su protests that there are more things we must see.

It's okay, I assure him. We can skip them.

He looks worried. He may fear losing pay for the day, which I want to reassure him would not happen, but I don't know that. And I know that if we don't finish the tour, his work ethic would make him feel that he'd failed at his job.

Sophie sleeps for a half hour. Then I convince her to walk. I can't possibly carry her all the way back to the car, and the tour group prohibits guides from carrying children, largely to preserve the guides' professionalism. Our only hope of getting back to the hotel is if Sophie can walk out of the park.

She manages about five minutes down the path before she suddenly bows her head and delivers the contents of her stomach onto the ground.

Just then, a cheerful group of British and American tourists surges toward us, waving madly. I recognize them from the airport baggage pickup.

"How are you doing?" calls an American couple while Sophie is midvomit.

"Um," I say, gesturing at her.

"Oh!" they cry. They stop. Everyone digs through pockets. Out come wet wipes and Kleenex and a peppermint. The group sweeps on past, waving good-byes and chattering enthusiastically.

I wipe Sophie off, meaning to leave the rest of the Kleenex covering the mess so that no one will step in it. Then, I assume, we will alert a reserve employee. But apparently these are American customs. Mr. Su ushers us away rapidly.

"We don't have to see the film," I tell Mr. Su as noisy groups of schoolchildren straggle by in their sweatsuit uniforms, the children's arms laced through the straps of their backpacks. "Hello, hello!" the children call to us.

"Hello, hello," I say as Sophie and the children size each other up.

At Mr. Su's insistence, we take refuge in the empty theater. I figure that the film will give Sophie a chance to gather strength for the rest of the walk to the parking lot. She promptly goes to sleep again, at least until hundreds of children crowd in, bringing with them a roar of voices. They jiggle and elbow, jab and jockey, press and propel each other into rows of seats. Then more children flood the aisles. They bounce around, popping up and down, peering over at us, nudging each other and then calling, "hello," part friendliness, part proof to their friends of their bravery. A cute boy with glasses checks Sophie out.

The film flickers. One hundred shouting, squirming children drown out the Chinese narrator, but all I really need are the English subtitles. The narrator discusses at length panda copulation and procreation. Voices die down and giggles sweep across the auditorium. "Oooh!" the children shriek in unison at the birth of a slimy baby panda. "Aaah," they breathe at the sight of a cute cleaned-up baby. These kids seem just as likely as Sophie's classmates to put chopsticks up their noses.

All afternoon, we sleep in shifts. Sophie naps, then wakes when I lie down. I get up, and she drops right off again. We can barely rouse ourselves to meet Mr. Su for dinner.

I've been trying to persuade Sophie that we should try American fast food just once in China. Tonight, Mr. Su and I decide, is a good one for a quick meal at the McDonalds across the street from our hotel.

The cheeseburgers and fries taste pretty much the same, just less salty. We visit a grocery store for oranges and chocolate, and Sophie asks for packages of chrysanthemum tea and rock sugar to take home. Mr. Su decides that we need to try KFC, a Chinese favorite, and so at the two-story restaurant he buys us a few samples to snack on later. He asks if there's anything else we need. I have plenty of Tylenol, the only painkiller Sophie can take, but I'm almost out of ibuprofen and cough drops. Grocery stores don't even carry over the counter drugs, but Mr. Su assures me that there's a pharmacy nearby.

Fifteen minutes later, we arrive at a drugstore, a maze of low counters piled with boxes of medicines, no bottles or tubes.

I explain to Mr. Su what I need. "Ibuprofen?" I say. "Advil? Painkiller? For headache?"

Mr. Su seems puzzled. Judging by his perpetual confusion at our maladies and his oblivion to germs, I've already concluded that he has a robust immune system and never suffers from backaches or an upset stomach. Or headaches, apparently.

Mr. Su speaks to the pharmacist, who holds up an asthma medication.

"No," I say.

Strolling along the wall thoughtfully, the pharmacist reaches for a box to show me. It's acetaminophen.

"Close," I say. "Ibuprofen?"

The pharmacist nods. He triumphantly produces ibuprofen. We're all grinning from ear to ear—me, Mr. Su, and the pharmacist—pleased at our feat of communication.

"What else?" Mr. Su asks.

"Cough drops?" I say. "Like hard candy, for cough?"

This one is easy. The pharmacist quickly lights on some herbal drops. I go pay then bring back my receipt to collect my purchases.

I'm glad I think to ask Mr. Su to read the ibuprofen directions, since it turns out these pills are twelve-hour time-release capsules, not the every-four-to-six-hour doses I'm used to.

Next door is a bookstore, brightly lit, tables of books stretching to a back wall of loaded shelves. I long to go in, but Sophie looks beat. Back at the hotel, her fever is down, but it has been replaced by stomach cramps and diarrhea. Tomorrow morning, we're supposed to board a flight to Hangzhou, the city where I met Sophie. Back then, I was so absorbed by my sick baby, I remember traipsing through a beautiful park, taking a boat ride, and walking along the water, but the landscape was all a vague backdrop for my baby's red face and angry wail. I've been looking forward to being there again, actually seeing it this time.

But at 7:45, Sophie wakes wheezing. I fetch her inhaler. She's sure she's going to throw up again. I think back to her asthma attack years ago in Northern Virginia, and then the next year, when she again became severely dehydrated. I need to find something to restore electrolytes, but if I had so much trouble explaining ibuprofen, how I will I ask for Pedialyte or Gatorade? And now, only a few hours before we're due to board a plane, I too have mild stomach cramps and diarrhea.

I'm packed and ready to go at 9:30, but Sophie won't get up from her bed. "I can't," she says. That fall in Virginia when she was five, she'd sit up and then slide back down to her pillow, saying, "I can't get up. This is terrible," and it turned out she was in the midst of a serious asthma attack. The next spring she stretched out on the carpet and refused to move, and she was finally diagnosed with severe strep throat. At eight my bouncy child collapsed onto the couch, subdued, motionless for hours; she had pneumonia. When this child who rarely stops talking and squirming goes still, I've learned to take her seriously.

And so I resign myself. I will not be meeting my pants in Hangzhou today. We will not be revisiting the place where we first met. I ride the elevator down to break the news to Mr. Su.

"Sophie is sick," I tell him. "We can't go."

Mr. Su is alarmed. "She must go to the hospital."

"Oh, no," I say. "She just needs rest. And something to prevent dehydration."

"We must take her to the hospital for an IV," Mr. Su says.

In Hangzhou ten years ago, I took Sophie to a hospital, more like a clinic, for a rash, diarrhea, and an upper-respiratory infection. We were sped to the front of the line but still waited for hours, me sitting in an uncomfortable plastic chair holding my squirmy baby. Eventually we saw three different doctors in succession and obtained a new prescription from each doctor for each separate symptom. A baby in our group who had pneumonia was sent for an IV to a room of beds with bloody sheets. While I know hospitals may vary, the last thing I want to do is repeat that experience. Not to mention that I'm not sure I could get across that Sophie is allergic to aspirin, ibuprofen, and penicillin.

"Let's find a sports drink," I say. "Then we'll see."

Mr. Su phones the tour office in Beijing and puts me on with Jenny. "Do you need to take Sophie to the hospital?" she asks. It takes me several more minutes to convince her that I should try other things first.

Mr. Su, Mr. Huang, and I find a large selection of sports drinks at the grocery store, all with Chinese labels. "Gatorade?" I say. "Electrolytes?"

Mr. Su and Mr. Huang scan the shelves. "We will have to take her to the hospital," Mr. Su quickly concludes.

"They must have something," I say. "Ask if they have Pedialyte. A drink for babies when they are dehydrated."

Mr. Su consults with a clerk. "We will have to go to the pharmacy," he says.

Sophie has already been alone in our hotel room for forty-five minutes. A trip to the pharmacy will take another half hour.

Just then, Mr. Huang exclaims, "Gatorade!" I turn to look at him in surprise. This is the only English word I've ever heard him speak. And sure enough, he is pointing at bottles with Chinese writing but the familiar orange lightning bolt slashing through the middle. Unmistakably Gatorade. I buy two bottles.

And so begins a long, long day. Through the windows, I can see the street below and the steady flow of bikes and cars and people on foot. Longingly, I look down at the buildings: restaurants and shops, the bookstore and bridal boutiques and cell phone dealers and studios specializing in wedding photos. We are cooped up in a hotel room, me on the fourth day of wearing the same pants, rain tapping against the window, a vacuum cleaner overhead.

We're on one of the few nonsmoking floors, but it's sandwiched between two smoking floors. In an ashtray beside the elevator, a row of cigarette stubs poke out just beneath the "No Smoking" sign. Funny how the inescapable smell of tobacco smoke makes me feel even more hemmed in, as if the walls are contracting around us.

〜

A glass of Gatorade later, Sophie is weak but on the mend. I'm relieved to escape the hotel room to meet Mr. Su and obtain some lunch. He has insisted on returning to walk me over to KFC, and he urges me to sit down while he orders food. This was supposed to be his day off, but he is so conscientious about his job, he's going out of his way to take care of us. I point out what we want—a chicken sandwich, two pieces of chicken, fries, and an egg tart.

"And what for you?" Mr. Su says.

"That's for both of us," I say. His skeptical expression is back. It's a Chinese custom to order many dishes, which in the case of Chinese food are low-calorie and healthy. But American junk food combined with Chinese tradition can create dangerous habits.

While I wait for Mr. Su, other mothers beam as I admire their offspring. They catch my eye and smile, the universal sympathy that passes between mothers. Then a boy Sophie's age spots me. His eyes widen. He nudges his mother. He points right at me and says something.

His mother glances at me apologetically and then addresses him. He lowers his finger but goes on staring at me. Then a giggle bubbles up. He points at me again and doubles over, consumed by merriment. His mother grabs their tray and tugs him away, sending me a mortified look. He allows himself to be pulled along, but he keeps turning back, guffawing at each glimpse of me.

Mr. Su brings me bags of food. He announces that he will meet us again later to take us somewhere for dinner.

"It's your day off," I protest. "We can find something."

After he repeatedly insists and I repeatedly protest, we agree on a compromise. Right now, he will take me to a restaurant and write down our order, and Sophie and I will return and present it later. We weave through unfamiliar streets, jogging over a block or two, zigzagging back toward the hotel and then into a building like a bank with a big plate-glass window. We climb some steps to a carpeted restaurant with soft music playing. At a desk in the lobby, we turn through a menu, past the bee pupa, silkworm pup, and tasty web duck. All look pretty much like they sound—a plate of bees, a plate of worms, a dish of webbed feet.

I arrive back at the hotel with a thin piece of paper covered with characters, a list of carefully selected beef, chicken, and vegetable dishes. I'm pretty sure that I will never be able to find that restaurant again.

I hold down my sandwich that has carrots, peas, and corn baked into the chicken patty. Sophie is amused by my account of the laughing boy.

"Maybe he thought you were Colonel Sanders," she says.

"Because of my jolly, aged face?" I ask.

"Your glasses. And short light hair." She dissolves into giggles that are reminiscent of the boy's. She's obviously feeling better. Not well enough to go for a walk, though.

I finish the two books I've been reading during the last few days, then have to unpack my luggage for more reading material. I'm restless, afraid that we're not going to make our scheduled orphanage visit. Sophie has to have felt pretty awful to have missed any of our trip; it's unlike her not to even be up for a walk. All day I've been confident that she'll be well enough to travel by tomorrow, but now I'm starting to worry.

What if we can't visit her home province? Who will be more disappointed, Sophie or me, if we can't go? Some children don't really want to go back to the welfare institute where they spent their early months, but she has never hesitated when I've asked if she wants to. The answer has always been yes. Until now, I haven't admitted to myself quite how much this matters to me, too.

I don't have high expectations. I don't expect any dramatic discoveries or life-changing revelations. I don't expect to unlock the mystery of my child's origins. I just want to try to find someone who remembers her, someone who fed her or jiggled her or changed her diaper or made her laugh or soothed her when she cried. Secretly, I wish to find someone who remembers her, maybe even someone who loved her. I know that a lot of families, going back, share my own modest hopes but never get the reassurance they desire. And I have to brace myself for that possibility. But to travel all this way and not get to go at all, to not even see the place where my daughter slept—I can hardly stand the thought.

By mid-afternoon, if I were at home with a sick child, I would be restless and despairing. I'm surprised that I don't feel that way, not yet, at least. Stuck in here long enough, I imagine I will reach the state I did sometimes when Sophie was a toddler and a preschooler, when I became half-insane at times, held captive by parenthood and winter. It didn't start out that way. When Sophie was a baby, I felt hemmed in by a job where I wasn't happy, but at least I was free throughout the winter to pull Sophie in her little red wagon around the South Carolina town where we lived. Even in January, the cows were out, a pasture full of them, and they mooed at Sophie. She bellowed back, low in her throat, with a firm mastery of their language.

Talking to cows on a sunny winter day felt weird, like we'd bypassed a whole season, leaving ourselves nothing to anticipate. Still, I was completely unprepared for the confinement of winter when we moved to Pennsylvania.

Every morning in those first couple years, snow swirled like dust when you shake a rug, quietly painting between shovel lines, growing from yarmulke to chef's hat on the fence posts, etching every small twig on the tree outside the landing window. Icicles drooped from the roof in multiple layers with the ancient complexity of stalactites.

Back when Sophie was still too little to help, I swung a shovel every morning at the long skeletal fingers with knoblike joints, elongating as temperatures rose, pointing at the ground more bonily, more grotesquely, each day. They tinkled as they broke along the tips, one after another in a music of falling ice, leaving a series of square chunks still clinging to the roof like a row of piano keys. Driving Sophie to school and then myself to work felt like steering a boat. We swayed gently from side to side, gliding peacefully along the slick surface.

It was like living permanently in a Christmas card: beautiful and soothing if terribly, terribly confining. Sophie was so young, and I had no one to talk to much of the time, and I found myself making metaphors obsessively, needing to find connections, to feel connected to something.

And yet the snowplows kept making their rounds and everyone zipped through the hills, undeterred. They seemed so bold in contrast to the South Carolina neighbors who hunkered down with cases of bottled water and loaves of white bread at the first rumor of a snowflake sighting in Charlotte. Relocating to live among this hardier stock, I thought, would make me hardier, too.

And maybe it did. Or maybe a day in a hotel room in China with a sick child cannot begin to approximate those winters, when I was nearly eaten alive by restlessness and boredom and my child's needs. We retreated for whole weekends to an upstairs room outfitted with games, Band-Aids, coloring books, videos, and a space heater. Snow rained down outside. Our room was cozy. At first I felt self-sufficient, if maybe a little lonely, but my dread hummed underneath everything as the space heater kicked on and its coils turned red. I wanted to go somewhere, do something, travel, run. After a long bout of bronchitis, barricaded by sluggish despair, I gave up on shoveling snow in a cold that relentlessly tickled my lungs. The post office threatened to report me to the city for not clearing my walk in a timely manner, an offense that could lead to fines and jail time.

I am so glad that those days are over. I remember when Sophie was a year old, soon after we'd arrived home from China, a day-care worker said to me, "She'll make a good little companion for you." I was appalled that anyone would imagine I'd gone through the whole lengthy, complicated, frustrating adoption process just to have company. Especially when, at the time, this baby seemed like a pretty poopy, hungry, loud, demanding companion. A dog or a cat would have been much easier. But now, as Sophie flips channels on the TV, I am surprised to realize that, even sick, she can be a funny, entertaining companion. At home, we never channel surf; we don't get that many channels, and we rarely have time for such a completely unstructured activity anyway. So skipping from channel to channel, trying to figure out what's going on, feels like an exotic game.

Sophie stops to watch a Chinese cooking show, or so I assume as a man speaks informatively while seasoning soup and scooping up a spoonful. Next to him, a woman in a chef's hat glows supportively. But suddenly she begins to yell at him and storms out in tears. A soap opera, not a cooking show after all, we conclude.

I wish Sophie felt better, but otherwise, I'm kind of enjoying our day together. We needed rest. The tour of China has so far required the same enormous structure, scheduling, and discipline as our daily lives at home. Sometimes it seems we are always running on wheels like hamsters, trying to achieve good grades and evaluations and scores and publications, adhering to meaningless rules and caring too much about arbitrary reward systems, never relaxed, forgetting the happiness of just reading a book, just talking, playing a game, watching a show, and accomplishing nothing. Just a few years ago, all I wanted to do was escape winter days in our upstairs room. Now, I sort of wish for them again. To step off the wheel into a low-pressure life where neither of us has anything to prove.

Sophie skips through channels to another soap opera. Or maybe it's a very long towel commercial. Everyone onscreen wears towels tied around their necks like scarves, turbaned decoratively on heads, wrapped around their midriffs, twisted like bandages around their wrists, flying like capes behind them.

"Feeling any better?" I ask Sophie, who lies on her stomach on the bed, an improvement from groaning under the covers.

"A little," she says.

On TV, grandmotherly women in pretty sparkly evening gowns hold up plain sheaths against their bodies. They seem to be saying, "I know I'm wearing a glamorous gown, but oh how I long for the days when I could fit into an ugly girlish cotton dress like this."

Sophie switches channels to a recap of Olympic swimming competitions, then zips on to a game show with a timer that sounds like a thumping heart. Contestants stand stiffly, staring at the audience, doing nothing, which suddenly pays off splendidly: bells ring and the audience leaps up, flinging hands into the air, cheering. Music swells, floodlights color the stage, and confetti pours down.

Sophie surfs on to what appears to be a unisex beauty contest. Men strut in white Fruit of the Loom briefs and women prance around in floral pink swimwear and high heels, daisies tucked into their hair. Sophie remains so still, I crane my neck to see if she is awake. She is, riveted by cut Chinese men flexing their muscles, demonstrating their arm spans, and showing off samurai moves.

I never regretted becoming a parent, yet I felt as if I'd become irrelevant to the rest of the world during those first winters in Pennsylvania, derailed from the career track I'd thought I was on, unable to maintain much of a social life, staring out our landing window often at a tree that held snow in branches like steady arms that managed not to bow under all the weight. I was mesmerized by the snow, falling on and on like a dreamlike drift of dandelion seeds, uncontained.

The days went on and on back then as we chugged along the mindless track of mealtimes, nap times, bath times, bedtimes. Somehow, so gradually it took me a while to notice, Sophie started to color inside lines and carry tunes, achievements of which I was dubiously proud. Then she lit on a picture of a cow. In a flat kid voice with no resemblance to the passionate full-throttle bellow of her younger self, she said, "Moo." That was it—just "moo," and some deep dormant grief stirred in me at that leap between pure experience and the translation of it.

Winters that seemed like they would go on forever now seem so long ago. Now I'm actually feeling nostalgic for that hard, hard time, those late afternoons when Sophie was little and sun colored between the blind stripes on the floor, when finally winter light antiqued early evening, holding snow in its restless swirl like dust in a sunbeam. We'd go out for brief walks, mostly excuses to drink hot chocolate afterward, making our way over thick slush under a dirty top sheet of snow. New flakes settled on top.

At least three layers of snow covered every part of the earth, and when Sophie and I used to walk, it was with at least three layers of clothing over every inch of skin. The cold muffled sounds, subdued smells. I heard, far away, the slow rumble of a snowplow, which pushed heaps of snow up the street and deposited them at driveway entrances. I kept wondering: how could I believe that becoming Sophie's mother was the richest thing I'd ever done, yet still feel that I might disappear under all those layers of snow and sweaters and love and boredom, of yearning for something more every day?

Those years, I always felt torn, always felt as if I wanted something that I couldn't have. At home, I longed to flee. When I fled, I missed Sophie desperately. When she was five and the snow started early, I didn't think I could face another winter in our upstairs room. My first two books had just been published, so I organized a little tour. I would be traveling eight times. Sophie could come sometimes, but not others. Being apart occasionally would be good for us, I told myself; we had been apart only five nights in four years.

"I'm not going away to college," Sophie announced one day. "I'm going to live with you forever."

My little swell of hope was immediately quenched by a pang: even while I felt confined, I had started to dread that terrible severance when my child would grow up and leave me. The inevitability of that hollowed me out and left me breathless. It reminded me that I needed to leave sometimes myself, remember who I was before this attachment dissolved me altogether.

Sophie watched me pack for my first trip without her. "My heart has two parts," she said coolly. "One part will miss you, and one part won't."

"It's okay to feel that way," I managed, taken aback, more shaken and hurt than I thought I should be. Maybe because she'd pinpointed exactly what was taking me away from her: my four-chambered, two-part heart, desperate for freedom while longing to stay put.

In the morning, as I zipped my suitcase, Sophie said, "I've changed my mind. I'm going to miss you with my whole heart."

I drove across upstate New York missing her while blowing snow alternated with sunshine and a kite-tail of birds flapped above. A week later I missed her as I reviewed a presentation in a bed and breakfast in Missouri, my electro flame flickering brightly, creating the illusion of a cozy fire but putting out no heat. I missed her the most when I was fenced in all around by noisy crowds at a Chicago conference. The only quiet place I could find to call her was a public bathroom, but toilets kept flushing, drowning out the end of every sentence. The next day I never heard the cell phone when her babysitter tried to call because Sophie was sick.

One more trip, I told her two weeks later. After this one, I wouldn't travel without her for a long time. She didn't believe me. She dawdled until she missed her bus. Frantic, with three hours to pack, organize my talk, cover my classes, and get to the airport, I scolded her. She disintegrated.

A bereft child can be as paralyzing as a natural disaster. I tried not to flick up my watch as I rocked her in the La-Z-Boy and sang lullabies.

Turn around and you're one
Turn around and you're three
Turn around and you're earning your Ph.D.

I sang, and her tears stopped. She even laughed once.

"When you didn't answer the phone last time, I thought you were dead," she said. "Whenever you go away, I can't sleep. I'm afraid you'll die and leave me all alone."

We talked. Our talk wound down. I recited a list of things we'd do together in the summer. She recited a list of things you should never flush down the toilet. Then I took her to school, where the secretary wanted to know why she was late for the fifth time that year. How could I explain the havoc my travel had wreaked? Could I offer *emotional crisis* as an excuse? *Fear of mortality?*

"She wasn't feeling well so I let her sleep," I responded feebly.

"Slept in," the secretary wrote on Sophie's late slip.

That night, the school sent a note home citing district policies on attendance. There was a vague threat about truancy court and an injunction that "slept in" was not an acceptable excuse.

But I wouldn't get this warning for a couple of days. About the time Sophie got out of school, I was in a plane above Nashville, surprised to see not rigid white islands of ice but instead water that shimmered like silk, creasing and shining with every breeze.

I called Sophie every day at the same time. She sounded younger on the phone, her voice impossibly small and sweet. "Are you calling from a bathroom?" she asked.

When I remember my wanderlust, I understand how important it is to encourage Sophie to make her own escapes someday, to travel and to see new places, so that someday when she settles down, she will feel more settled in her soul. I have always struggled with this, with being content, with enjoying the moment rather than worrying about the next item on my to-do list or planning the next trip.

When Sophie was six, I cut back my traveling but still left a couple of times for job interviews, not sure that I wanted to stay in the cold, wintry place where we'd landed. While I was away, Sophie kept bursting into tears at school. She took off the locket that had once belonged to my mother and clasped it in her fist. On a tiny piece of paper, she drew a small picture of me. Later she unlatched the locket to show it to me. She had given me a big smile, a rounder face than in real life, short hair, earrings, and glasses.

After that, it would be a couple of years before I would travel again, to teach twice a year in Kentucky, feeling, always, as if I'd run away from home, loving the energy of the work I was doing but fighting a queasy stomach churning with guilt and a terrible longing to be home with my daughter again. Always that exhilaration at war with guilt and longing, my split self. Even now when I'm away, sometimes Sophie will say on the phone, "I'm not homesick, I'm momsick." In my hotel room, often I am homesick, daughter-sick. I sing lullabies on the phone, my words carried to her after that slight delay that makes cell phone conversations so unsatisfying, the timing and rhythms of interactions off. *Where are you going, my little one, little one,* I sing over the phone while she drowses on the other end.

I'm surprised right now, in our hotel room in China, not to feel the age-old tension between my desires. Our bedclothes are all askew, the glasses tea-stained, the trashcans overflowing, the Kleenex boxes empty, and the room musty, the air conditioning barely covering the faint, sour smell of illness. But just as long as we can leave tomorrow, I feel no need to be anywhere else. My mother's death has made me think a lot about what matters to me, how I really want to spend my time. Not in busywork or meaningless competitions or meetings or dashes from one thing to another. "I like downtime," Sophie often reminds me when our schedule gets too hectic. So here we are. Hanging out, reading, writing, talking, channel surfing. When we go home, we will take more time to just do this, I think.

By late afternoon, we've found a new game. Sophie chooses a TV show, and I write an interpretation of what's happening on the screen. I read it to her and we laugh uproariously.

A knock at the door interrupts a commercial announcing the opening dates for *High School Musical 3* in Indonesia, Thailand, Hong Kong, and Singapore. I leap to my feet at the rapping: at last. Housekeeping. Clean glasses and towels, fresh Kleenex and toilet paper. Now if I can just explain to the maid what we need.

I point at the beds and shake my head. Then I gesture enthusiastically toward the bathroom. The maid steps tentatively into the room and points at our messy beds. I shake my head again, hoping that a movement from side to side means *no* in China as well as in the U.S. "Don't need," I say. I try to explain that we can't leave, can't get out of her way. "Sick child," I say.

She looks confused.

I slap my hand to Sophie's forehead, meaning to pantomime taking her temperature. In my eagerness, I instead I whop her in the head. Sophie flinches, and the woman looks alarmed. She glances at the phone as if wondering if she should call the Chinese equivalent of Child Protective Services.

Instead, she hastens to replace our towels and supplies, peering at me occasionally as if I am from an inexplicable species.

By 4:25, my stomach cramps have abated, but Sophie remains relatively immobile. She has lost so much weight, her pants slip right off her hips. I go to check e-mail after first extracting my jacket from her, since she has turned it into pajamas, a leg tucked into each sleeve. By the time I return, she's taken over my bed, sprawling across it with books and crumpled Kleenex scattered about.

I present our dinner choices. The Chinese restaurant Mr. Su recommended, if Sophie is up to the walk and I can find it. KFC again. Room service, which offers preserved chicken claw with wild chili, marinated duck gizzard, and spicy diced rabbit with red chili oil.

While Sophie ponders the options, I peruse a hotel pamphlet. The chef here can prepare "all kind of great delicacy that you have no need traveling world over," I report.

"What do you think?" I ask Sophie.

"Not the restaurant," she says. "Not KFC." This is how she makes decisions: process of elimination.

I hand her the room service menu and turn through pamphlets about scenic spots we've missed in "Splendid Chengdu." There's DuFu's Thatched Cottage, home of a Tang Dynasty poet, a "Saint in the world of verse." There's the Memorial Hall of Li Bai, the greatest romantic poet in Chinese history, his home now a "bright pearl." And who knew that Chengdu also boasts the only Salt History Museum in the world?

Sophie has tossed aside the menu and is watching a horror movie on the Star Channel. She also has mustered enough energy to clip her toenails.

In my bed.

We settle on pizza for dinner, a mix of corn, mushrooms, and curiously bland meats in a region known for its spicy cuisine. Sophie eats instant soup from a cup. Dying for something hot to soothe my throat, I tear into some hotel-provided jasmine tea only to find that it's loose, not in a bag, and without a teapot and strainer, I'm not sure how to fix it. A friend tells me later that you're supposed to strain it through your teeth, a bit of wisdom that probably wouldn't have helped even if I'd known it.

On TV, a beautiful woman pouts, then lashes out in an emotionally tortured tone before fleeing the scene, followed by her devoted, bewildered boyfriend. A boy arrives urgently at the home of a fiercely defiant girl in a sundress. He produces a picture of her when she was fat, and she covers her face with her hands and races from the room.

Sophie and I go for a short walk, just down to the gift shop, to test her stamina. A saleswoman follows us, rushing forward if we let our gazes settle on any object, much less if we actually touch it. The woman immediately picks up the item in question, points out its unique features, describes the process of manufacturing it, and offers a special price, just for us, until I long to flee like a tortured woman in a Chinese soap opera.

"Maybe we will come back later," I say, and make a dash for the exit.

"How do you feel now?" I ask Sophie.

"Not the exact thing as good," she replies, her nice way of saying *incredibly lousy.*

My lazy, contented feeling is beginning to evaporate. All I want is for her to feel better. Mostly because we've got to get packed if we're going to make the orphanage visit, but also because I'm down to twenty-eight cough drops and only one tea bag, my pathetic defense against the bronchitis that keeps trying to take hold. I can get tea in the restaurant or the plane and from room service, and I can drink plain hot water to soothe my throat, but at the rate of one cough drop per hour I'm going to need a guide's help to locate more by tomorrow.

One day confined to a hotel room hasn't been so bad. In fact, when I look back on it later, it will be one of my best memories. But two days in a hotel room? I'm starting to get nervous. If we can't travel tomorrow, we will head home in two days, disappointed at going all the way to China and never being anything but tourists. The village where Sophie was born, the city where the welfare institute resides, the buildings themselves where she lived are like black-and-white pages from a coloring book. We may have to go back to the U.S. with still only those outlines, without the colors that will help us to finish the picture.

When Sophie was little, I wasn't the only one with the occasional impulse to run away. Once when she was six, Sophie announced gravely that it had come time for her to leave home. After lunch the next day, she said, she'd be setting off to live in the woods.

"I'll be sad, but if you must. . ." I answered, matching her serious tone, playing along.

For two hours she bustled around upstairs, packing her Hello Kitty suitcase on wheels.

As a young child, my own mother used to threaten to run away from home, and her mother said only, "If you must." Obligated to make good on her threat, my mother stole off to hide behind the barn until dusk, when the smell of cornbread and her fear of the devil who lived in the woods drove her home again. There, her matter-of-fact mother placed before her a steaming bowl of beans flecked with bacon.

"I'm going to run away," I once raged at my own mother.

"Be careful," she replied serenely.

I remember this now with surprise: how secure I was in my sense of home, knowing my threats were make-believe, that no one would really let me go. Still I stormed off with my book and crouched behind the shed, imagining that I really belonged to another family. I didn't know any real orphans, but I'd read about them: Moses, Anne of Green Gables, Heidi. Orphans who foraged for berries and nuts in the woods were the stuff of fairy tales. I imagined being one of them, plucky and independent, making my own way.

But my daughter really has lived in an orphanage. I don't know what it means to her when she threatens to run away.

All over the world, parents of adopted Chinese children tell versions of the same story: once there was a man strolling to work, mounting the police station steps, when a sound caught his attention, a tiny cry, and there, before him, was a bundle of ragged blankets, or maybe clean, new ones with satin edges, and in it, a baby. I picture this man in a blue patrolman's uniform, thumbs hooked in his holster, whistling, although this is an absurd image straight from the comics page: who wears a holster to work, anyway? Do Chinese policeman carry guns or wear blue or whistle?

Anyway, maybe it wasn't a policeman at all but a grandmother stopping by to report a stolen bicycle. In others' stories, it wasn't on the steps of a police station, but instead on a sidewalk or at a market. And maybe the baby was a year old and had a cleft palate, or maybe she was three days old and jaundiced, or maybe she was a newborn with soft nails and the remnant of an umbilical cord, but the point is, she was a baby, swaddled in blankets or bundled in rags or wrapped in newspapers, squalling angrily, with an operatic shriek or a thin, hoarse wail: the baby who would become our baby.

Long ago, reading Bruno Bettelheim's *The Uses of Enchantment*, perhaps the section about Little Red Riding Hood or the one about Hansel and Gretel, I was struck by his claim that fairy tales capture the two greatest human fears: being abandoned or being devoured.

Like a lot of adoptive parents, I cringe at the word *abandonment*. The Chinese government does, in fact, call it that when a mother leaves her baby behind. "It's worth noting that parents in China who take their children to the doorstep of a police station—or even more blatantly, to the front door of the Chinese Center of Adoption Affairs—with every intent of getting them to care and safety, are said to 'abandon' their babies," Karin Evans writes. In some places, parents don't have the option to legally relinquish a baby for adoption, or, in more careful current lingo, to make an adoption plan. In such places, abandonment may be more like the Western act of placing a child for adoption than like throwing a baby away.

And yet, on adoption listservs, the idea of abandonment has provoked much debate. Some parents claim that the characters for *abandonment* more exactly translate to "left to be found." Karin Evans argues that "delivered to safety" is a more apt term than "abandonment." But many parents counter that such translations represent bogus, romanticized views, attempts to soften a harsh reality. Maybe so—but the evidence suggests that the harsh reality is less about the inhumanity of individuals and more about the brutality of governments. It's a reality in which desperate parents with few choices must confront official policies that force abortions and sterilizations and encourage hidden children. While I believe that honesty is essential to

our children's long-term psychological health, while I don't believe in gloss-
ing over our children's pasts, the insistence on interpreting the word *abandonment* in a Western context strikes me as ethnocentric and inaccurate,
no more informed than the statements of strangers who approach adoptive
parents in public to cluck their tongues at the way the Chinese "throw away
their girls."

Once, at a McDonalds, confronted by such a comment by a guy in line
ahead of me, I plopped my toddler onto the counter and launched into my
usual lecture on the social, cultural, political, and economic forces that lead
to the painful decision to give up a child when relinquishing a baby for adoption is illegal. I mentioned the one-child policy and steep fines for additional
children, the lack of a social security system, and entrenched customs that
could cause parents without sons to be destitute in old age. I told stories
about Chinese women whose eyes fill with tears when they see foreigners with
Chinese babies.

The man who'd made the idle comment stood there, his own eyes glazing
over. He eased away nervously. It was clear that from then on, he'd think twice
about offhanded comments to strangers. Sophie, then three, appeared to be
listening intently.

The speech had really been for her, anyway. I didn't know what she would
make of all of this someday, but I wanted to give her all the information I
could so that she would have the tools to make up her own mind. But even if
we present our children's stories with as much compassion as possible for the
birthparents, even if we believe that babies are quite deliberately left in public
places where they will be found and cared for, even if we acknowledge that
birthparents find the loss of their children painful and that they've put forth
every effort to ensure their children's care, those children understand earlier
and perhaps more deeply than most of us that any bond can be broken, any
love lost.

As a parent, I'm always anxious about the medium between neglect and
smothering. But secretly, like most people, I suspect, I also still carry Little
Red Riding Hood and Hansel and Gretel inside me, their fears stalking me.

The day after Sophie threatened to run away, I was reading the Sunday
paper when she came downstairs, her suitcase bumping along behind her.

"It's time for me to go," she said.

I was surprised. I thought she'd forgotten. "I wish you'd stay," I answered.

"I'm afraid I have to go," she said woodenly.

"Well, if you must. . ." I pretended to return to the newspaper as she wheeled her suitcase to the back door. Sending me one more long look, she went out. I heard her suitcase clank down the back steps.

Still in my socks, I hastened to the front porch, intercepting her as she rounded the corner. The air smelled damp, and it was still a little chilly. Melting ice dripped from the gutters. Cold from the porch boards seeped right through my socks. When Sophie saw me, she parked her suitcase in front of the steps and flew up into my arms. The prodigal daughter had come home. I would put rings on her fingers and sandals on her feet, slaughter a fatted calf, and throw a feast.

But she pulled away and turned back toward the steps.

"I wish you'd reconsider," I said. "I wish you'd live with me."

She shook her head, plodding back to regain her grip on her suitcase and resume her departure.

When Sophie was a baby, one of my students gave us Margaret Wise Brown's *Runaway Bunny.* The young bunny keeps threatening to run away, to become a trout and swim away, to become a rock high on a mountain, to become a sailboat and sail away. The mommy bunny serenely replies that she will become a fisherman and fish for him, a mountain climber and climb to him, the wind that blows him where she wants him to go.

I'd always found this book a little creepy, the omniscient overbearing relentlessly smothering stalker bunny mom kind of disturbing. It reminded me a little of the poem my mom wanted read at her funeral:

> Do not stand at my grave and weep
> I am not there, I do not sleep.
> I am a thousand winds that blow,
> I am a thousand glints on snow. . .

My mom thought it was beautiful. I wasn't so sure I wanted to feel like she was following me every time I saw the sun on ripened grain or felt the gentle autumn rain. My mother believed that it was her job to raise us not to need her anymore, and I'd always accepted that summary of a mother's role. I was afraid of becoming a control-freak mom who was everywhere, all the time.

But now as I stood at the kitchen window, watching Sophie's progress down the sidewalk, I reconsidered my interpretations of *The Runaway Bunny* and my mother's funeral poem. Sophie's footsteps slowed. She came to a stop. She stood there and stood there. She jerked forward one more step. Stopped. Another halting step.

It was like watching her batteries run down, movements sluggish, then nonexistent: she was frozen in place.

I paced, anxiety mounting. Should I let her go on with the game or make her come home? She wouldn't go far, and maybe she needed to feel independent. No, she needed me to insist that she come back.

By the time I made up my mind, it took an unbearably long time to tug shoes onto my feet and get them tied.

I'll never know what to make of her sad resolution that day she ran away. I'd traveled some that year. Maybe she was thinking, If you can go, I can go, too. Or maybe she was just seized by cabin fever. When I ask her now, she says she doesn't really remember.

On a weird recent day, the sun had shone for a half hour then been replaced by big sloppy globs of snow. It was like that all day: sun, snow, sun, snow. "It's like living in a snow globe," our friend Scott said. "The big sadistic giant keeps suddenly saying, 'Oops, it's time to overturn the world again.'"

But the day that Sophie ran away, the damp warmth felt more lasting, and cars, colorless all winter, white with salt and brown with grime, emerged from car washes as shiny as jewels. And as I watched her stalled on the sidewalk, suitcase behind her, my throat constricted for the day I really would watch her go. The creek behind our house had burst its banks in a rush so loud I kept thinking it was raining. Sophie wasn't going yet, I thought, not for years. First there would be bees floating above geraniums and melted popsicles, sandals gritty with dust under our toes. I hastened down the sidewalk to reclaim my child.

"Where are you going?" a neighbor called to her from his porch. "You look like you're headed to the bus station."

She stared at him, mute.

I thought of the man or woman who had found her only a few short years ago, who'd slung her up into his or her arms and started a process that led to me. I hoisted her up as if she were still a baby, hefted the suitcase with my other hand, and took us home.

We unpacked together. To live in the woods, Sophie had collected four pairs of jeans, a baby quilt Ruth had made her, a hairbrush, and a dozen books, including *The Runaway Bunny*. We sat down to read it, and I resigned myself to saying the things I realized she wanted to hear. Except that I also realized that I meant them: that if she'd run away to live in the woods, I would have to go live in the woods with her. That no matter where she went, I'd find her and bring her home. For years I'd held something back, and now I felt the tension slacken, just a little, as I gave myself, my self-protection, up. It wasn't that I hadn't committed myself for years to being fully and completely her mother. It was more that in that moment, I gave up worrying about the consequences to myself.

And later I will think of *The Runaway Bunny* when I come across a passage in Xinran's book, her letter to adopted Chinese children everywhere about their birth mothers: "I believe she never left you; she just became part of the mountains and the seas, of the wind that caresses your face, helping you feel the change in the seasons. She brings you peace with the night-time moonlight, and the rich textures and colors of life in the sunlight by day." And I allow that knowing your mother's goodwill is always with you can be comforting.

Looking back, the act of picking my child up and carrying her home seems like a weird reenactment of the day that the Man handed me this baby, Ni Qiao Qin, and I took her home with me.

"Did you fall in love with me at first sight?" Sophie asks sometimes.

"I was way too terrified," I answer, adding that it didn't take long before I knew viscerally that I was attached to her forever, a certainty that came before love. And so for ten years we have told and retold the stories, lived and relived our meeting, and affirmed and reaffirmed that I would make the same choice all over again. Along the way, we have also entrenched our myths, including the ones I've embellished over the years: that my daughter had been found on the steps of a police station the day she was born, according to a line on her official documents. That ten months later, she was delivered to me by a man to whom she was deeply attached, a man who knew how to make her laugh, a man to whom she clung. But he and I didn't speak the same language, and there was no interpreter nearby, so I never found out his name.

If Sophie is sick for another day, if we are stranded in Chengdu for another day, we will be able to keep our myths. I try to believe that this could be a good thing, preferable even, but I don't. I'm relieved that, though we move slowly the morning after our long day of being confined, Sophie feels well enough to go down to the breakfast bar. The chef there only makes fried eggs.

"Scrambled, please," I said one day, and he smiled and fried me an egg.

"Omelet?" I tried the next day, and he smiled and fried me an egg.

Today I pantomine breaking an egg and emptying the shell onto the griddle. I fling my hands around in a stirring motion. The chef smiles and flings his hands around in a stirring motion. I nod feverishly. He nods back. He smiles big. He cracks an egg onto the griddle and just when I think he's going to fry it, he begins to whip it around with his spatula, dancing, his motions exaggerated. He grins at me. Voila! A scrambled egg.

Sophie is so impressed by this, she makes me repeat the scrambled egg dance so that she can have one, too. I gesture madly and the chef stirs even more wildly as he fixes an egg for Sophie.

Sophie is eager to eat again. She holds down her breakfast. We are able to meet the guide sent to escort us to the airport, Vivian. "How is Sophie's ear?" Vivian asks me.

"Her ear is fine," I say. "It was her stomach."

Vivian looks puzzled. I gather that ear infections are common in Chinese children. But this seems to be a culture where no one ever gets a stomachache.

"Did she go to the hospital?" Vivian asks.

"No, she just needed some rest," I reply.

"I thought she went to the hospital," Vivian says.

We make it to Hangzhou, where we are whisked into a van by our new guide, Grace, and transported another hour to Yiwu City by our new driver, Mr. Yu. There is still no sign of my pants.

Grace points out the beautiful farmers' houses along the highway, with turrets and towers and cupolas on top. I spot one crowned with a wire sculpture that reminds me of a hood ornament. "They are only allowed to build their houses so high," Grace says, "so everyone tries to show their prestige by building things on top." These are the first single-family dwellings we have seen in China. I stare at house after house. One house has a cupola. The next outdoes it with two cupolas. The next has a cupola and a tower.

Sophie is from a province that not only harbors a clear competitive spirit but has far more space and money than do other places we have been. This is my daughter's birthplace, I keep thinking, distracted as the countryside hurtles by. Somewhere nearby are my daughter's birth parents. Grace tells me that the city has a population of 350,000, similar to Wichita, where I lived for my first twenty-one years. Now I can visit my hometown for weeks and never run into anyone I know. This puts into perspective the narrow likelihood of locating the Man, much less my child's birth parents.

As we drive to Yiwu City, we talk about tomorrow's orphanage visit. I explain to Grace what we hope for: to see Sophie's file, to see her finding spot, to identify, maybe even meet, the Man. An alarmed look crosses Grace's face when I mention the file, and she doesn't seem to hear the rest of my list. "I don't know about the file," she says. She pulls out her cell phone and makes a quick call. She talks rapidly into the phone. Closes it just as speedily and turns to me. "You can ask," she says, "but it's a new director, so you probably won't be able to see her file."

"Don't other people ask to see their children's files?" I ask. I thought this was a pretty standard question, the least of my requests. On the Internet, people are always comparing notes—did you get to see your child's file? What was in it?

"No," she answers.

That night in our hotel, I prepare Sophie for the next day, maybe also trying to prepare myself. We will drive to the orphanage, I explain, and meet with the director. We will ask to see Sophie's file, and he will probably say no. We'll ask about the Man, but the director may not know him, or the Man may be long gone, or we may find the Man but discover that he doesn't remember Sophie because it was so long ago. More likely, I think but don't say, people will pretend to remember her and smilingly offer vague generalities about a good baby.

We will offer the yearbooks we agreed to deliver on behalf of families who have adopted from Yiwu over the years. Families from all over the world annually send photos of our children to Ralph Stirling in Washington State, and with the assistance of other Yiwu families, he assembles posters and these yearbooks. After we hand over the books, we will tour the baby room, have lunch, go shopping for a gift for the orphanage, take a few pictures of the police station steps, and return to our hotel with hours to kill. Maybe we will shop for souvenirs in the late afternoon. Tonight we'll probably go to bed early.

I am so convinced by my cautious description of our day that I don't bother to pack the things I typically carry with me—cough drops, a hat, and wet wipes. We'll be indoors all morning and back here soon enough.

When the orphanage director doesn't bother to remove his sunglasses before he proceeds to turn down our every request, the visit feels even more anticlimactic than I feared. We might as well have stayed in Chengdu, channel surfing. An hour after arriving, Sophie's eyes have glazed over, and I want to retreat, too, rather than go on making stilted conversation with this unyielding administrator. A nap sounds really appealing.

Words swirl around us. No, we cannot see the file. The Man no doubt left here long ago. It will not be possible to identify or locate him. We stare drowsily at the oranges and small, green applelike fruit in the middle of the table. I know we should eat some to be polite, but after a big breakfast, we are not at all hungry. We are startled by the sudden motion of Mr. Yu jumping up and abruptly leaving the room.

That's when I struggle to come up with proper, impersonal questions to ask, ones that Mr. Li answers briefly and informally: there are eighty children under the supervision of the orphanage, but many have been sent to foster homes in the countryside. Thirty percent will be adopted. The children go to the local schools. I nod and desperately try to think of a way to get him to elaborate. As a last-ditch measure, I pull out the yearbooks. He studies each page for a long time. He almost cracks a smile once or twice. That's when Mr. Yu bursts back into the room, talking fast and pounding his arm. That's when everyone starts talking at once and gesturing and laughing and rushing off to get maps. That's when Grace finally tells us that Mr. Yu has consulted with orphanage staff members and learned about a disabled girl who used to help care for Sophie as well as identified the Man and found a staff member who comes from the same village.

"It is very far," Grace says. And then she asks the fateful question. "Do you really want to go look for the man?"

"Yes," Sophie says, and so I, too, say, "Yes."

Grace tells us that it will cost an extra fifty dollars for the van.

"That's okay," I say, and the next thing we know, we've all piled into the van and headed off on a wild ride through the countryside to look for the Man.

We pull onto the shoulder of a dusty road. Below us, beside a pond, a woman lowers a pair of pants, pushing the clothing into the water, then lifting it, now heavy, to flatten it on a rock. Water laps peacefully as she dips each garment. As we get out of the van and walk away, loud noises erupt: whop, whop, whop. She has laid out all the wet laundry on rocks and is beating it with a stick. The sound carries across the otherwise silent village.

Grace opens an umbrella to protect herself from the sun, and we head down narrow roads the width of alleys between old brick and plaster buildings with ceramic roofs. Yellow flecks of rice have been spread out to dry along the walks. A woman in a broad-brimmed straw hat rakes them, creating furrows between the long rows. We take care not to step on them.

The Man has a name: Lu Xing Qian, Mr. Lu. Grace fills me in as we walk: he is a wealthy merchant from Yiwu whose wife once worked at the orphanage. *Wealthy* means that he owns a shop, two cars, and a house in the city. He also maintains an apartment in this village where he is building a retirement home. Startled, I ask Grace to repeat and spell his name.

When my social worker called ten years ago to tell me the name of my baby, she said that it was Ni Qiano Qian. The name sounded vaguely Hispanic to me, not Chinese. My friend Sara, who'd studied Chinese, agreed that something was off, but she rifled through her Chinese-English dictionary, trying to look it up. I expected to hear that my daughter's name meant something like "Beautiful Flower" or "Lovely Blossom." Dubiously, Sara said that the closest translation she could find was "small fleck of rice in the front hall." Later, I would come across the Chinese saying "Girls are maggots in the rice," and I would think, well, at least that original translation of my daughter's name suggested that she was the rice, not the maggot.

The name, and the translation, turned out to be wrong. My daughter was Ni Qiao Qin, which means "smart and musical." Had the original name reported to me been accurate, my daughter and the Man would have shared a middle name, Qian. Well, maybe. Depending on the tones, Qian could mean a number of different things; it might not be the same word at all. But the coincidence adds to my feeling that this man is the closest thing to a blood relative that Sophie may ever know.

Mr. Feng goes to knock on the door of Mr. Lu's building. We wait on the sidewalk. I will the door to open, but it doesn't. A scrawny black lab skitters from the entryway. "He's not home," Grace tells us. "But this is his pet dog."

It has never occurred to me that Sophie could have been exposed to a dog before she came to the U.S., since pet dogs are not as common in China. Ten years ago, when I met my baby in a hotel room in Hangzhou, while two other families cooed over their babies and flashes popped and Sophie howled, a social worker who understood a little Chinese exchanged a few words with the Man. "He often took her home to visit his family," the social worker told me. The Man said something else, and the social worker faltered. "No, wait— maybe not," she said, turning away to oblige a couple's request for a picture with their new baby.

This seemed to me to be important information, but when I asked the social worker about it later, my question was met with a blank stare. The next day, during a brief interview with the Man, I asked our interpreter to find out if it was true. She regarded me impatiently and refused to translate, as if she just didn't deem my question to be anything more than idle chit-chat. When you have to translate every word, you start to measure which things are worth saying. So much goes by the wayside.

Sophie has loved dogs since she was a baby, going straight to them as if recognizing old friends. I just assumed she had a mysterious natural rapport with animals. But now as the skinny lab follows us from a distance, nose close to the ground, toenails clicking on the sidewalk, I wonder if Sophie once played with this one. It doesn't seem like a young dog to me, it's so thin and a little swaybacked, but it's too far away and I don't know enough about dogs to recognize if it's old enough to have been around ten years ago.

Mr. Feng is undeterred by the empty apartment. He briskly leads us on, down more roads, around more corners, past trees and crops and silos and cell phone towers and houses crowded together. The only traffic is the occasional motorbike. There is none of the hum and roar of airplanes and cars and appliances and radios that underscores the air of cities, just this remote silence.

Finally we reach the construction site of Mr. Lu's new house. It's a depression in the dirt with steel rods shooting out, a crane perched alongside, bricks stacked on the edge. No one is here. Mr. Feng climbs over hills of gravel and heads down a slope toward a brick building with a picture of Donald Duck painted on the side. I jump at a sound, a flap of wings as a rooster leaps from the fence behind me. And then, up through the hills of gravel, comes a triumphant Mr. Feng, followed by two people. I recognize the woman from photos of the orphanage staff. The Man is the picture in my hand come to life, his kind face a bit more aged, his waistline slightly expanded.

By American standards, he is muscular and tan, his stride so athletically long and quick it is almost a jog as he approaches, beaming up at us. I'm not sure how old he is, maybe in his fifties or early sixties. I hand him the picture to preempt any confusion, refresh his memory, maybe offer him a little assistance so he can at least pretend to know who we are. But he returns the photo with barely a glance. He does not need a picture, this gesture seems to say. Of course he remembers Ni Qiao Qin.

"He recognizes you," Grace tells me. "But not her. She has changed so much."

Now it is time to inspect Sophie. She has become used to this ritual. She stands patiently, slightly bemused, as everyone congregates to admire her and pronounce her a "very nice girl," according to Grace's translation. Everyone is laughing and talking. We smile a lot. We pose with the Lus and take pictures. Sophie seems at once so young and so old: quiet and shy, yet poised, carefully polite.

Then Mr. Feng and Mr. Lu decide that we will all have lunch, and so we crowd into the van, seven of us now, and drive to an open-air restaurant, the roof held up by bamboo posts. A waitress brings Sunny D for Sophie and me and mugs of beer for everyone else. For a good fifteen minutes, our hosts and driver and interpreter all toast us and one another, refilling our glasses constantly. Our stomachs are sloshing with Sunny D by the time the mayor of the town arrives at our table to thank us for visiting and propose a toast. We smile and raise our glasses again.

We drink tea and eat sunflower seeds, piling up heaps of snapped shells while everyone else talks like old friends. I want to ask, What do you remember about Sophie? Why were you the one who brought her on the train to me? Had you ever taken her home to visit your family? Did you have a dog? Were you sad when she left? I want to tell him how much that baby missed him, how she wailed and refused to sleep for weeks, how, despite her grief, she decided on the second day that I was hers and that no one else was leaving her again. From then on, she never let me out of her clutch. I wonder how to say all this, our different languages and cultures and experiences creating a dense forest, with few tools to cut a path.

But we manage to hack through a series of rudimentary questions and answers, learning that the Man has a thirty-two-year-old son and a five-year-old grandson who live nearby. The Man used to stop by the orphanage after work, and while he waited for his wife, he played with the babies. Sophie preferred him to everyone else. Every day, she waited for him to come. Soon he came especially to see her.

Grace is worn out from translating all of this, and the food starts to arrive. I sneak out my plastic fork, but I am not sneaky enough. Everyone stares and howls with laughter. Sophie sighs. Normally she would glare at me, but right now she is being too guarded and polite to display her embarrassment at her mom's limitations. Everyone else all starts talking at once. In any language, this is good-natured ribbing, and I am the target. I just smile.

The Man signals to a waiter, and soon two silver forks appear in a bowl of boiling water, presented to me as if I am royalty in a fairy tale, putting my flimsy plastic utensil to shame. I laugh and thank the waiter and my hosts. Sophie eyes me scornfully, horrified that there are two forks, suggesting that she has also been taken for an inept American.

Now a waitress brings a platter of flat green vegetables the color of spinach. "All the dishes here are local," Grace says, searching for another word. "Organic."

"What's this?" I spoon some vegetables up for Sophie and me.

"Leaves from the trees," Grace says.

Another dish arrives, a heap of greens with the stringy appearance of cooked spinach. Spinach, it seems, has become my all-purpose reference point. "What's this?" I ask.

"Seaweed," Grace announces. We each scoop some up while Grace exchanges a few words with Mr. Feng. She turns back. "But not from the sea," she says. "From the mountain."

Oh, I think. Weeds.

A waitress places a platter of meat on our turntable, topped by two claw-like shapes.

"And that?" I ask.

"Chicken." Grace looks puzzled at my ignorance. But of course: those are the chicken's grizzled feet right there on top.

We try some weeds from the mountain and leaves from the trees and chicken and sweet and sour pork with the bones still in. Next comes fish head soup. The Man keeps an eye on Sophie's plate, refilling it regularly. She gamely eats whatever he gives her.

Grace chats with the others, occasionally passing on to me tidbits of information. Mr. Lu remembers bringing Sophie to Hangzhou on the train, she says. He accompanied two staff members and two other babies. Yes, I say. Good memory.

I want to ask why it was Mr. Lu who brought Sophie to me rather than a staff member, but I'm not sure how to word the question so that it doesn't sound like a complaint. Grace looks tired after four hours filled with walking in the heat and driving and translating. So I try to decide, just as I did ten years ago, on one question that will yield something meaningful for Sophie, who doesn't know what to ask either.

Ten years ago, I had approximately ten seconds to ask Mr. Lu a question. The interpreter wanted to get on to the important interview with the former orphanage director. We were in an office swarming with babies and new parents and grandparents and government officials. Parents changed diapers on polished walnut conference tables. Babies ate Cheerios from plastic baggies and threw stuffed animals on the floor and cried.

"Please just one question?" I asked the interpreter, and she cut her eyes toward the Man and sighed.

"What would he like me to tell her someday about him?" I asked.

She rolled her eyes at the sentimentality of adopting parents. Clearly reluctant, she addressed Mr. Lu, who answered briefly.

I wanted him to say that she was special to him, that he would always remember her, that he hoped she would grow up smart and strong, some words of affection or wisdom.

The interpreter turned to me and said in a bored voice, "He says, thank you for adopting her."

Ten years later, here I am again, searching for the one right question, looking for an answer that will assure my daughter of her enormous worth. But the sun and all the food have turned me sluggish or maybe just resigned, knowing that few of us ever really find any such question or answer. So when Mr. Lu says what I've been waiting to hear, it nearly slips by, like one leaf fluttering to the ground in a landscape of trees, one fleck of rice in the front hall, shaken off by a shoe, threatening to go by the wayside.

"When she left," Grace says to me, "he cried and cried."

I'm a little startled. Mr. Lu is beaming at both of us, and Sophie's mouth quirks up in a slow smile. She may have caught his words, but I'm not sure if she absorbed them. Her smile seems more a polite response to his benevolent gaze.

I try to remember how he said those words, whether he was looking at me or Grace or Sophie, whether he was smiling or his eyes were sad, but the moment went by so fast, I missed it.

"She was sad, too," I answer. "She missed him."

The moment passes quickly as waitresses clear our table and bring takeout containers because, Mr. Lu explains apologetically, he and his wife do not like to waste food. I reassure him that in the U.S. we also take leftover food home. For a second we bond over a common philosophy about waste.

"He says that Sophie is lucky to have a mother who brought her back," Grace says. "He says that you are both lucky."

Sophie turns to me. I nod. We are.

"I have to go to the bathroom," Sophie mutters to me, and then heads over to the toilets, stopping to pet two puppies tied outside. She disappears inside and hastily reappears, calling to me, frantic. It turns out that when she entered the stall, a lizard ambled out of a crack in the wall and stared at her.

As I stand guard against reptiles, I realize how little I really know about Mr. Lu. I would like to ask Mrs. Lu questions about working at the orphanage. I would like to know what Mr. Lu sells in his shop. I wish he knew that the baby he once played with makes good grades, plays the clarinet, does gymnastics, and loves dogs. What he knows is that she is happy and healthy. What we know is that when she left China, he cried and cried.

We pile into the van and head through the clouds of dust we kick up to drop the Lus off at their construction site. We call out our goodbyes, promising to visit again, maybe in less than ten years. And then we drive on down the highway, past haystacks sculpted like little huts and road workers in baseball caps and the occasional yellow hard hat and the True Love Textile Company. Sophie is lost in her own thoughts. After a while she starts to nod off, and I drowse, too, in the hot wind blowing through the van.

Half-asleep, I imagine I am holding something, a souvenir of some sort, and then I jolt awake. My hands are empty, but they feel full, as if I now have something tangible, solid, and three-dimensional, to take home: the certainty that my child was loved before I met her. There's so much we will never know, but we know this, and for now that is enough.

Chapter Ten

October 2008

"The art of losing isn't hard to master," I've recited often to Sophie, at her request. She's been brought up on Elizabeth Bishop's villanelle as if it were a nursery rhyme, and for some reason, it appeals to her. Maybe because she loses everything. Her beloved stuffed dog, her library books, her favorite earrings, a key down the vent. But things always turn up, and so she likes the breezy tone of Bishop's "One Art." But I remember best the ominous final lines that strip back bravado to reveal loss's raw reality.

I have recurring dreams in which I lose my wallet or forget what I did with my daughter. I have trained myself to wake quickly from these, back to a world where what was lost in dreams has been miraculously restored. Where the moon casts a soft light on my daughter's cheek. Where she breathes quietly in her sleep.

My own mother lost a baby, her first child. My sister was born with a heart defect and lived only six hours. She never had a name. Her gravestone simply reads, "Infant Daughter." "But what would her name have been?" I used to ask my mom, who gave only vague answers. I kept hounding her until she said, irritated, "I don't know, maybe Carol." Deep down, I always suspected that my mom was hedging because she'd meant to name that baby *Nancy Grace,* and I would have been someone else.

My mother never forgot her first, lost baby, though she revealed to me only glimmers of the despair she'd once felt, the fear that she'd never have another child. Then my brother was born, and I followed, and soon after that, my brother developed a rare blood disease. My mother talked sometimes about holding her pale, lethargic boy, sitting with him for hours and then days in the hospital. She held him still so the nurses could take blood, and the memory of the betrayed expression in his eyes stabbed her for the rest of her life. I have a vague recollection from later when my brother and I were toddlers, of her carrying a teapot from the camper stove to the table. "Watch out or I'm going to spill this on you," she said to my brother when he hopped down from the bunk and landed too close to her feet. Then she tripped, and the hot water sloshed out, burning his leg. I remember the chaos of my parents rushing him to the sink to pour cool water over the burn, murmuring soothing words, checking and dressing the wound. But my brother refused to speak to my mother for hours afterward. It turned out he thought she'd been threatening him. He thought she'd meant, "If you don't stay out of my way, I'll punish you by purposely burning you." It took much cajoling to convince him otherwise.

My mother worried about this her whole life, too. But she didn't mention until I was in my twenties any of the ways she believed she'd failed me. She'd always felt bad, she said, because she hadn't nursed me. It turned out that when my brother was ill, she quickly realized that she couldn't take care of us both, and I was put on formula and farmed out to aunts. "You were like Topsy," my mother often said sadly. "You just grew." My mother had to choose between the sick baby and the healthy one. I don't know, if I were faced with the same dilemma, that I would choose any differently. The more I know about the terrible choices of so many birth mothers, the more I can put aside my childhood resentments, the more I can understand my own mother, the more I hope I can help my daughter understand both of hers.

A homeland visit is inevitably a journey about loss. What has always lurked in the background is now foregrounded: the loss of a family, a country, another possible life. The reality of loss has been especially vivid for us so soon after my mother's death. But finding Mr. Lu reminds me that for every loss there is something to be found. Not that I expect to find anything else on this trip. That just seems greedy.

So I only nod when, on the drive back to the orphanage, Grace tells me we probably won't be able to find Sophie's birthplace. "That's okay," I reply. There has clearly been some error in translation here. I haven't been expecting to find Sophie's birthplace. "I just want to see the police station steps where she was found," I explain to Grace. This seems to me a fairly modest request, but she furrows her brow in what is beginning to seem a characteristic worried expression. She goes on to tell me that Sophie is from the western part of the city. Once a small village, that area has largely been taken over by tall buildings.

Sophie was the one who most wanted to meet the Man. But I am the one who most wants to see the police station steps, this place that represents another link in the chain of Sophie's past. In the absence of much information about her as an infant, I hunger for whatever small detail I can get, even if it's just knowing whether the stairs are made of wood or concrete, whether there is a simple railing or an ornate one, whether the building is small and ramshackle or large and bustling and impersonal.

Earlier, I asked Sophie if she wanted to see the police station. I was willing to forego it if she didn't. Jane Liedtke, the director of the group that has organized our tour, Our Chinese Daughters Foundation, cautions in her article "Walking down the Village Path" that parents should not treat the finding spot as a photo shoot, a Kodak moment. It is the place where, after all, our children were severed forever from their birth parents, and it is important to tread lightly. But Sophie said yes, she was interested in seeing it.

Grace's expression does not relax as we return to the orphanage. We pull through the gates again, under gold characters spelling out, I assume, *Yiwu City Social Welfare Institute.* We park between the office and residential buildings, in front of a playground built with donations from adoptive families. The playground remains empty on this warm day, freshly painted blue and yellow and red criss-crossed metal bars untouched.

On closer inspection, I realize that I have no idea what one does with these. They look to me like the exercise stations we've seen in small parks in China where older people gather. I'm not sure that this equipment would be fun for children. There are no slides, swings, seesaws, merry-go-rounds, sandboxes, jungle gyms, none of the apparatus that I associate with childhood and much of which is manufactured in China. The playground itself is built on a tiled space, no grass to break falls. But then I realize I am once again viewing the area through my American expectations. These tiles appear to be a resilient rubber, probably safer in the long run and more suited to drainage.

Back inside the office building, we are taken to see Mr. He, the assistant director, who is young and warm. He smiles nonstop as he shows us the shrunken copies of posters of adopted Yiwu children that plaster his walls. I present him his copy of the yearbook, and he gets all excited that I too know Mr. Stirling, the dad from Washington who keeps Yiwu families connected, even if my acquaintance with him exists only on the Internet.

Despite the seemingly firm proclamation from Mr. Li that we can't see Sophie's file, Mr. He hands it to me and allows me to flip through it. Mostly I find copies of documents that I was given ten years ago, medical reports and adoption paperwork, nothing new or interesting. The only unfamiliar paper is covered with handwriting. When I adopted Sophie, I asked the former orphanage director if she had been found with a note. At the time, American adoptive parents commonly had a romantic image of thin red paper pinned to our babies' collars, bearing a scrawled plea or promise, "Please take care of my baby," or "I will never forget her."

The orphanage director assured me that yes, there had been a note, and that it had been placed in Sophie's file, available for her to see someday when she returned. In the intervening years, I have learned that such notes rarely exist.

Because Americans wanted the notes so badly, orphanage staff sometimes forged them and stuck them in the babies' files. Those files have since been purged of these false notes. So I'm pretty sure that this, a whole paragraph of characters, is more likely a police report or informal record of some sort.

Mr. He takes the file from me. He and Grace read the paper, pointing at words, checking it over periodically as they converse. They seem deeply engaged but don't translate the conversation. Something important seems to be happening, so I don't interrupt, even though I want to know what they're saying, even though I would like a copy of this note. Since we weren't supposed to see the file in the first place, I don't want to press our luck. Someday I will ask, but not now.

After a while, Mr. He puts away the file, and we adjourn to the orphanage's living quarters, walking across the courtyard past the mysterious, empty playground. We are not allowed to take pictures in the residential building. We climb gray concrete stairs and pass through a knee-level gate into a room where a few children toddle around while two older girls sit writing at a small table.

"Ni hao!" calls a little boy, and two others wander out of the gate and head straight for the stairs. They are shooed back into the play area. The older girls mutter to each other and never look up from their table. I wonder if they feel resentful toward privileged foreigners parading through their home, reminding them of what they don't have.

Some of the children who are still here are waiting to be adopted, like one little girl who toddles through, laughing, a caretaker holding her hands to steady her. "Did you see our daughter, Jillian?" her mother will write to me when we return home, and I will be happy to have this small image to report of her laughing child-to-be. Less than a year later, after Jillian comes home to the States, we will meet her and her family in Washington, D.C., Jillian transformed into an American child, shy around the strangers she didn't even notice that day in China.

Some older children who remain at the welfare institute have physical disabilities, which I can only guess is why they have not been sent with the others to foster care in the country. They are growing up in the orphanage like the one-armed girl who, Grace has told us, once cared for Sophie. Now a married woman with a baby of her own, she is not around today, but I hope that someday we can track her down, too. I am eager to know more about her life and hear what she remembers about Sophie.

We are led across the playroom to the stiflingly hot baby room. The walls are lined with cribs. They bisect the middle of the room, uninterrupted rows of them. Babies lie on their stomachs on the sheets, listless, except for the ones in the arms of several white women, who tote them around or stand swaying gently. One of the women comes up to me and says, "Where are you from?"

I'm surprised to hear quick, offhanded English. "I'm from Pennsylvania in the U.S.," I say.

"We're from Minnesota." She looks amused. "We're traveling to orphanages to do physical and occupational therapy."

The English language has come to seem like a cage, one so tight I can't move much in any direction. Now I stare, puzzled, at this woman who is inviting me to break out, be free, climb the hills and sail down the valleys of my own language, dive into a colorful underwater world of subtexts, fly through the air performing linguistic feats of big words like *physical* and *occupational* and *therapy.* But I feel as stymied as when I am faced with a Chinese meal and no silverware or serving utensils. "I have been using simplified English so long, I am not sure I can break the habit," I say.

"I know what you mean," she says, but she's with a whole group of nurses with daughters from China, and she sounds perfectly natural in contrast to the robotic speech that keeps coming out of my mouth.

I want to hold a baby, but how do I choose one in a roomful of babies without enough adults to hold them? I walk along, looking at the little ones flopped on their sheets, not sleeping but eerily still, eyes glazed with boredom. One or two babies cry, a squeaky, unaccustomed sound as if they don't expect their noise to garner any response. Most of the babies don't bother. They are eerily silent. Sophie is also eerily silent, hanging back and looking around uncertainly, shy around all of these babies.

A boy cries huge tears like Sophie used to, and one of the nurses goes to him. What about all of the ones who've given up, I wonder, who don't seek attention because they won't get it anyway? How do I pick up one of these babies and ever put it down again?

A little girl with wild dark hair and layers of clothing under her pink polyester shirt creeps around the rail of her crib. Sophie comes to stand beside me as I lift the baby up. She stays very quiet and still, bundled in several layers of clothes in the heat. "You were all bundled up like this when I met you," I tell Sophie. This is why she still runs so hot, I think; she was overheated the first few months of her life, stifled by too many clothes. At least the cribs are bare, without blankets, though ragged ones have been piled on a table. Sophie always kicked off blankets when she was a baby, so that if I wanted to ensure that she'd be warm, I'd dress her in fuzzy footie pajamas. She didn't like them. Even in the dead of winter, they were too hot for her.

Sophie watches as I carry my tiny, silent bundle facing out so she can look around. We circle the room, passing baby after baby. There is an occasional small rattle affixed to a crib rail, but those are the only toys I see. If Mr. Li were a child development specialist and not a government official, this room would be filled with bright toys, I think. How hard would it be to give these babies something to look at and chew on and squeeze?

This seems like a terrible life, endless hours of confinement without breezes or songs or conversations or the smell of bread baking or the freedom to move around, to observe and examine and discover the world. Did my own daughter really lie here for ten months, her days broken up only by light and dark, the occasional bottle or caretaker to change her diapers? No wonder she looked so forward to the Man's visits. No wonder she didn't want to sleep for weeks after I first met her, grieving over the loss of familiarity but also suddenly wildly overstimulated and so eager to make up for lost time, to see and hear and smell and taste and touch things.

A small Chinese girl has entered the room and reaches through the slats of a crib to pat one of the babies. "Hello," I say to the girl, who looks about three.

"She's sixteen," a nurse informs me, clearly cautioning me against the baby-talk tone in which I greeted the girl. I realize that she's probably so small due to dwarfism and that she likely encounters what must sound like condescension way too often. I quickly shift into a normal, grown-up voice. She doesn't speak English; she just looks at me impassively.

I continue to circulate with my immobile but curious baby whose eyes keep moving, taking things in silently. A baby girl flings herself toward us as we pass, nearly tumbling over the bar of her crib. "Whoa," says one of the Minnesota nurses, rescuing her. A baby boy grabs my hand and tries to nibble on my finger. I nod at Sophie, who holds out her hand and lets the little boy gum it. She laughs and takes a step back.

I would like to stay here all afternoon holding babies, but Grace says that we have to go locate Sophie's finding place. I feel regretful as I gently lower the little girl into her crib. She again accepts her fate silently. We say good-bye to the babies and the nurses from Minnesota, preparing to go on tracing Sophie's life backward, from the Man with whom she once shared a bond to the room where she once slept, and now, after all, the place where she was found on the day she was born. Reluctantly, I leave the babies behind in their prison of heat and boredom.

But then we're back in the van, bumping and skittering along rural roads, the van weaving like skis over moguls, on our second wild and unexpected journey of the day. Mr. He, the orphanage's assistant director, has come along to point out the way to Mr. Yu. I ready my camera and steel myself for the cold concrete steps and big plate glass window of a police station, or the ornate gates or wooden door. I just want to be able to picture it accurately in my mind, this first knowable link in the chain of Sophie's history.

Mr. He points and talks rapidly: turn here, turn there, there was water, a pond, maybe it was here, no here.

Grace translates fragments. That's how I know we're looking for a pond. A police station next to a pond? Or maybe the station has been torn down? This building has played such a monumental part in the history I imagined for my child, but I never pictured it next to a pond. I envisioned it on a busy street, maybe near a market.

We park and hop out of the van onto a dirt road on the edge of a village. Mr. He leads us to a stretch of green, scummy water that looks more to me like a flooded area than a pond. There is no bank. The water just ends in tangles of weeds near a couple of pine trees that stand next to phone towers and low brick houses beside a row of four-story apartment buildings. Mr. He says a few words and then shakes his head.

"This is like the pond where Sophie was found," Grace says. But it's not the right one, I assume, because there is nothing that looks like a police station in the immediate vicinity. Two bikes stripped of their paint have been left parked at the water's edge, and someone has hung laundry to dry on a rope strung above a huge rock.

We troop on into the village, where the buildings are old, like the Hutongs in Beijing, plaster or brick with elaborate iron gates over wooden doors, or, incongruously, entrances with no doors, just bright floral or striped blankets hung before them. The streets are narrow as alleys and dusty, mostly unpaved. We walk through an open-air market, where plastic buckets, Styrofoam coolers, bushel baskets, and smaller hanging baskets are piled with vegetables and fruits. We pass heaps of green onions tied in bunches, containers filled with nuts and pink apples, bananas hanging in clusters, cloth goods spread out across tables, dusty heaps of thin paperback books. Umbrellas shade the merchandise, and paper lanterns and balloon animals hang from the ceilings. We pass open-air rooms that appear to be bars, where people play pool and snooker. Pool balls clack against one another.

I hold my camera low, snapping pictures. Sophie's brow furrows. At home this would be an all-out scowl, accompanied by her snarling at me to put my camera away. "Stop taking pictures," she hisses at me now, but then her desire to appear polite seems to win out over her American preteen tendencies, and she just turns away. I'm torn, feeling that I should honor my child's wishes but that in the long run she will wish for pictures of her village. So I go on snapping the button, being careful to appear respectful and to be as unobtrusive as possible.

Grace explains to us that this village was very different ten years ago. Many of its residents have gone to the city to find work, and most of the population here now consists of renters who have let the buildings go. That's why we see crumbling walls and graffiti, Chinese characters scrawled across the plaster. On a concrete wall, four rows of big black letters and numbers march along, reminding me of clues in the Nancy Drew computer games that Sophie and I sometimes play together. Nancy is always stumbling upon cave walls with writing scrawled across them like L3R9F15, which tells you that to navigate the cave you make three left turns and nine right turns and then go forward fifteen steps. As we come upon this wall in China, I have a brief feeling of being in my own live-action computer game, tracking clues to solve a mystery, if only I knew how to decipher all of these characters and numbers.

Briskly we continue past a China Mobile shop, another unexpected detail in this rustic setting, and stop to consult with a couple of men. Mr. He and then Grace and then Mr. Yu address them. The strangers glance over at Sophie and me. One calls to a passing woman, who turns back and listens thoughtfully. She is tall, in her twenties, less casually dressed than the others, who wear jeans or khakis, T-shirts or polo shirts, and sneakers. She looks like she just stepped out of a business meeting in her black suit that nips in at the waist and black leggings. With great authority, she gestures and then sets off down the street in her high-heeled black pumps. We follow. Two more people join us. Everyone seems to be debating something. The woman tosses her flipped-up short hair and points and keeps going. We stop at a building with a sign in Chinese posted on a wooden door, like an eviction notice. Two mops hang next to the door.

"This is where the man who found you lives," Grace tells Sophie. "He rents out the house now because he does business in the city."

I glance at Sophie, startled. The man who found her? There is a record of the man who found her on the police station steps? Surely he would have taken her right inside and turned her over to authorities. I imagine him rushing home to tell everyone that he had found a baby. The story must have circulated for days.

More conversation ensues, or maybe it's an argument, or maybe everyone is making jokes. It's frustrating to have no idea. The young woman in black tosses off a comment to the group before she turns abruptly and leads us past more crumbling brick-and-plaster buildings, around more corners, through a narrow corridor into a courtyard. She yells up at a man on a balcony. He yells back. A grandmother with a baby rounds the corner. More people gather. They stare and gesture at Sophie, who accepts their attention and curiosity with quiet dignity.

She is being a model child, very, very calm, gazing quietly at everything, taking it all in, saying little. At home she would be complaining by now that she was bored, or hot, or tired, or hungry. She would be tugging at my sleeve, asking a million questions, the way she does when I'm on the phone and she's not part of the conversation. "What?" she would keep asking. "What happened?" Here, she stands and listens, and when others look at her, she meets their eyes with her own level gaze and then politely glances away.

"They remember the baby," Grace says. Sophie and I look at each other.

"You," I say.

"I know, Mom," she says, without her usual impatience.

I've had a false idea that because China is such a big country and because there have been so many abandoned babies, no one will remember just one. But statistically, in fact, finding an abandoned baby is not a daily event. It makes a lasting impression on the finder. Discovering my daughter was not a mundane, easily forgotten event in anyone's life, a thought I find comforting.

If the villagers remember the baby, I think, maybe they also remember a pregnant girl or woman. Maybe when they look at this beautiful child, they note her resemblance to a woman or a man or another child here. I know that there is a danger that an abandoned child's return can get birth parents in trouble. Alternately, a newly discovered connection to an American family can raise a family's status. Of course I don't know whether either will happen in this village. I only hope that, somehow, word will reach Sophie's birth parents that their baby came back today. I hope that word will reach them that she is healthy and strong, smart and beautiful, safe and loved.

The man comes down from his balcony.

"This man is the father of one of the men who found her," Grace says. "There were two."

I am even more mystified. Two men found my daughter at a police station, and it was the talk of the village?

As the conversation continues, I assume that they are all comparing notes, debating the location of Sophie's finding spot, but I'm not sure. They could simply be discussing the weather, making flirtatious banter, or engaging in small talk, although that's unlikely. It's disorienting not to know what's going on but even more disconcerting not to understand the general tone and direction of the conversation.

Everyone keeps casting surreptitious looks at me. They stare at Sophie openly. She smiles politely and looks a little self-conscious while I steal glances at each of their faces, recording in my memory these people with a connection to my baby. The father of a man who found her, with a wide flat face and a pot belly. The elegant businesswoman who has taken charge, model-like with her slim waist and hands, her pretty oversized features, her fashionable dress and the clear confidence that inspires others to treat her with deference. The grandmother who shifts the baby she holds to one side, using the other hand to gesture. The baby who hangs limply over her arm, starting at the ground, unprotesting as the gestures grow more dramatic and he flops up and down. This baby has a big round head. I want to touch the fuzz of hair on top.

The conversation seems to go on and on. There is much pointing and shaking of heads. The father keeps sneaking glances at the child his son found many years ago. And I keep trying to concentrate, to trace with my eyes the spaces between bricks with the mortar missing, the grandmother's small silver earrings, the numbers that appear to have been stamped all over the wall behind her. I have to remember this, all of this. If it is ever possible to legally track down Sophie's birth parents or a sibling, she will want as much information as possible. And pictures, too, pictures of all these people and places, because we never know who might be able to help us. I reach down with my camera and keep clicking the button. Mostly I don't even check to see what I'm photographing. I just hold the camera off to my side and snap picture after picture. Sophie narrows her eyes at my camera but says nothing.

Maybe, I think as I listen, no one is quite sure where the police station was located, which seems odd. I guess that it has been torn down. The grandfather points in one direction, but the grandmother points in another, and the woman in black shakes her head as if she's disagreeing with both of them. In fewer than ten years, everyone has forgotten where the police station was? After what seems like a very long time, we take our leave. We walk some more.

Then Grace says, "This is it. The pond was where the high-rise stands now."

"But where was the police station?" I ask as we gaze across the street at a new apartment building constructed on what appears to be an old foundation made of crumbling bricks. In contrast, the high-rise, which actually has only two or three floors, is freshly painted orange with pink trim around its big shiny windows. Next to it, barely showing behind a wall, stands a small, older structure with a flat roof that is longer than the building it covers. In front of the wall, heaps of broken blue glass glint in the sun. A woman in a straw hat rakes at the rubble, moving broken glass from one pile to another. Maybe, I think, that building was the police station. It seems like a strange home for law and order, with all the broken glass heaped in piles that are almost as tall as the raking woman.

Grace helps us piece together the story, and only then do I realize that there does not seem to have been a police station at all, at least not initially. Those steps have loomed so large in my imagination, even now it takes me a few seconds to let the image go and replace it with new ones.

Early one June morning ten years ago, two young men rose early and came down to the pond to fish. And there, in the tall grass, maybe among reeds and rushes, they found a baby girl. My girl. I am in awe of how biblical, how mythical, an ordinary life can suddenly become.

"She left me here?" Sophie says. She has been so placid all morning. Suddenly, she sounds alarmed. "She left me to drown?"

Women in rural areas have commonly drowned baby girls immediately after birth, but usually at home in buckets or bowls of water, not in public places like ponds. Xinran writes about the water kept beside the beds where mothers give birth. If the baby is a boy, the water is used to wash him. It is called "Watering the Roots Bath." If the baby is a girl, the water is called "Killing Trouble Water." It is used to drown her.

But this is not what happened to my daughter. It was a summer morning, and a pond is a place where fishermen arrive early, before the markets open, before the police station turns on its lights, before the unpaved walks have been trod by people on their way to work. It was a summer morning, and someone knew that by a pond, this baby would be found.

Anchee Min tries to recreate what happens to many birth mothers as they leave their babies: "She wanted what was best for you for the last time. She might have traveled as far as her money allowed her . . . where she would lay you down and hide you inside lotus roots or celery leaves. I am sure she would watch from a distance, hiding herself behind a crowd or in a bush. There she would experience a kind of death. She would suffer until someone picked you up and yelled. She would try, try hard not to answer the call—*whose child*—not to run toward you. She would bite her lips until they bled. For her you will forever be 'a broken arm hidden in her sleeve.'"

I was told that my daughter was found on the day she was born. I assume there was some evidence that she was a newborn, something about her umbilical cord or skin tone or head shape, but I don't even know if this is true. I don't know if her birthday is really the day we were told. But if her first mother had just given birth, would she have traveled, be in any shape to crouch behind a bush, to wait and watch? And yet there are so many stories about mothers waiting and watching.

I'm not sure if Sophie really wants me to take a photo, so I stand gazing at this site, picturing two men, maybe in their twenties, maybe even younger, moving through the dark, carrying bamboo fishing poles. Maybe they also had a bucket of worms; perhaps they'd brought a packet of seaweed-wrapped congee for their breakfast. I imagine them in rubber boots, stepping through weeds along the water's side, looking for a good rock on which to perch or perhaps wading out to stand and cast their lines. Maybe the moon was still full in the sky, like in the silk picture we bought at the factory in Beijing, the shimmery, silvery blue and gray scene of the edge of a pond. Or maybe the sun was starting to appear on the horizon, the sky lightening. And then there was a sound, the low keening of a newborn that might have seemed at first like a distant radio and then the cry of a hurt animal coming from the weeds. Was the baby, not yet named Ni Qiao Qin, not yet known as Sophie, perhaps with an unknown name chosen for her by her birth mother, floating in a basket like Moses, or had she been swaddled in blankets and left near the shoreline?

One of the men must have stumbled over her and leaned down to peer, startled, at the baby's face. One of the men must have scooped her up. Did the two men abandon their fishing and take the baby home, calling as they went, "A baby! Come see!"?

In the 1990s, Xinran writes, with tightly controlled media and widespread poverty in rural areas, people there had no TV or phones or money even if there were movie theaters, so their entertainment was what happened on the street. Finding a baby was an event. Did the women in this village exclaim and cuddle the baby and check her diapers and give her a bottle? Is my view of all of this too romanticized, too sentimental? I remember when I adopted Sophie, everywhere we went, Chinese women came forward who wanted to hold her and play with her. Why would it have been any different here in this village?

At what point did someone call the police or take the baby to the station, where someone else reported on the official record that she'd been found on the steps? Or was that some kind of clerical error or shorthand that somehow got transferred to her abandonment papers? Did that same person scrawl the note in her file that gave more specifics about who had found her and where? We may never know the answers to these questions. We may never trace my daughter's origins beyond this place where a pond used to be.

Grace urges Sophie to cross the street and stand in front of the apartment house. Sophie says nothing, obeying, standing there smiling and detached. I hurriedly, dutifully, take a picture, though I feel weird about photographing what Jane Liedtke calls the scene of a crime.

We turn back for what I assume will be a long walk through the heat to the van. But we arrive within a few minutes, even though it's seemed like we've tramped all over this small village. As we climb into the van and head back toward the orphanage, a song loops through my head, the Paul Simon song Sophie used to make me play over and over. I used to hear the verse about the baby girl found among the reeds and rushes, the baby with the clear eyes and the silky brown hair, and think of Sophie.

I used to picture my own baby, who was also found, who also had bright, bright eyes and soft, dark hair. But I didn't know that she, too, was found among reeds and rushes, that the silvery silk picture we bought in Beijing could have been her finding spot. I listened to the song for years never knowing how those lines paralleled her story. I bought the picture in Beijing with no idea how it would echo my daughter's beginnings.

Sophie will never say much about that day. She'll write about it in a school essay a month later: "My favorite thing was that I got to see the village I was born in. It smelled funny in some ways and it was mostly rented out. I also got to meet the dad of the son that found me. This is the best place that I have traveled to so far."

Unlike many adopted children, Sophie had never fantasized aloud about her origins. She was practical, never telling me that she imagined that her birth parents were royalty and that she was a princess, that her birth parents were rich and wished to bestow their fortune on her, that they were celebrities, movie stars or famous athletes. If she has ever idealized her birth parents, imagining flawless beings who would let her do whatever she wants, she has not shared these thoughts with me. The only wish she has expressed is the wish to know them. She will mention that in her school essay, too. "I was devastated when I had to go back to the U.S.," she'll write. "But now I'm planning to go live there soon someday back home. And maybe find my birth mom. I hope that my mom can still visit."

I can't know entirely what seeing that village meant to my daughter. As soon as we get back into the van, she sinks into default travel mode and nods off. Or maybe pretending to sleep in vehicles is her way of obtaining some privacy to think. I'd like to do that, too. I'm awed by the events of the day. I have an endless capacity to be amazed by the mere act of seeing things in which I'd previously only believed in a hypothetical sort of way.

I wasn't always that way. I was such a different child from my daughter, who isn't sure that she believes in God. I harbored wild fantasies and a restless need to be understood. Nobody ever told me I had a choice about what to believe, and so I believed in God and stability and permanence. I believed that things would stay where you put them, and so if I lost something, I looked for it. Sophie is much more philosophical. She assumes that things will either return to you when they're supposed to or stay lost forever. There's nothing you can do about it. If you find it—your necklace, your key, your birth village—cool. If not, whatever.

Or at least this is the face she presents to the world. When she can't find a book, a necklace, a glove, she doesn't even look. "Where's the last place you remember having it?" I'll ask, but she's impatient with retracing steps or visualizing her movements or talking them through. She shrugs, she refuses to play. Maybe it will turn up, maybe it won't. Searching seems to her a wild, haphazard waste of energy.

I have always believed that if you looked hard enough, you would find things, and yet I'm perpetually surprised to actually find them. Often, recovering lost things feels miraculous to me, the same way a baby throws plastic keys away and seems surprised and delighted to discover that they're still there on the floor. Sophie's village is like a lesson to me in object permanence, a reminder that our pasts are not abstractions. Today we have stepped unexpectedly into the concrete, one step closer to the miracle of ordinary reality: that my daughter came from a real place and real people. Until today, this was like a fact I read in a book. Today, it's shaped itself into an astonishing certainty that I turn over in my mind again and again, thinking about this part of her that isn't connected to me at all.

Later we drive to the wholesale market to buy gifts for the orphanage. I wanted to purchase an air conditioner for the baby room, but Mr. Li said no, someone had already done that. The air conditioner is currently in storage until the baby room can be remodeled. I will find out later that it has been in storage for more than a year while babies whose hair is damp with sweat toss and fuss.

We are driving fast and wildly once again, since the shops will close soon. We pass median strips crowded with pots, a profusion of flowers bursting out of them. I like the idea of filling my yard with pots of flowers, hundreds of pots, although it seems so much more temporary than planting the flowers in the ground.

At the wholesale market, a mall-like building lined with stall after stall, we hurry, hurry, while a woman cleans the floor, a river of dirty black water washing ahead of her mop. Mr. Li told us that we should buy diapers, but Grace thinks that that's an awful lot of diapers, so she suggests we buy toys instead. I veto stuffed animals. I want toys that are safe for babies to chew. I want toys that can be washed. I want toys in lots of colors and shapes. Sophie likes this idea, and we find a stall full of bright-colored plastic toys, stacking blocks and rings, tool sets and xylophones, cars and dolls. Sophie and Grace and I all circle, pointing. "That," we say, and "five of those" and "ten sets of those." The stack grows as we pick out hundreds of dollars worth of toys.

But the market does not take credit cards, and they are about to close. A man who works there dashes out with us to the van and hops into the front seat to direct us to a bank, where I stand in line to withdraw cash. We drive the man back to the market, where I pay. Around us, other proprietors close up their stalls.

We stop for dinner at KFC. Outside the front door, an employee entertains the small children of customers by giving them a group dance lesson. The row of toddlers solemnly follows along. We watch and eat our egg tarts and then drive back to the orphanage to meet the delivery truck.

When we knock on a door at the administration building, a family looks up, blinking, from a dark room where they are sitting on couches watching TV. The night manager of the orphanage directs the delivery guys to carry the crates of toys up to the playroom. The buildings are dark and quiet, but two older children emerge, excited, to help Grace and the staff check the packing slip against the boxes' contents. The children unwrap toys, chattering enthusiastically. The staff members nod and smile.

"They like your gift," Grace says.

The baby room is open, unmonitored right now by any adults. Sophie and I slip inside, past each sleeping baby. One with a Band-Aid on its head nods against the mattress, a movement too lacking in energy to qualify as head banging. I don't know if this baby, with snot stuck to the end of its nose, is a boy or girl. "Mamamama," it cries. I pat its back and whisper soothing sounds, and it quiets. Sophie has been watching me with a look I can't decipher. All day, she's been distantly polite to me, as if I'm a slightly embarrassing stranger. I remember feeling obligated to apologize for my mother's own bumbling ways when I hit adolescence. Now, though, as I calm this fretful baby, Sophie looks surprised, I think, and newly respectful.

"Can we slip this baby into my backpack and take it home?" I ask. Sophie looks around furtively, like she believes I mean to do it.

As a single woman, because of the new regulations, I could never come back to China to adopt another baby. But for a second I wish I could sneak this one away, this baby with its own unknown story. I wish I could spirit away to loving homes all these babies with pasts and futures we will never know. Out in the playroom, Grace has confirmed that all of the toys we paid for are here. Now the children and staff are wrapping them up again, repacking them in cartons, whisking them away to the storeroom where I fear they will sit for months, maybe even forever, next to the air conditioner.

I pat the sleeping baby, wondering who this child will be someday, adopted or fostered by a Chinese family, taken home to the Netherlands or Australia or Great Britain or the U.S., learning a new language, no longer having to pound its head and call for a mother. Until then, I can't even give this baby one small thing, not even a bright blue plastic ring, a green block, a red hammer. I think how grateful I am for every tidbit of information, every person who may have passed through my daughter's life during the ten months she was here, every small piece of evidence that someone cared for her, connected to her, took time for her.

And so I stand and soothe this baby, this baby that I wouldn't recognize if I ran into it on a street someday. I pat the baby's back and murmur, imagining that a few seconds of attention, a moment of locking this baby in my memory, can make any kind of difference.

Epilogue

The morning after the orphanage visit, we walk along the tracks at the train station, searching for Platform 2.3, which sounds like something out of *Harry Potter*. We are continuing to retrace Sophie's steps, moving through a compacted version of her first few months, though by now those steps are completely out of order. We've seen the place where she was found, the baby room where she slept. We've met Mr. Lu. And now we're on a train from Yiwu City to Hangzhou, the same train that Mr. Lu boarded with Sophie almost ten years ago to bring her to me.

I wonder if Mr. Lu looked out the window and saw the same things I see; I wonder how much this landscape has changed. I don't feel like taking any more pictures, but I want to fix this ride in my memory. I start jotting down a list of things that blur by my window, the same buildings and landscape that must have rushed by Mr. Lu that day. Apartment buildings clustered together amid the spread of countryside, jagged mountains in the distance, peaking and dipping like ocean waves, like narrative arcs, like the trajectories of our lives. Ruined apartment buildings with no windows. Occupied ones with billboards painted on the ends facing the tracks. An old graveyard on a hill in a country where cremation is now mandatory. Brick farmers' houses with shiny windows, blue and green glass, tiered balconies, gothic turrets and gables, triangular roofs. Clean lines of earth, a small pond, a tilled field, narrow rows of green growing things, a block of seedlings, angled, geometric and precise, charming. Balconies with boxes, strings of laundry, pots of flowers, wooden birdcages, blankets hanging over rails.

There's so much we can't know, but the miracle, to me, is how much we've been able to discover, how many scraps we now can piece together. Each small bit of information, each picture I take, each detail I jot down, feels like another girder or cable or anchor in a bridge I'm building. Right now, that bridge may be merely decorative, as fragile and ornamental as one on a Blue Willow plate. But I keep writing things down, hoping that finally what we piece together will have enough substance for my daughter to cross over freely. Sophie's irritated with me. She wishes I'd quit taking pictures and notes. She's tired and cranky.

A portable CD player plays and replays Chinese children's music. The chorus repeats a thousand times. *Lao shi ni, lao shi ni,* it sounds like. A steel building stands next to a pond surrounded by weeping willows. An elegant pagoda on a mountain precedes a wire radio tower. Sophie goes to sleep. We arrive in Hangzhou, dispense passengers, acquire more. The family across the aisle, two parents and a young child, get off, and is replaced by two old women. Sophie opens her eyes and stares, turns to me as if something magical has happened, this transmogrification of a young family into two elderly women.

Mr. Lu got off the train here many years ago when he brought baby Ni Qiao Qin to me. But we stay on, waiting for it to pull out of the station and clatter on to Shanghai, where we will catch a plane for home.

My pants meet me in Shanghai. By now, Sophie has such a craving for a grilled cheese sandwich that I assemble a makeshift one from the breakfast bar: I cover a thick slice of bread with some fancy cheese, the first cheese I've seen in ages, and slide it into a toaster oven. Sophie looks skeptical at the result but wolfs it down. We spend our last day in China buying gifts at the market, taking a taxi past Shanghai's tallest building, which our guide compares to a bottle opener. Later, at our hotel, we ride the glass elevator, shooting pictures of Shanghai from each floor of the twenty-one-story building, making our own flip book of rising and falling through the sleek metal landscape, big fancy concrete superhighways clover-leafing and winding through the city below us. We buy prawn-flavored Pringles and lime Propel at the convenience store, and Sophie fixes me tea labeled "Sweet, leafy goodness."

"I don't want to leave China," she says over and over. "I want to stay here."

But of course we have to go—back home, back to school, back to work. It is noon China time when we arrive in Buffalo, midnight there. We are wide awake for the drive home to Bradford. Our house feels cold and empty. We unpack as the furnace kicks on. At 3:00 A.M. at the Yummy Bacon-Wrapped Steak Store, we buy the ingredients for grilled cheese sandwiches, then go home and fix them. The house begins to smell like heat and food again, inhabited. We tumble into our beds.

Only a few days later, we stay up to watch election returns. "In ten seconds, the polls close on the West Coast," says Tom Brokaw.

We count down: "Ten-nine-eight-seven-six-five-four-three-two-one!" we shout.

"It is now eight o'clock on the West Coast," Tom Brokaw says, "And Barack Obama is the forty-fourth president of the United States."

Sophie doesn't want to watch the inauguration in a noisy cafeteria with classmates who are capable of putting chopsticks up their noses. That morning she accompanies me to work instead, and we watch it together, on a big screen on campus.

The moment that Obama becomes president, a quartet goes through the motions of playing a piece taped earlier, "Air and Simple Gifts." Yo Yo Ma and Itzhak Perlman and two others weave together two pieces, one of them the song that the trash truck played in China as it went round and round Xi'an:

> 'Tis the gift to be simple
> 'Tis the gift to be free. . .

And I think that maybe, with our first African American president, the U.S. will look more like home to children like mine.

I read Sophie some testimonials of parents whose children have gone on homeland visits. "I've been touched by Jesus!" she responds wryly, back to the wisecracking, feisty child who disappeared for a while when we were in China. That's what these stories sound like to her, miraculous conversion narratives. Going to China wasn't about closure for her so much as about opening up a whole new world, making both her own past and her future more concrete.

If we hadn't gone to China, a lot of things might have happened anyway. Sophie might still have taken Mandarin classes for two years and begun to sign her school papers in Chinese. A teacher insists that she sign her name in English, too. "If you don't, when you get to middle school, no one will know whose paper it is," she says. Sophie knows there will not actually be any other Chinese children at her middle school, but she dutifully signs the names side by side. On tests, on papers, at the orthodontist, she writes both names, claiming both of her identities.

If we hadn't gone to China, she still might have decided two months later to return to competitive gymnastics. She attends a meet after one team practice, before she knows the beam routine. The coach has to talk her through it. A minute after the final bell, she finally completes the dismount.

Soon after, given a school assignment to dress as someone from pioneer days for a field trip to an old village, she appears at my bedside in the middle of the night, saying, "I know. I'm going to be an Indian." This is the first time I realize she has been worrying about this, about going as a white pioneer when she feels a greater identification with the Indians. I help her make a headband with a feather. I find a pair of moccasins and some fringed cloth to cut into a dress. Her teacher, the fifth-grade teacher Sophie loves, protests. She tells me that she wants the children to wear costumes from the "olden days." I try to convince her that Indians existed in the olden days, too. Gradually, though grudgingly, she backs down, and Sophie goes as the only Indian in the fifth grade. I don't know if the teacher ever understands how important this is to her, but in the end, she gives Sophie an A for social studies.

And in the end, the first low beam score and the final high social studies grade are beside the point. Maybe, even without China, my daughter would have had the courage to risk failure and to be true to herself. She would still win sometimes and lose others, and maybe she'd still enjoy herself either way. But I can't help but think that she has a new security about her place in the world and a renewed confidence in herself. I know this might have happened even if we hadn't gone back to China. Even if we hadn't gone to China, she probably would have made good grades, taken up the violin, and become a state balance beam champion with the same routine on which she scored a 4.8 out of 10 in her first level 4 competition. Naturally, I imagine, even without the China trip, her nervousness about storms would have faded, her vision of China eventually would have become more complicated, and she would have become calmer, if still mercurial, as she matured.

So the only thing I can conclude with absolute certainty is that if we hadn't gone to China, we wouldn't have a dog. All my life, I've found dogs to be slobbery, annoying creatures. Then I adopted a child who loved dogs, and in China, after seeing Mr. Lu's scruffy black dog, I started getting all sentimental about the possibility that Sophie had, as an infant, been attached to this dog. And so now I promise her a pet, and eventually we drive to Connecticut to pick up our supposedly hypoallergenic goldendordoodle. Soon, like parents since time immemorial, I am rising early to let the dog out, walking the dog, and feeding the dog. Sophie spends her time goading the dog, rolling on the floor with the dog, and yelling at the dog for running off with her beloved stuffed dog, Zeke aka Ozzie Osborne.

In the summer, we travel to Spain. It turns out that Sophie hates planes but loves traveling, and now she wants to live in Barcelona as well as Beijing; she wants to live everywhere, learn more languages, maybe join the Peace Corps someday. She gets all pumped up when she talks about this. She talks fast and breathlessly about the whole world that's opened up to her. Well, she says, maybe not the Peace Corps. Especially if it means living in a mud hut without refrigeration. I remember the Canadian mother at the Tang

Dynasty Show: "She's ten. Things change." She was right, and I'm just trying to keep up.

Sophie wins her first all-around in Greensburg, Pennsylvania, the town where my McCabe ancestors settled when they emigrated from Ireland in the 1800s. Sophie doesn't know this. She flies across the gym to me, waving her trophy. "I watched Chinese gymnasts on YouTube last week, and today, I tried to be like them," she says.

Obsession with Chinese culture gradually gives way to gymnastics culture, which is its own world, even small-town, lower-level YMCA gymnastics. It's inevitable, given the time we spend on practices and meets and team parties and fundraisers. Now everyone around me is talking about front hip circles and kips and deductions and vault scratches. As with dance, it seems to me that the community becomes more important than the competition or performance, the way the whole team cheers the first time a teammate lands her back handspring in competition, the way a whole gymful of parents from different teams claps rhythmically to keep a girl from having to complete her floor routine in silence when her music fails. We watch our girls learn to fall and get right back up, salute the judges through tears after a teammate's injury and go on, get really good at one level's skills and start all over again at the next level. Our girls may wear sparkly suits and jeweled warm-ups, but they can also hoist their body weight above a bar.

Back when I was working on my doctorate, I read a lot of studies from the 1990s about the alarming loss of voice in adolescent girls. Carol Gilligan and Lyn Mikel Brown, Mary Pipher, and the *AAUW Report on the Status of Women* all addressed the phenomenon of girls who, at the age of eleven, were "articulate, resourceful, and knew their own minds," but by adolescence, had become silent and reluctant to speak up about their beliefs or desires, gradually disconnecting from their own opinions and experiences.

More recently, I've encountered studies suggesting that children adopted from other countries and cultures tend to maintain a strong interest in their origins until adolescence, when their attention turns to fitting in. This is why homeland visits are recommended by the age of ten, so children have a chance to explore those aspects of their identities before the distractions of hormones and social anxieties.

I don't know whether it's possible to combat these tendencies; maybe they're normal developmental stages. It remains to be seen what kind of difference homeland visits make to children adopted from other countries. Someday, they will write their own stories. For now, I see my daughter increasingly torn about when to speak up, when to stay quiet. In the sixth grade, she gets a role in a school musical, a character whose lines are largely in Cantonese. She plans to wear her dress from the Tang Dynasty show, but then comes home upset that the teacher has added a coolie hat to her costume. And she's worried that she's going to be made up to look like a doll. Say something, Mom, she says.

So I mention to the teacher the China Doll stereotype that objectifies many Asian girls, ask if Sophie can't wear the same amount of makeup as the other, white, characters. And can she just wear a hair clip she bought in Shanghai, not the hat? The teacher is very accommodating. Sophie spends hours trying to master the Cantonese tones and the lines of her songs. I am proud of her, performing a solo up on stage in front of filled auditoriums, and have to suppress my laughter and exasperation that the other Chinese characters are all wearing kimonos.

The drab gray, snowy landscape to which we returned gradually becomes a green and blooming world, the mountains woolen again, as if someone laid over them a nubby, lumpy homemade green sweater. Choruses of leaves flutter. In the breeze, one leaf strokes the porch rail like a slow hand petting a cat. By now, we are back to being too busy, between my two jobs, my writing, Sophie's gymnastics and music and school, the house, and now a dog who drags me out of bed too early every morning and licks all the windows and sheds everywhere when her coat gets too long and fluffy and goes wild in snow, churning up all the neighbors' yards. I am back to my old worries about tasks and deadlines and schedules.

One morning I am cleaning the kitchen when chaos erupts on the north side of the house. A crow caws from the tree outside the landing window, and another screams from the garage rooftop. Crows keep swooping low over the yard and bamming into the railing of the kitchen porch.

I follow the cacophony to the porch window and peer out to find a crow that appears to be stranded on the railing, edging its way along the thin metal as if perched on its own balance beam. It has a slightly fluffy, downy look, but this bird is surely too big to be a baby who hasn't yet learned to fly. It turns to look at me through the window, lifts its wings twice, and then just stands there. I open the door and step outside. It watches me approach but still doesn't move.

The crow in the tree above goes wild, flapping past the porch and then looping to beat by again, close enough that I can feel the wind stirred by its wings. The garage crow joins in, also winging crazily past the porch, reminding me of the frenzied flight of lost bats. I retreat into the house and back to my work. Two hours later the crow is still edging its way along the railing while the other crows caw madly.

Everyone I ask—a friend, a neighbor, finally the state game commissioner—worries that the crow on the porch has an injury or a virus. They lecture me about the ugliness of nature, assuming that the crows flying by are picking on the weaker, outsider crow. I glance out again. The porch crow has moved from the railing to the top of the trash can and sits all plumped out there like a pillow, making itself comfortable.

As I sit down to mark papers, I think of these events as just a story I'll tell Sophie when I pick her up tonight from gymnastics practice. But the crowing in the yard distracts me again. I look up "crow behavior" on the Internet. I learn that fledglings leave the nest at this time of year, that they can be quite large and may not obviously be babies, and that the crows that dive-bomb passing people are usually parents, protecting their young from predators.

So, I realize, for five hours now, these shrieking crows have been warding away danger, bearing with a baby who has not yet learned to fly, berating and admonishing intruders like me that might threaten the baby, maybe also scolding the baby or urging it: "Just fly. At least give it a try. Don't just sit there!" I know that nature can be harsh and brutal. Sophie saw a baby crow fall from the same tree a few weeks before and hop around fluttering its wings. The Internet tells me that if the nest is too full, parent crows will kick out a baby or two, and that's likely what Sophie witnessed.

But what I've been watching is something altogether different. It's parental concern and protection, encouragement and nagging, the wisdom of knowing the right time to push the baby to fly on its own. I peer out the kitchen window again and am almost disappointed to find my porch and yard still and empty. Nothing on the trash can lid or railing. No sign of a floundering baby bird in the yard.

As I leave to go pick up Sophie, a parent crow remains perched at the peak of my garage roof, strutting a little, I think, as it caws loudly. Crowing. I imagine it proclaiming to the world that its baby has flown. I'm probably getting it all wrong again, but this time the squawking sounds triumphant, like a boast, like a gloat, like a basking in parental pride, glorying in the flight of the baby bird. The garage crow is all puffed up, like I feel when Sophie gets her cartwheel on the beam and then proceeds to do cartwheels on curbs, walls, and railroad ties as we walk our dog. I want to crow like that when she learns to play "Simple Gifts" on the violin, when she discovers Paul Simon and comes home from school all excited. "My teachers have *heard* of him!" she says, awed that his music is more than just another of her mother's arcane interests.

The image of the crows stays with me, not just because of all my anthropomorphic metaphors for my own parental struggles or the reminders of how easily we can oversimplify what it means to be an outsider, but because for one afternoon, they slowed me down. They slowed me down like long winters during Sophie's preschool years had, like that long day in Chengdu. The crows distracted me from meaningless achievements or petty competitions, derailed my intense focus on ticking off things from my to-do list. Someday, I think, I will spend my days like that, not rushing, just watching the world and thinking about it. I understand that that's what I really want for my child—to care more about the process than the result—and that going to China made me more sure of that.

We talk a lot about the importance of choosing battles. When Sophie complains to me about a requirement in band class, I say, "Do you want me to protest? Do you want to choose this battle? Is it worth it?"

We are sandpapering holes in her bar grips. A heap of white leather sawdust grows on the tray as I twirl holes with fine sandpaper, clearing spaces for her small fingers.

No, she decides, this battle isn't worth it. We twist and turn the sandpaper. Our progress is slow. The conversation turns to how to respond to racist or ethnocentric comments.

"There are bigger places where people get it, but there are also thousands and thousands of small towns just like this one," my daughter says, poking her fingers through the holes and wiggling them. "Sometimes it's better not to say anything." The grips are still stiff, but the finger holes are big enough that now she can break them in. I watch her try them on, wave her stiff hands, and don't know whether to find her insight extremely wise or deeply heartbreaking. Or both.

When I was in elementary school, every Thanksgiving we sang, "Over the River and through the Woods." While we no longer rode in sleighs through the white and drifted snow to see our grandparents, my own heritage was still close at hand. I lived a car ride away from relatives, the bridges we crossed so much smaller than those that many of our children have to build.

The Blue Willow pattern is thought to be a hybrid of two cultures, invented in England but derived from an old Chinese design. According to a Wikipedia entry, the original Chinese design had no bridge with people on it. That was added later. Like the bridge that went over the river in the song of my childhood, I cannot picture the fragile, curving one in the Blue Willow pattern long or strong enough to span the distance between two countries and two cultures. Our children will have to invent their own.

Sophie and some friends get together for a sixth-grade assignment, to build bridges out of edible substances. Kids bring creations to school made of ramen noodles and peanut butter and pretzel rods, hard candy, cereal, marshmallows, and gumdrops. Sophie's group constructs theirs from rock candy, Rice Krispie treats, and pretzels. Each group stretches their bridge between chairs, and the teacher drops weights on it to see if it will hold.

"We won," Sophie says that night, serenely sucking on a big chunk of the purplish-blue rock candy. "But don't get too excited. A lot of people won." She goes on eating it for days, this hard and sweet and indestructible piece of bridge that she and her friends have built—the first, I hope, of many.

In gymnastics, levels 5 and 6—the top compulsory stages—have the same vault, a simple handspring over the vault table, performed in four stages: preflight, support, second flight, and landing. I watch girl after girl explode off the table, trying to keep their arms and legs straight, to stick the landing. Sophie fractured her foot the very first time she did this vault. It took eight weeks to heal. I always feel a little nervous when she takes off running for the springboard. I keep this to myself, this and my trepidation about the bars. Recently, one of her teammates missed her jump to the high bar and broke her arm.

Is the legendary confidence of gymnasts, the demand it makes of its practitioners to repeatedly conquer their fears, worth it? I don't know. I hold my breath as I watch my daughter complete her front hip circle and perch there in a split above the low bar, toes pointed delicately in a remnant of dance. She squats onto the low bar, assessing the high bar above, focused, measuring the distance, calculating her movements. My heart always pounds in that moment before she throws herself into empty space, toward the high bar. In that split second, I clench my sweaty fists, waiting, waiting, releasing a huge, relieved sigh every time she catches herself coming down.

Note on Sources

A number of secondary sources provided valuable background for information about China, homeland visits, and issues related to domestic and international adoption. *From Home to Homeland: What Adoptive Families Need to Know before Making a Return Trip to China,* edited by Debra Jacobs, Iris Chin Ponte, and Leslie Kim Wang (Yeong & Yeong, 2009) is a wonderful and varied collection of articles that offer tips for homeland visits and discussions of their importance and effects. Several of these articles were especially helpful to me in establishing background information about homeland visits, including pieces by two anonymous writers as well as those by Jane Brown, Robin Carton, Jenna Cook, Iris Culp, Sandra Lundy, Sheena McCrae, Joyce Pavao Maguire, Iris China Ponte, Leslie Kim Wang, Serena Fan, Tony Xing Tan, Xiohui Fan, and Andrea Williams. Jane Liedtke's article "Walking down the Village Path" is also reprinted in this collection.

While I have not directly quoted from it due to confidentiality policies, the Yahoo group Adoptionparenting has also been a rich resource for general information about many of these subjects as well. Becca Piper's series of articles, "The Gift of Identity through Journeys of Discovery: Do Kids Need to Know the Past?" (http://www.AdoptiveFamilyTravel.com) offered further perspective on similar issues.

I also consulted Karin Evans's *The Lost Daughters of China* (Jeremy P. Tarcher/Putnam, 2000) for background information about issues related to China adoption, as well as Kay Ann Johnson's *Wanting a Daughter, Needing a Son: Abandonment, Adoption, and Orphanage Care in China* (Yeong & Yeong, 2004) and Richard Tessler, Gail Gamache, and Liming Liu's *West Meets East: Americans Adopt Chinese Children* (Bergin & Garvey, 1999). Penny Callan Partridge's poem "For All the Little Girls from China" appears in Evans's book, as does Anchee Min's "Letter to All the Lost Daughters of China." Xinran's *Message from a Chinese Birthmother: Stories of Loss and Love* (Chatto and Windus, 2010) is a riveting read that gave me insight into the plight of Chinese mothers forced to give up their children.

I learned a great deal from several works that offer the perspectives of U.S. birth mothers whose children were adopted domestically, including Ann Fessler's *The Girls Who Went Away: The Hidden History of Women who Surrendered Children for Adoption in the Decades before Roe vs. Wade* (Penguin, 2007); Meredith Hall's *Without a Map: A Memoir* (Beacon Press, 2008); Mary Bloch Jones's *Birthmother: Women Who have Relinquished Babies for Adoption Tell their Stories* (Chicago Review Press, 1993); Linda Bach McKay's *Shadow Mothers: Stories of Adoption and Reunion* (North Star Press, 1998); Margaret Moorman's *Waiting to Forget: A Motherhood Lost and Found* (W.W. Norton, 1998); and an anthology edited by Nancy Robinson, *Touched by Adoption* (Green River, 1999).

I found Larry and Quinn Herzberg's *China Survival Guide: How to Avoid Travel Troubles and Mortifying Mishaps* (Stone Bridge Press, 2008) a charming and helpful set of tips for traveling in China. Lonely Planet's *China* (1998) was also entertaining and informative.

In Chapter 5, the discussion of media portrayals of adoption includes references to Jay MacDonald's interview with Scott Simon, author of *Baby, We Were Meant for Each Other* (*BookPage*, September 2010); "China's Horrific Adoption Mills" (*New York Times*, January 11, 1996, section A.25); "Saving the Orphans" (*Time*, January 22, 1996, 40); "Made in China, Loved in America" (*McCall's*, June 1997, 66–67); and "Why Are American Babies Being Adopted Abroad?" (*People*, vol. 36, no. 22, June 6, 2005). Background for chapter 6 includes Beth Lloyd's report on "China's Lost Children" (ABC News, May 12, 2008, http://abcnews.go.com/International/story?id=4774224&page=1ABC News Report); "The Dying Rooms," now available on YouTube (http://www.yidio.com/the-dying-rooms-24/id/2701484978); "The Lie We Love" (*Foreign Policy*, November/December 2008); and "A Family in China Made Babies Their Business" (*Los Angeles Times*, January 24, 2010). The *60 Minutes* story on Vy Higginson and Marion West can be found at http://www.cbsnews.com/stories/2007/10/05/60minutes/main3334427.shtml.

About the Author

Nancy McCabe is Associate Professor and director of the writing program at the University of Pittsburgh at Bradford and a faculty member in the brief-residency MFA program in creative writing at Spalding University in Louisville, Kentucky. She is the author of two previous books, including the adoption memoir *Meeting Sophie* (University of Missouri Press). Her work has also received a Pushcart Prize and made the Notable List in *Best American Essays* four times. She lives in Bradford, Pennsylvania.